"NIEGGRI" in MOSCOW under GORBACHEV
My life as a foreign student in USSR

CONTENTS

Acknowledgements   5
Introduction   7

A. FROM MALI TO MOLDAVIA   9
1. Cold war   9
2. On to Kishinev   27
a. Getting there   27
b. Dorm life   45
c. Nationalism   68

B. EDUCATION   78

C. THE TEMPTATIONS   99
1. Contraband   101
a. From Europe to the Soviet Union   111
b. From the Soviet Union to Europe   119
c. From the Soviet Union to the third world   126
2. Boulafs   136
3. Vodka   148

D. EASTERN JIM CROW   161
a - "Fucking Niggers"   166
b - SOBs chasing Soviet girls   191
c - Rich daddies' kids   197

E. GORBACHEV AND I   206

F. The XTRA-FILES   288

AKNOWLEDGEMENTS

This account of my journey to the former Soviet Union was made possible by the unconditional love and support from my family, my wife Jennifer and our two boys, Moussa and Gagny Eli. You made it happen.

I dedicate it to my late mom Fanta Doucouré and to all those who are denied access to a decent life by dishonest leaders.

Love,
Dad

I would like to thank Katherine Walters Brick, author of *The Enchantment of Miranda, The Girl Who Grew Back'*, for her invaluable assistance.

Введение

INTRODUCTION

As a student in the former Soviet Union from 1986 to1992, I recount here how foreign students from around the world got to go to Moscow, live among an extremely hostile indigenous population and graduate or not, as circumstances permitted.

In the 1960s, developing countries were the political battleground of the cold war between the West and the communist bloc, led respectively by the United States and the Soviet Union. Many countries tried to benefit from that protracted war by letting both sides in and then watch them outdo each other in aid. Unfortunately, the colonial powers did not have the interest of any colony in mind as they invaded and subjugated the native inhabitants. After essentially "raping" the entire African continent for centuries, Europe in the early 1960s was losing its grip. It did all it could to hang on to most of its former territories and to also counter China and the USSR.

At the same time, the United States also started to get a foothold on the continent in an effort to counter the communist ideology that seemed to resonate with many newly independent countries, among them my native Mali.

That competition for space and influence between the

powers in the early 1960s, charted the course of history for each and every country that later broke out of bondage. Subsequently, these circumstances directly paved the way for my trip to Moscow on a scholarship, twenty-six years later.

Landing in Moscow from West Africa was a cultural and physical shock, as I and many fellow students frantically tried to make sense of our new environment. At the same time, the Soviet Union, with Gorbachev as general secretary, embarked on the most consequential political transformation of the 20th century - Perestroika. These six years changed our lives alongside the alteration of the Soviet society itself. We became inside witnesses looking through the lenses of an outsider.

As foreign students, we faced horrible situations well known to our embassies, but never shared with us all prior to our trip to Moscow. We were blindsided by the realities on the ground due to the incompetence of our diplomats in Moscow and the numbskulls at the Malian departments of Education and Foreign Affairs. Their uselessness cost lives, and when things broke down, there were no consequences for those charged to look after students' welfare abroad.

Here is how the course of my life radically changed along with the earth-shattering end of the cold war then that of the Soviet Union itself.

Real identities are hidden and the stories could be those of each and every student in the former Soviet Union.

I
ОДИН

A. FROM MALI TO MOLDAVIA
1. Cold War

"Gentlemen, the policy of colonial expansion is a political and economic system that can be connected to three sets of ideas: economic ideas; the most far-reaching ideas of civilization; and ideas of a political and patriotic sort.

"In the area of economics, I am placing before you, with the support of some statistics, the considerations that justify the policy of colonial expansion, as seen from the perspective of a need, felt more and more urgently by the industrialized population of Europe and especially the people of our rich and hardworking country of France: the need for outlets [for exports]. Is this a fantasy? Is this a concern [that can wait] for the future? Or is this not a pressing need, one may say a crying need, of our industrial population? I merely express in a general way what each one of you can see for himself in the various parts of France. Yes, what our major industries [textiles, etc.], irrevocably steered by the treaties of 1861 into exports, lack more and more, are outlets. Why? Because next door Germany is setting up trade barriers; because across the

9

ocean the United States of America have become protectionists, and extreme protectionists at that; because not only are these great markets shrinking, becoming more and more difficult of access, but these great states are beginning to pour into our own markets products not seen there before. This is true not only for our agriculture, which has been so sorely tried and for which competition is no longer limited to the circle of large European states. Today, as you know, competition, the law of supply and demand, freedom of trade, the effects of speculation, all radiate in a circle that reaches to the ends of the earth. That is a great complication, a great economic difficulty; an extremely serious problem. It is so serious, gentlemen, so acute, that the least informed persons must already glimpse, foresee, and take precautions against the time when the great South American market that has, in a manner of speaking, belonged to us forever will be disputed and perhaps taken away from us by North American products. Nothing is more serious; there can be no graver social problem; and these matters are linked intimately to colonial policy.

"Gentlemen, we must speak more loudly and more honestly! We must say openly that indeed the higher races have a right over the lower races.

"I repeat that the superior races have a right because they have a duty. They have the duty to civilize the inferior races... In the history of earlier centuries these duties, gentlemen, have often been misunderstood; and certainly when the Spanish soldiers and explorers introduced slavery into Central America, they did not fulfill their duty as men of a higher race. But, in our time, I maintain that European nations acquit themselves with generosity, with grandeur, and with sincerity of this superior civilizing duty. "I say that French colonial policy, the policy of colonial expansion, the policy that has taken us under the Empire (the Second Empire, of Napoleon III), to Saigon, to Indochina (Vietnam), that has led us to Tunisia, to Madagascar - I say that this policy of colonial expansion was inspired by the fact that a navy such as ours cannot do without safe harbors, defenses, supply centers on the high seas. Are you unaware of this? Look at a map of the world.

"Gentlemen, these are considerations that merit the full attention of patriots. The conditions of naval warfare have greatly changed. At present, as you know, a warship, however perfect its design, cannot carry more than two weeks' supply of coal; and a vessel without coal is a wreck on the high seas, abandoned to the first occupier. Hence the need to have places of supply, shelters, ports for defense and provisioning. And that is why we needed Tunisia; that is why we needed Saigon and Indochina; that is why we need Madagascar... and why we shall never leave them! ... Gentlemen, in Europe such as it is today, in this competition of the many rivals we see rising up around us, some by military or naval improvements, others by the prodigious development of a constantly growing population; in Europe, or rather in a universe thus constituted, a policy of withdrawal or abstention is simply the high road to decadence! In our time nations are great only through the activity they deploy; it is not by spreading the peaceable light of their institutions that they are great, in the present day.

"Spreading light without acting, without taking part in the affairs of the world, keeping out of all European alliances and seeing as a trap, an adventure, all expansion into Africa or the Orient - for a great nation to live this way, believe me, is to abdicate and, in less time than you may think, to sink from the first rank to the third and fourth."[1]

This March 28, 1884 speech by Jules Ferry, former prime minister of France, describes in elegant terms the mindset of a bigoted and insecure power seeking to undertake self-serving adventures. His xenophobic comments won him a lot of cooperation from fellow European imperialists. Later that year, Portugal would sponsor a conference in Berlin (The Berlin Conference: November 15, 1884 – February 26, 1885)

---

[1] *Jules François Camille Ferry, "Speech before the French Chamber of Deputies, March 28, 1884," Discours et Opinions de Jules Ferry, ed. Paul Robiquet (Paris: Armand Colin & Cie., 1897), -1. 5, pp. 199-201, 210-11, 215-18. Translated by Ruth Kleinman in Brooklyn College Core Four Sourcebook*

to discuss the division of Africa. The goal was to literally divide the continent in spheres of influence, subjugate the native populations, and seize natural resources.

If this sounds familiar, it should, because we still deal with the same mindset under different circumstances two centuries later. In the mid-twentieth century, the United States and Turkey joined talks with twelve European countries that already controlled most of the continent at the time. After three months of bartering over somebody else's territory and resources, the "superior race" displayed its superior and disgusting immorality by agreeing to the political and economic "gang-rape" of Africa.

In the case of West Africa, secured by the French at the Berlin conference, that meant subduing a series of kingdoms and empires headed by powerful warriors. Among them the Ghana, Malinké (Mali) and Songhai Empires that controlled Saharan trade and were in touch with Mediterranean and Middle Eastern centers of civilization.

The French military penetration of the Soudan (the French name for the area) began around 1880. Ten years later, France made a concerted effort to occupy the interior. A French civilian governor of Soudan was appointed in 1893, but resistance to French control did not end until 1898, when the Malinké warrior Samory Touré was defeated after seven years of war. [2]

In 1895 the AOF (Afrique Occidentale Française) or French West Africa was created in order to officially and efficiently administer the conquered grounds. This colonial Federation made out of eight occupied territories will provide France with everything she needed for two generations, even warriors during the two world wars. Shamefully the African vets from those wars would later be denied their pensions, French citizenship and other basic rights to this day.

By 1958, separatist trends throughout the continent were bubbling, forcing colonial powers to consider peaceful

---

[2] *Paul Halsall July 1998 [halsall@murray.fordham.edu] Internet Modern History Sourcebook Project.*

alternatives. Feeling that rising tide, France tried to preempt a substantial independence push from its sub-Saharan colonies by making some cosmetic changes. At that point, it considered its territories as France too and allowed its subjects to be represented at the National Assembly in Paris. My own maternal grandfather, Amadou Doucoure, thus became a French Senator of the fourth republic for a decade (1947-1958) and took multiple trips to attend the assembly meetings in Paris. Documents from his files on the French Senate website show that he pushed for universal health care, labor rights, war veterans' pensions, compulsory education and equivalency between diplomas in France proper and in French territories. Surprisingly today, battles are still being fought over some of these same issues here in the US and around the world (http://www.senat.fr/senateur-4eme-republique/doucoure _amadou0122r4.html#1940-1958).

France bought itself some precious time by that last move, in order to be in a position to still shape the future of an independent French-speaking-West Africa.

Under President De Gaulle and fearing the red penetration by the Soviet Union and China, the French government tried to persuade newly independent countries not to fall for the appealing anti-Western Soviet propaganda. So, after the 1958 constitutional referendum, the Government of France recognized two republics: Sudan and Senegal. [3]

In spite of the growing push for independence throughout the continent, Senegal decided to remain closely associated with France. Because of three hundred years of French influence and control, metropolitan Dakar (the capital city) had enjoyed a privileged position. It had long been allowed an elected city council, and its inhabitants were the first to receive French citizenship and representation in the Assembly. Senegalese troops also were among the first to rally around the free French government during World War II.

Sudan (future Mali), on the other hand, ruled by one party, the US-RDA (Union Soudanaise-Rassemblement Democratique

[3] *Department of State Pub: 8056, P-3 U S Department of State – Bureau of Public Affairs - Office of Public Communication -Washington, DC April 1993 - Managing Editor Peter A. Knecht, Editor: Anita Stockman*

Africain), and its leader Modibo Keita, wanted its total independence from France.

Despite these differences, on April 4, 1959 the two republics, Sudan and Senegal, expressed a desire to join together and form the Mali Federation. In December 1959, General de Gaulle announced that France would support Mali's independence, and offered French assistance to help develop local institutions and establish a reciprocal association with France. The three parties, France, Senegal and Sudan, even set future goals:

1. Independence for Mali in 1960 and the development of firm foundations for future political existence;

2. Continued fruitful association with France;

3. The development of a Eurafrican community of friendship.[4]

Everything seemed to be going as planned, and the honeymoon was about to start. The Mali federation obtained its independence on June 20, 1960 with Keita as president. The two Senegalese leaders, Senghor and Dia, were at the top of their popularity and about to write a page of history, should the Mali federation survive. This success would set an example in the region and bring peace and cooperation between former colonies on one hand, and with the West, led by France, on the other. The United States saw this as an opportunity to enter this former French Sub-Saharan Africa.

Unfortunately, in August 1960, exactly two months after gaining its independence, the Mali Federation collapsed, unable to overcome its internal political divisions. The competition for influence and power between the two leaders led to the dismantlement of one of the most promising unions in the postcolonial era. As a result, two independent countries were formed instead: Senegal and Mali, with their respective heads of state, L.S Senghor and M. Keita.

Mali officially got its independence on September 22,

---

[4] *Thomas P Melany, Pres. Consultants for Overseas Relations, Inc.150 Nassau Street, New York 38, N.Y. BEekman 3-1966. Information bulletin #1 April, 1960. P-1 sent to The Honorable Joseph C. Satterthwaite, Assistant Secretary of State for African Affairs; Department of State 5120 Upton Street Washington 16, D.C*

1960. Keita, at the head of the only organized political party (the US-RDA), established himself as the uncontested leader of the republic. Disillusioned by the reality of Mali's new status with France, he pivoted East to the chagrin of France and the West. Keita and his government accepted the promise of Marxist solutions to the country's difficulties, and advocated state Socialism as the only course of economic development. Mali would subsequently withdraw from the Monetary Union backed by France in 1962, jeopardizing its financial stability.

This surprising Malian policy worried most in the West and attracted others. The communist bloc (USSR, its Eastern European allies and China) multiplied its aid and promised much more collaboration to come. To keep the republic from completely switching sides, France engaged in a covert battle. Some of president Keita's close advisors were even offered two white women in order to convince him to focus West. Mali found itself in the middle of a nasty political game with some potential benefits.

The US and the Soviet Union, at the pinnacle of their cold war now gnawing the continent, were contemplating the dismantlement of the colonial era. Eager to secure a wider sphere of influence, the two superpowers courted Mali in order to steer it away from each other.

The Soviets were making their way in through sympathy to the causes of newly independent countries that were determined to fight neocolonialism, imperialism, apartheid, and impose self-government principles. China, as the underdog, sent a large number of specialists to Mali and offered to build a textile plant.

Parallel to the superpowers' camps and the commonwealth-like relations, newly independent countries tried to congregate around the Non-Aligned Movement (NAM). This organization was founded in Belgrade in 1961, and was largely the brainchild of Yugoslavia's President, Josip Broz Tito, India's first Prime Minister, Jawaharlal Nehru, Egypt's second President, Gamal Abdel Nasser, Ghana's first president, Kwame Nkrumah, and Indonesia's first President, Sukarno. All five leaders were prominent advocates of a middle course for states in the developing world between the Western

15

and Eastern blocs during the Cold War.[5]

The third rail became a necessity for those countries wishing to avoid the inescapable fatal choice between East and West. This non-aligned movement, or the third-world, meant to help tread the middle road between communism and capitalism, the two world "default systems" at the time. This tremendous and sometimes unbearable pressure, compelled Mali's new leader Modibo Keita to give an earful to all flatterers as the non-aligned movement was about to meet in Belgrade (ex-Yugoslavia). Struggling with the issues at hand, he summed up the state of affairs a year into independence as world powers put forth their offensive charms:

"To us, neutralism means to assume our responsibilities, all our responsibilities, in order clearly to define our position on any problem brought to our attention and to suggest a solution of our own concepts. How can an African country be neutral in the face of French aggression against Tunisia? How can an African country be neutral and trying to be an arbitrator in the Franco Algerian conflict? All peoples are entitled to freedom. All people are entitled to govern themselves freely. The Algerian people want to govern themselves that is the underlining principle of Universal Morality. We are with the Algerian people and against the French government. The Angolan people are struggling to liberate themselves from Portuguese domination. Following the same principles that cause us to be pro -Algeria in the Franco-Algerian conflict, we side wholeheartedly with the Angolan people against the Portuguese government. As for disarmament, we shall study all the theses that have been formulated. Whether they come from East or West, we shall come to a decision, in a completely objective manner, in favor of the solution that appears to us to be the most logical. With respect to nuclear tests, we shall also study the theses formulated, and we shall give our support to the one that is most consistent with International logic and morality. This is what positive neutralism and a policy of non-alignment means to us. It may happen, however, that in our action for the liberation of colonial peoples, and with respect to

[5] http://en.wikipedia.org/wiki/Non-Aligned_Movement#cite_note-2

the problem of nuclear test and disarmament, our position will coincide with that of such and such a camp. That will be the result of chance and not of any alignment whatsoever regarding the positions of that group.

To us, positive neutralism also means having no prejudice against any country until either it or its government adopts a position, with respect to African and International problems, that we can condemn because we consider it contrary to the interests of the African peoples and to International morality.

To us, the policy of nonalignment means also corporation with all nations, whether of East or West. We appreciate a country that helps us without conditions or that helps us without trying to guide us by remote control more than a country that helps us because we support it in the United Nations or elsewhere, when a certain problem is brought up. This can be demanded of other countries, other peoples, but it is futile to try to demand it from the Republic of Mali. Thus, we have had to apply this principle at the United Nations, and we have galled the Western bloc in connection with its position regarding anti colonialist struggles, or we have not agreed with representatives of Eastern countries regarding a certain solution to be given to a certain problem.

This is what positive neutralism means to us Malians. But, there is a field in which there is no bargaining, no neutrality, and that is when the right of colonized people to free themselves from all domination and govern themselves is involved. There, we take sides; we are on the side of the colonized people striving to free itself from the colonial power that, in violation of universal laws, wants to continue its domination.

We shall cooperate with all peoples, but especially with those who will accord us our rights and who will accord them to all men in all respects. To those who claim that we will lean toward communism, or capitalism, we shall answer that we shall not consider these words as simply words but that we shall judge both capitalists and communists strictly in terms of the behavior of each of their advocates towards us and our problems, towards our aspirations. We shall denounce and combat neocolonialism to the bitter end. We denounce not only neocolonialism; we also denounce and condemn the aim of the powers that express their determination to dominate the developing states politically and economically. We denounce and condemn imperialism for its contempt for men and institutions that refuse to expose its view.

We shall not judge powers in term of the relative strength of their forces, but only in term of the meaning they give to freedom. Our friends will be those who oppose the domination of one people by another. Our friends will be those who give their unconditional support to the struggle for liberation being waged by oppressed peoples. Our friends will be those who do not impose any conditions on us, who do not ask us to align ourselves with them on any position.

Many rumors are circulating about the conference of nonaligned countries. What we can say here and now is that the Malian delegation to that conference will pronounce itself clearly, in your name, on all the vital problems: anti colonialism, disarmament, nuclear tests, world peace, peaceful coexistence, the Berlin problem, and the reform of the United Nations.

As far as we are concerned, it will not be the creation of a third bloc that is involved, but a question of affirming quite clearly that no regime can be imposed on the world. We shall point out that the Third world can and must make its impartial contribution, with strict objectivity, to the search for a solution to the problems that concern all of mankind. To us it is clear that international peace is the best guarantee of our development, and we shall not fail to stress our disappointment at seeing the serious disagreement between two blocs, which, just yesterday, were fighting side by side against Fascism, and Hitlerism. We know that those who have suffered from the war do not want war. We also know that those who grow rich on war are the only ones to want war. Mali's position will be clearly defined at the Belgrade conference.

After our opinion has been expressed objectively, we

shall see who will then want to continue cooperating with us." [6]

The speech clearly sums up the mood and the propensities of third-world Africa in 1960, the Year of Independences. That year seventeen other countries of the beleaguered continent would get their so-called economic and political independence. It also crystallizes the need and necessity for such a movement, which would ideally allow its members to stay in balance and avoid another horrible subservience.

Besides the burning desire of new African nations to decide, speak and stand for themselves, two other major disputes were vital to the continent: the Arab-Israeli conflict and white minority rule in Namibia, Zimbabwe and South Africa. Diplomatic relations and friendships in the early sixties also depended primarily on countries' positions regarding these boiling questions.

This edgy atmosphere, coupled with cold war animosities, led to an interesting political courtship on the world stage. Each faction had its own goals and subtle ways to achieve them: the two superpowers were trying to get in, the ex-colonial powers were negotiating a hate-free stay, and the ex-colonies were shaking off the immoral looters.

With the cold war raging on, the two biggest players provided support in many different areas: economy and trade, diplomacy, military, and education/ training.

The Soviets saw in Africa and its newly independent countries a great potential for the international communist movement. They were counting on potential conflicts of interest between Africa and the West, which would play to their advantage. Their key policy was to expand their presence by multiplying contacts and aid. They charmed with obsessive compassion to the causes and problems the newly independent countries were dealing with.

Politically, they paid special attention to Mali, Ghana and Guinea, who's radical and aggressive anti-Western policies

---

[6] *Department of State, Division of Language Services, Chapter on Mali's foreign policy.LS # 42732 R-XXXII / R-XVIII French.1-5 pp. Translation of President Modibo Keita's speech: Policy of Nonalignment and Positive Neutralism. August 20, 1961.*

offered the USSR its first footholds in sub-Saharan Africa. The Soviets declared that these states were suitable candidates for the status of national democracy, a formula contrived to permit the close association of certain states with the bloc, even though they were not under communist control. The unprecedented invitation of the governing parties in Mali, Ghana and Guinea to attend the 22nd Congress of the Soviet Party underlined Soviet hopes of bringing the radical African states into the communist fold by absorption. [7]

Leaders in Mali found the centralized, authoritarian Soviet regime more suitable to their needs, familiar as it was to the governing style of previous kingdoms. Malians embraced the system and lost no time importing ideas and potential solutions from Moscow, where democracy was characterized as an unaffordable luxury.

Government organizations started in the cities: communities took turns cleaning, organizing meetings, etc. Soon, governmental policies became more personal and ideas like sharing the same meal and eating from the same plate became popular. The militia also started to ID people at night and began to beat and jail couples that did not have their marriage certificate on them. Women wearing short skirts were taken to the militia headquarters and, as punishment, received salt in their genitals. A climate of fear and intimidation ensued; prompting people to take a second look at this new political direction the government was embarking on.

Economic aid and assistance were the main inlets for the Soviets with struggling countries like Mali, which were in dire need of capital investment funds, unavailable from domestic savings. The bloc took advantage of the situation and made mouth-watering offers of trade, aid, and technical assistance. Mali's acute economic difficulties, due in large part to its exit from the monetary zone sustained by France, made it vulnerable to these tempting offers. By 1961, the total trade between sub-Saharan Africa and the Soviet bloc amounted to

[7] *National Intelligence Estimate Number 11-12-62, 5 December 1962. Trends in Soviet policy toward sub-Saharan Africa. P-5. Submitted by the Director of Central Intelligence, Concurred in by the United States Intelligence Board as indicated overleaf 5 December 1962*

$140 million, compared to $85 million in 1959. Mali sold about 85% of its then principal crop, peanuts, to the bloc, and planned the same for 1962. In exchange, the bloc traded machinery, oil, and industrial materials against larger quantities of cocoa, copper and coffee.

Civil air services quickly became part of the equation. Soviet and Czech aircrafts started to operate in Mali and Guinea, and Soviet maintenance crews were soon replaced by Malian and Guinean nationals in training. By June of 1962, the bloc had 1600 technicians on assignment in six sub-Saharan countries receiving bloc economic aid, 160 of them in Mali.

A number of East Germans, Czechs and Bulgarians were actively involved in the establishment of an information service, a news agency, and a Mali state trading company. They took on large projects for maximum political impact (such as dams, factories, stadiums, bridges etc.). A gold mine in the South and the Olympic stadium in the capital Bamako were some of their first proud endeavors.

The bloc proposed to lend $550 million in credits to the region. Mali was to receive $78 million from the Soviets and $19.6 million from the Chinese communists by June 1962. Later on, they accorded a moratorium on Malian debt payments until 1970.

In military assistance, while the bloc aimed for a lucrative market and strong political establishment, the Mali government looked to secure its own base. The bloc provided most of the equipment for the 3,300-man force in Mali. By June 1962, there were 25 Malian military personnel trained in the bloc and a total of $2 million in military aid agreements. In equipment, between September 1955 and June 1962, Mali received 30 armored personnel carriers, 47 artillery pieces, 100 vehicles, 5 transport aircrafts and 2000 to 3000 pieces in small arms.

Another scheme of penetration onto the continent was the cultural exchange programs. As of mid-1962, the Soviet Union and the Eastern European satellites had signed 25 cultural pacts with nine African states. Although they varied in scope, most of them provided for academic scholarships, cooperation in cultural and information fields, exchanges in

21

printed materials, radio materials and films. In addition, communist-supported local organizations were recruiting at the grass roots level. [8]

By June 1962, 55 Malian students were being trained in the USSR, and another 110 in its European satellites.

On the other side, the US was entering the African arena cautiously due to its ties to Western countries being driven out, but with some clear goals. Mali was then seen as a major leader in the region because of its dominance in pre-colonial West Africa. The principal objectives of US assistance to Mali were to lessen Mali's political and economic dependence on the communist bloc and encourage development of firmer ties with the West. Stated specific objectives were: to moderate the political and economic radicalism of the Malian leadership; to counteract the influence of the Soviet bloc and Communist China; to encourage restoration of cooperation between Mali and France; to promote closer relations among Mali and moderate West African states and constructive Malian participation in West African regional organizations and projects. [9]

In order to achieve this set of goals, the US quickly approved military efforts in Mali. Immediately in 1961, a year after independence, a US Mobile Training Team (MTT) went to Mali to organize and train a roughly 225-man parachute company. A second parachute MTT went in 1963 to conduct replacement training and a refresher course.

A third and final MTT was scheduled to arrive in Mali in January 1965 to conduct Jumpmaster and refresher training. However, the MTT was temporarily postponed pending clarification by the US of reports that Mali might have sent volunteers to assist the Congo rebels. The late reports were not confirmed and the approval for the third MTT was sent to the US Embassy in Bamako on April 9, 1965. However, the GOM (Government of Mali) delayed accepting the third MTT for various reasons.

---

[8] *National Intelligence Estimate 11-12-62 trend in Soviet policy toward sub-Saharan Africa. pp. 6-9.*
[9] *National Intelligence Estimate. Draft Weber: EW: 10-28-65. MALI – CASS, P.1*

Within months, the Malian chief of Staff submitted an oral request for:

1. The previously planned third MTT program (parachute maintenance training for 8-14 men; refresher training for 177 parachutists; jumpmaster training for 12 men; and judo training for 12 men;

2. A new basic parachute-training program for 200 additional candidates.

The US embassy strongly recommended that both Malian requests be approved, stating that the requests were in accordance with their policy objectives in Mali and Malian internal security needs; were reasonable in content and scope; would be inexpensive and would fall within the present overall cost ceiling for the Fiscal Year 1966 ($ 0.6 million).[10]

In September 1965 and January 1966, Governor G. Mennen Williams, Assistant Secretary of State for African Affairs, visited Mali to enhance the US image. In November 1965, the US government agreed to supply two C-47 (DC-3 type aircraft) to the Malian army. In January 1966, ceremonies inaugurating the airport, power plant and paved access road at Timbuktu were held. President Johnson designated Charles M. Spofford of New York and Hans A. Ries of California to represent the US at the ceremonies. Another two loans for the Central Veterinary Laboratory and the Higher Teachers Training College would follow. [11]

In 1965, a confidential draft of the NIE (National Intelligence Estimate), described the situation in Mali and what the US future steps should be as follow:

"Since the breakup of the Mali federation and Mali establishment as an independent state in 1960, Malian leaders have charted a radical course both politically and economically. In foreign affairs, Mali has practiced a militant Nonalignment,

---

[10] *Office of West Coast and Malian Affairs, Bureau of African Affairs, Department of State US government memorandum, October 19, 1965. Sent to Governor Williams-Assistant Secretary of State for African Affairs, by Nichols Feld-officer of African Affairs, about Mali paratroop training Project. P.1*

[11] *National Intelligence Estimate situation report-sept 1965-jan 1966 – Mali, P-2, paragraph 6: US-Malian Relations.*

which often parallels Soviet or Chicom positions on world issues. On the African scene, Malian leaders have vigorously promoted African unity and opposed colonial and apartheid regimes.

President Modibo Keita achieved considerable influence and stature among African leaders through his mediation efforts in the Algerian-Moroccan border dispute of 1963 and to a lesser extend in the Nkrumah-Entente confrontation of 1965. Internally, Mali's single political party (the US-RDA) is a highly organized, authoritarian body whose influence extends to every village within the country's borders. In pre-colonial history, Malian tribes exercised a dominant influence in West Africa.

Economically, Mali's socialist option has resulted in direct state control over most sectors of the economy. State agencies and enterprises now account for over 70% of Mali's annual imports. To date, however, Malian socialism has produced few concrete results in the economic field and the credibility of its widely propagandized socialist road to development has suffered in comparison to the progress of more moderate West African nations.

Mali's economic resources are meager and at best do not hold out hope of impressive economic development. The most promising line of development is in the area of livestock production where Mali could become a significant factor in the context of a more closely integrated West African regional economy. However, since independence Mali has pursued economic policies, which have exacerbated its inherently difficult position. The withdrawal from the CFA monetary union in 1962 resulted in the termination of French budgetary assistance and marked the beginning of inflationary financial policies which have depreciated Mali's currency and kept the country in chronic balance of payments difficulties. In 1963 Mali entered into a stabilization agreement with the IMF (International Monetary Fund), which has now lapsed as a result of Mali's failure to carry out its economic and financial commitments. The main difficulty was inability to restrict inflationary financing of the government budget, including operations of the state enterprises.

Mali's efforts at economic development have been

heavily financed by the Communist bloc, France and the EEC (today's European Union). Smaller amounts of assistance have been extended by West Germany, the US, Yugoslavia and the UAR (United Arab Republic formed out of Syria and Egypt). The results of this substantial foreign aid have not been promising. Few projects have yet been carried through to successful completion. At the same time, because of harassment of the private sector and inefficiency on the part of state enterprises and government agencies, there has been a considerable decline in several areas of economic activity.

It seems reasonable to expect that Mali will continue to profess nonalignment in the world affairs and to advocate state socialism as the course of its own economic development. Within the broad limits of these concepts, however, there is room for a more pro-Western orientation and a more realistic approach to the country's economic difficulties. There is also some hope since Mali's ruling elite is far from monolithic. While some members of the National Political bureau appear committed to Marxist solutions to political and economic problems, others seem to favor closer relations with the West and with France, in particular. The continuing economic crisis appears to have strengthened the hand of those moderate elements, who were responsible for Mali's efforts to improve relations with the US. They would also promote the Malian goodwill mission to Washington, which signed an agreement under Title I, and II of Public Law 480 in July 1965. It is France, which would provide support for the Malian currency and draw Mali closer to the regional organizations of its more moderate West African neighbors.

Strategy:
The main lines of US assistance strategy toward Mali should be the following:

1. We should strengthen the bilateral US relationship with Mali through a small, but effective aid program and through the various other programs and channels available to the US;
2. We should counter Soviet and Communist Chinese influence to the extent possible without a substantial

25

increase in US assistance. In no sense should we seek as an end in itself to substitute US assistance for bloc or other Free world aid;

3. We should encourage the reestablishment of ties between Mali and France. In realistic terms of reducing bloc communist Chinese influence, the major substitute sources of aid are France, the EEC and international organizations. The key step in this process will be Malian reentry into the Franc Zone with its corollary implications for Malian economic policy.[12]

This growing antagonism in the competition for influence between the two camps created a profitable dilemma among the third world countries. With the two superpowers providing a wide array of assistance, the third world countries found that help was always right around the corner, in exchange for openness to certain ideas, products and other logistical needs of the superpower. Mali, as well as many developing countries, began to understand the rules of the game more than the main players themselves and sought assistance wherever they could get the most in return, regardless of political orientation. The strengths and weaknesses of the ideological competitors were well known and were played by African leaders to achieve their personal goals.

Mali leaned toward the communist bloc but remained receptive to the West, well beyond the fall of the Berlin wall in 1989.

It was in that environment of political gamesmanship that my own academic scholarship to the Soviet Union was offered. A direct consequence of the cold war, twenty six years after Mali's independence.

---

[12] *National Intelligence Estimate draft, 10/28/65 MALI – CASS. US ob jectives pp. 1-4. By Heinz Weber*

2 On to Kishinev
a. Getting there

In June of 1986, as the high school final written tests ended, students started to prepare for their oral exams. History, Economical Geography and English were the subjects to master. Everybody, somewhere deep inside, fantasized about a scholarship to study abroad.

It is the time of the year, every year, that Malians sharpen their already good general knowledge. They do so by discussing foreign affairs within small groups of friends called "grins" (chatting friends seated in the dooryard, boiling and serving Malian or Chinese tea, even to strangers passing by). At the grin, just like at the barber's or in a taxicab, one could hear all kinds of conversations about anything anywhere. From the prince of Brunei's fortune to Marilyn Monroe's affairs with the Kennedy brothers; from the neighbor's plan to marry a second wife to Lenin's impotence. Everybody had something to say about anything around the world.

One beautiful late afternoon, after a light rain had sprinkled the red lateritic roads, thus perfuming the neighborhood, our small grin gathered at my friend's door. When an acquaintance passed by, studies abroad became the predominant subject as somebody asked when the gentleman got back from Europe and if he ever graduated. Among us was a former student from the USSR who, in fact, did not graduate.

He began to explain why he could not stay in a country we always had reservations about. He said that he pretended to be mentally ill in order to be repatriated as soon as possible, less than a year in Kiev, the capital of Ukraine. He added that the city was like a big jail without entertainment, and that foreign students were spied on even in their rooms and bathrooms. "It is a dead place and that is why I came up with my cast iron alibi to escape. There were no nightclubs, movies or bars to frequent peacefully. Places that young adults cannot live without", he added.

He also mentioned a girl that we all knew, and described her agony. She was in the hospital and cried every night, demanding to be sent back home.

The grin dispersed soon after, and I will bet, each one of us had a little thought about the place and the remaining students.

A few weeks later, the results of the oral exams came out and we the graduates entered the "hope" phase. Everybody longed for a scholarship to pursue a degree abroad, preferably in the West somewhere. Scholarships would come from all over the world, since Mali remained non-aligned and in good terms with all sides of the world political spectrum.

With the cold war in mind, the USSR, its allies, the West and many other countries provided thousands of scholarships to the Malian government and to other organizations. They were the ultimate prize for every graduate.

Soon after graduation, I applied at two medical schools in France (Paris and Lyon) and also joined the ranks of those who converged on the Department of Education or several other organizations, handling scholarships. It still is one of the most stressful times of the year, as every student's future is on the balance.

After a few weeks in that scholarship quest, a first answer came from France. The Claude Bernard University of Lyon (A big southern city, where my brother-in-law lived), accepted my application and was expecting me in the first week of September. I was more than delighted to start my medical checkups and document my superb health, in order to secure my student visa.

One day, coming from the Department of Education and in a good mood, my younger sister greeted me and said: "Why are you working on whatever you are working on in town? You are going to Moscow." I still do not know what made her say that out of the blue, I got mad at her for the innocent gag and did not want to hear anything on the subject.

Then, one scorching night several days after the incident with my sister, I asked a friend for some cold water to drink. "Do you not want Siberia?" He replied, referring to the coldest part of the USSR. My subconscious instantly connected the two events, and made them sound like an omen regarding my next destination. An internal battle then ensued between my hopes and these unrelated coincidences. I tried to block it out by motivating myself with a potential departure for Lyon. As I got halfway through my medical tests for France, the government issued the list of scholarship recipients for the USSR. By destiny, my name was with those college-bound students, leaving to study Agronomy there. That was followed by a radio address requiring us to show up at the Department of Education in preparation for the trip.

My dilemma could not be worse, and my heart skipped a beat anytime my mind entertained an eventual trip to the USSR - the "big jail". Nevertheless, I was constantly reminded from within that I was leaving to discover something different, and best yet paid for entirely, compared to at least seven very expensive years in France.

We were not that rich by any stretch of the word, but we had everything we needed to be among the happiest kids on earth. My parents put everything they had into food, books and our education. Soccer was my love and I played it each and every afternoon. On weekends we would pick each other up on motor bikes (two of which belonged to my sisters) and travelled to different counties to test our talents. I even made my debut with a division I team of the capital, as I was contemplating a professional soccer career in France. Then, one day my mom asked me a poignant question: How would you live your life without a diploma, if you get injured playing at the professional level? I was not prepared for such blank question, and did not have a good answer for it. It did get me thinking hard about staying in school or turning pro.

A trip to France would have been quite a financial challenge and I am not sure we could have pulled it off.

In the end, financial considerations tilted the balance toward the mysterious but intriguing USSR, with a young and charismatic leader named Gorbachev. Paging through the list of scholarship recipients, I saw the names of many colleagues and close acquaintances from prominent families. That ultimately eased a bit my anxiety about the now inevitable journey that felt at times, like one without return.

By now all the grantees had been summoned to the Department of Education to start the long and painful paperwork associated with any trip abroad. The halls of the department looked like a market place, full of people looking for irresponsible clerks who had not yet made the decision to show up for work. Those who made it to work, wandered in other offices, chatting with colleagues about the latest soccer game. Others pretended to work, with their faces in a pile of insubstantial documents, and reminding students to be quiet or come back after lunch - a sure way to miss any decision-maker.

One bright side of my multiple trips to these departments, was the collateral friendships I was forced to make by running into the same students over and over again. Day after day, I would rub shoulders with the same people in the halls, clinics or at the photo shop. I ended up making a lot of new friends, rendering the whole process palatable. Within that huge crowd were other scholarship recipients going to the US, Bulgaria, China, Denmark, Egypt, France, Germany (East & West), Hungary, Italy, India, Japan, Malaysia, Libya, Morocco or even Syria.

Overall though, there were two kinds of scholarships, one through public schools, and the second through different organizations or unions (labor, women, youth etc.).

The Soviet Embassy asked us to provide fifteen pictures and fill out pages upon pages of documents. I was taken aback at first, but concluded that these were the Soviets we were dealing with, and one could always expect the unexpected from them. That attitude stemmed from the fact that an average Malian understood little about them and was always surprised by some of their comportments. Like this corner store owner who once asked if the Soviets were real "whites" after a brief encounter with one client. The latter asked if he could purchase more than one loaf of bread (because of the rationing in the Soviet Union) before putting them under his arm pits. Also odd, was the way they all dressed in the same khaki uniform, lived in the same compound and got bused to movies or their culture center, never individually.

Later on we went to a meeting with a representative from the Soviet Embassy. Through a translator, he said that we would get our plane tickets and entry visas at the airport right before the flight. Dates and names again were to be communicated by radio. He also warned us about the cold at that time of the year in Moscow, and added that upon arrival every student would receive a supply of winter gear. Changing majors would also be possible once there, but only through our Embassy and the Soviet Department of Education. He also warned that breaking laws, engaging in political activities and interference in Soviet internal affairs would not be tolerated. Then it was our turn to ask questions. I was particularly interested in the possibilities of travel within and outside of the Soviet Union, fortunately somebody beat me to it. Our host nodded and stressed that we, of course, would be able to travel with the permission of the Soviet government. Nobody questioned the conditions under which one could get such a permission. It just did not cross our minds due to the freedoms we enjoyed and took for granted, at home. After extracting more information here and there from former students and those vacationing home, I ended up with two unanswered questions: Is the USSR that bad? And if it is, why do we not see more students returning home like the one who faked an illness? Only time would tell me.

Soon, the dates and names were announced on the radio, and I was scheduled to fly out on August 28, 1986. Now certain of the inevitable, I started to give away some of my personal items, from soccer jerseys to jeans, books, cassette tapes or soccer magazines I had been collecting for so long. The rational being that I would find new and different items at

31

my new destination. That gesture would later cost me greatly.

A week before my departure, I started to pay my last visits to all my close relatives, friends and even acquaintances. At every stop, people wished me well and told me stories about a friend, a neighbor or their own child. Cases were very different, but more discouraging than appealing. Some students came back home very rich, some without a diploma, some mentally ill, some others with unfaithful spouses. Unfortunately many others returned in their caskets from unexplained deaths. Filled with doubts, stereotypes and conflicting information, I began to pacify myself from a religious standpoint by acknowledging the role of fate and destiny in all of this.

Finally, the D-day arrived. That Thursday, Aeroflot (The Soviet airline) had organized a special flight alongside the regular weekly one, to carry more students. The check-in time was 7:30 AM and the boarding was at 9:30 AM. I asked my friend to take me to the airport very early, anticipating any delay we might encounter.

I had my last breakfast with my mother and my stepfather in a very tense atmosphere. Knowing my mom, I was anxiously waiting for the last advice she had 'cooked' all night. As a teacher, she loved giving advices to anybody of any age, whenever she felt like it. She would not miss the slightest opportunity to steer people in the right direction. Some of our most dreaded moments were, when my friends and I would say goodbye to her, on our way out to the movie or to meet other friends. More often than not, we found ourselves spending an entire hour listening to what we thought were unwarranted lessons, but which I now know were worthy advices. I even remember a first cousin saying that he preferred to be spanked than to go through mom's hours of moral lectures. However, this time, right before my trip, she looked like she was the one about to receive some advice. Her eyes were turning red and her facial muscles simply could not hide her true internal feelings. Just before I finished my breakfast, she looked me in the eyes and said, "You are not a kid anymore, never forget where you come from (a great and proud family) and make sure to preserve the dignity of the family. Make her (family) prouder by graduating with good grades and do not let anybody lead you astray". My stepfather, a man of few words, was sitting across the table from me and mentally reviewing his own speech. Right on queue he addressed the problems of tobacco, alcohol and women. "Do not let anybody mislead you with the old rumor that you cannot make it through the winter without drinking alcohol," he added. "Moreover, as far as women are concerned, do not let them destroy you; secure your future and they will find you themselves". My mom then added a popular saying: "If you die because of one woman, hundreds will bury you". These were the last pieces of advice I got before my departure to the airport. My mom finally gave me her left hand, as we do in Mali whenever somebody travels far away and for a long period of time. She started to cry out loud, I then shook her left hand and got in the car.

At the airport, there was no place to sit down as there were more accompanying relatives than passengers. Some students came two hours after the announced time, convinced that Aeroflot is never on time, as others took their last pictures. At noon, I said good-bye to my second sister, her husband and some friends that could not wait anymore. The traffic by Aeroflot's counter was jammed and there was still no news about our special flight. At about 1:30 p.m. the Soviet diplomat showed up with hundreds of tickets and visas in his hand, followed by his interpreter holding a list only to disappear again. From time to time I would send my flight attendant sister to enquire, but she always returned with some vague information. I started to doubt everything regarding that Moscow trip and did not know what to tell to my remaining delegation. So we sat, stood, talked, took pictures and fell silent as we desperately waited for Aeroflot to get its act together.

Finally, our two stars came back out and started to read names, handing a ticket and a visa to the lucky ones. At the end of that process, half of the students stayed behind and was to wait until next Thursday. For them all the invested time, nerves and money went down the drain and the annoying part was still to come. In Mali, that extra week would feel like a year because of all the gossip from friends and foes alike, as one would face questions about staying behind. People would smile with the corner of their mouths and ask ironically, "Oh, you did not go, I thought you were there already, what happened?" Others with a big smile would tease by asking: "How are the Moscovites doing?" These are people you never expected to know much about your daily life. Nonetheless, after few years abroad, I came to acknowledge that this interest of one in another was a charming side of our culture. It makes you feel human, part of the society as a whole. You make news for a while; people get wind of it and have some fun with it. I would later crave that warmth in Europe and the US, where people do not even know their neighbors, much less about their cancelled trips.

We waited another three hours before starting to board right after the passengers of the regular weekly flight. Suddenly, the flight attendants stopped and ordered us to go to the other side of the plane, where all the suitcases were lying on the ground. We were each supposed to identify our luggage, because they had found a suitcase without a tag that had to be identified. For security reasons, that procedure was a must, but it killed another hour.

At last, we took off around 5 p.m. exhausted, hungry and dispirited. In the plane, a friend sitting by me pointed at some Russian signs overhead and said, "See those hieroglyphs, pretty soon they will be as familiar to you as your mother tongue." I did not have a clue about those signs, as I had chosen German as a second language in high school. However, his remark briefly loosened up an otherwise grim atmosphere.

After stops in Ouagadougou - Burkina Faso and Tripoli - Libya, the pilot gave us a very smooth welcome landing in the heart of the Communist bloc - Moscow. Through the windows, I could see several officers dressed in very beautiful coats, seeming to monitor something around. The picture reminded me of a high-jacked plane sitting on a foreign tarmac, and surrounded by guards while phone negotiations took place.

Next, in the hallways, I could notice one officer standing at every corner all the way up to immigration check points. The emotionless faces of the immigration officers fed my prejudice about the Soviets and secrecy.

Then, custom agents opened just about every piece of luggage on our flight without major incident. However, I could see an acquaintance being held back, while an agent pulled a colorful silky fabric out of his suitcase. He then started to measure the fabric by holding it up against himself with his arms stretched. My acquaintance seemed very nervous as he answered questions. The officer was shaking his head as if to say no. I later learned that the fabric was one that students would buy in Berlin or Paris and sell on the black market to Soviet dealers. They would then market it in the Southern Islamic republics of the Union, for a fortune. My acquaintance apparently lucked out because this was his very first trip to the USSR.

Finally, we all met in the lobby and got introduced to the Association of Malian Students in the USSR, headed by the cultural counselor of the Embassy. After a warm welcome, we got into two buses. Two of my flight- mates, Barry and Maia, sat near each other, and a guy I just met named Fidel sat next to me. He asked a ton of questions about my people back home in order to uncover any relationship we may have. We indeed found out that we were somehow connected through a family where he used to rent a room.

Between rounds of questioning from my new friend, I managed to think about this new world I was entering. My first impressions were that Moscow looked like any other world big city, clean with good roads. The cars seemed either very small or too big; reminding me of the huge American cars of the 80s we used to call "big boats." The Cheremetyevo International Airport in turn had nothing to envy from any European one, to the contrary it outclassed many of them.

Before my mind could move on to the next curious thing about my new world, Fidel butted in again. "What kind of women do you like?" he asked precipitously, before proceeding to show me some pictures from his wallet. "See this one, she is from Poland, this other one is from here and this one is from Czechoslovakia. I stay by her most of the time," he added. "This country is full of women. What is your type?" he asked again. "I do not know yet, we will see," I replied uncomfortably.

"Just keep in touch and I will introduce you to some lady friends, especially if you stay around here in Moscow," he added. I did not know what to say to a guy I just met literally minutes ago, who so casually opened his private life to me. His comments took me right back to those of a friend in Bamako about lots of women in the USSR. I started to ask myself if there ever were a country without lots of women, and why were people here so obsessed with that theme? Then Fidel began to enquire about Maia and the nature of her relationship with Barry.

When I got another chance to talk, I asked about the destination of the two buses, and our eventual fate beyond the airport. He explained that we were going to a hotel named "Hotel Universitaire" where all foreign students settle for couple of days before being sent off all over the Soviet Union, with some staying right there in Moscow. After a good hour's trip through Moscow, we finally stopped near a set of buildings with a packed courtyard. I was puzzled by the sight of so many people from different backgrounds. I have never seen so many different ethnicities gathered at one place. Some were wandering around, others were sitting on the brick walls or playing games, some others were still queuing with their luggage trying to get inside the "Hotel Universitaire." We were told to get our belongings from the buses and follow the guide. We entered the lobby to find more people sitting on their luggage, or leaning against the walls, trying to catch up on lost sleep. Expecting the same fate, we were told to hang around. We managed to settle somewhere in that bazaar-like atmosphere, psychologically ready to kill time. Barry, Maia and I then started to bombard Fidel with questions about himself, our future and everyday life in this part of the world. He said he was a student in Poltava, a small city of 50,000 inhabitants about 88 miles from Moscow. He knew a lot of people, said to have connections at the Malian Embassy in Moscow, which sounded like a good thing for anybody looking to change majors. He talked about travels to all the big cities in Europe (Berlin, London, Paris, Helsinki etc.) and the kind of business all students do to make ends meet. He knew almost all the students we asked about, and even tried to call some of them.

He enlightened us about the rate of the Russian ruble against the Dollars, how easy or hard it was to travel and what was available or not in the Union. Then, Fidel got to the core subject - our near future. He repeated that we would be staying for about two days and then be sent off to other parts of the country. There, in those villages, cities or towns, we would stay for a year to learn the language. Then we would either be sent somewhere else for the next five university years, or stay in the same town, if one's major was available there. We started to enquire about the best places of the Soviet Union to live. Fidel insinuated that it would depend on who would be there to hang around with, and what one enjoys as favorite pastime, before changing the subject. He then left with Maia to call some people they both knew so that they could come and visit. It was about three when Barry and I went back to our stuff in the lobby, where the crowd seemed to have grown. We saw new people coming and some still getting keys to their rooms. Then, a long-time soccer buddy of mine named Morrison showed up in time to lower our adrenaline level. He had just gotten back from Berlin and was heading in the next few days to Kishinev (Republic of Moldavia) where he was studying. We started catching up so entertainingly that we forgot about our situation. Then two sisters that I knew since Bamako also came just to see who else made the trip, and promised to take me to the Kremlin.

In the midst of the fun, we finally got called to get our keys. I shared a tiny room with four other students, possibly from Laos or Vietnam. We could not speak to each other, but some international signs helped break the silence. I put my belongings under the bed, took a quick shower and laid down to ponder. With closed eyes I felt homesick, regretful and a bit sorry for myself in this new milieu. I was already missing everything and everybody back home. In this new world I was nobody, just another digit at the mercy of the system. What a contrast with my joyful town and high school years, when I was a semi popular rising soccer star. To break the sorrow, I decided to get out and find my colleagues. Once reunited in the lobby, we set out to find the others and make plans. At every floor and right by the elevator, was a lady seated at a table to check documents. She stopped us by yelling in Russian, and the only word we could understand was passport. We handed ours over and she showed us the way. We could not believe that an ID was needed in the same hotel between floors. Some said that this was just a side of the monitoring machine we were going to encounter from now on. That reminded me of the notion David referred to at the grin back in Bamako, about students being spied on even in the bathrooms. We shrugged and decided to later meet in the lobby in order to go eat supper at a state restaurant.

On our way there, we met two officers who looked at us, said something to each other and laughed at us. I got upset but could not do anything about it, not even confront them because of the language barrier.

The next morning, many Malian students came to meet their friends. Morrison showed up as promised, and we gathered in the lobby. He told us as a mentor that, there was not much to do or buy in the country. So, foreign students would travel to Europe to stock up on basic necessities like toothpaste, breakfast cereals, perfumes, underwear, etc. I asked about soccer gear like what I had just given away before leaving. He said that was a big mistake and now I would have to wait until winter break to place an order with somebody going abroad. Or, I would have to wait until the summer break to go myself. When I asked about the possibility of traveling myself next winter, he replied that the Soviets did not allow new students to travel right away. He added that the Soviets have their own sports gear that no one wanted; they are very ugly and poorly designed, he stressed.

Morrison reiterated that we would soon be sent all around the country to different cities and towns. "There are some ghost cities you do not want to go to," he advised. "Those cities or villages are like prisons, the Soviet Union itself is like a big prison; so imagine a prison within a prison. These 'prisons' are mostly in the southern Soviet Republics or areas toward Siberia in the far East. You should refuse to go, if by misfortune you get sent there this afternoon or tomorrow morning. Baku in Azerbaijan, Tashkent in Uzbekistan, and Dushanbe in Tajikistan among others, are impossible places

38

for foreigners. In case of emergency, you will rot there before anybody could help. These 'ghost cities' are hostile to humanity, period."

"In case you are scheduled to go to one of them, you will have to refuse categorically. Be psychotic, hysteric and crazy; they might change your itinerary. This old trick worked for some people before, and you will not lose anything by trying." This is serious stuff I thought and did not want to even imagine myself in the circumstance. I only wished none of us would have to go through that nightmare.

Already in the afternoon, some girls came rushing into the lobby with a list. They started shouting the names of some cities followed by those of foreign students expected to go there. A dead silence reigned inside, while those who had already learned their fate, cried or celebrated outside. It was like learning the results of a critical exam. My heart was racing and my legs could barely support me. Suddenly, I heard my name for Kishinev; "You are going to Kishinev, the capitol of the republic of Moldavia," repeated the announcer. It was the same Kishinev where Morrison said he resided, and would be going in few days. I felt blessed and briefly forgot about my colleagues. After processing the news, I wandered around looking for them. I could not find anybody in the lobby, so I decided to check in their rooms. Rushing from the elevator, I almost ran past the concierge on the floor in my haste. She yelled at the top of her lungs, "Passport! Passport," and tried to physically stop me. I gave up and handed over my document. Down the hallway, I pushed the door open while knocking and found a small crowd trying to comfort Maia. She was sitting on her bed, her big eyes full of tears, were ruby red. She remained silent and seemed filled with hate. Barry told me that they both were being sent to Baku, one of the 'ghost cities' of the Union to be avoided at all costs, according to Morrison. Barry was baffled by Maia's tears and did not seem to care about this verdict that could change their lives. When asked, he said, like a big optimist, "I have never been there, so I will go check it out," with the smile of a con man.

Fidel then decided to try to do something about the "tragedy" at hand. He went downstairs with Maia to make some calls. He pretended that not only could he change her destination, but better yet, he could arrange for her to stay in Moscow. Maia looked perplexed and Fidel's failure to get in touch with anybody at the Mali Embassy was tearing her inside. He was going back and forth, citing names of head honchos that would not have any difficulty changing her destiny. He would return from the pay phone shaking his head and whispering some words. Then he would say that the cultural counselor was on the other line, or away from his desk. Our poor friend put all her hopes and dreams in Fidel and was petrified by the prospect of going to Baku.

My train to Kishinev was scheduled for seven o'clock the next day, with our bus leaving the hotel for the rail station by 5. In the morning the two sisters came to get me and Barry for a tour of Moscow. We badly wanted to see the Kremlin and Red Square we heard so much and knew so little about. We hopped on a bus to the nearest metro station, and I could not believe what I saw down under. The stations were very deeply dug, and the gigantic escalators were about two hundred feet long, transporting hundreds of people at about a 45 degree angle. The stations were all in marble, very clean and spacious without a single graffiti or advertisement. I was later told that the subway system was purposely designed this way to serve as shelters during wars or other calamities.

The long trains were as spotless as the stations, without a single beggar in the long and winding corridors. We also saw many militiamen at their headquarters at each and every station, keeping the peace. I was very impressed by the state of the Metro network and could not help but compare it to the smaller, and graffiti-laden French Metro system.

We got out right next to Red Square and took an unforgettable guided tour of the place. We then decided to wander around Red Square when suddenly, a young Soviet man approached us and started to point at Barry's black leather jacket. Our friends interpreted it all, and said that the man just wanted to buy the black leather jacket for about 400 dollars. Barry converted that into French francs and decided that the amount was too low. The young man started bargaining, but our friends told Barry that it was illegal to sell imported items to the

Soviets. The poor man insisted, and followed us a little way on the bridge, risking his own safety, before giving up.

Our delightful tour of the city had to be cut short in order to catch the bus to the rail station. At five o'clock, our driver was not there and I started to panic again, reliving previous episodes. By five-thirty we were almost certain that our bus was not coming anymore. I feared that missing this trip could send us to one of the dreaded ghost cities. Nobody could tell us what was going on, or what would happen if our bus did not show up at all.

Finally, the bus pulled in and the race against time begun. The driver was humming something, making signs to hurry while grabbing people's luggage. In this chaos, we managed to say goodbye to the others, promising to use the Embassy to get in touch. We waved through the window and soon disappeared in the traffic, which was now our enemy to overcome. A heavy silence settled over the bus. The immensity of the city, and the rush hour were too challenging for our already-edgy driver. Everybody was silently and helplessly waiting for the next event, whatever that might be.

After racing between cars and navigating through shortcuts, we finally arrived at the Kiev railroad station. By the time the driver threw all our belongings out on the platform, and pointed his finger toward our train, it was already moving. We ran as fast as possible and jumped on board the last car and started moving toward the front. The conductors were gesturing for us to go further because we did not even know the number of our compartments.

Some passengers looked shocked, while others were laughing at us. We decided to keep going toward the front of the train until we saw some empty compartments. Passing from one car to another turned out to be very dangerous. The heavy and greasy green doors at the end of each train car slowed us down considerably. One had to pull them open with one hand and carry the luggage with the other, while literally standing on a small metallic platform. While on that tiny swiveling bridge, I could see the rail road rocks flashing by. The deafening rumble of the diesel engine and that of the wheels against the rails in that no-man's-land, was terrifying and made my heart pound out of my chest.

We repeated this same maneuver over and over again. One little misstep could have led to serious injuries or death. Ironically, it was precisely there that we would also go pee when toilets were busy or locked at night by the conductors. Because of the rush to the rail station, nobody had gotten a ticket or even a simple letter saying who we were and where we were headed. After a long and awful quest, we finally reached some unoccupied compartments that we gladly claimed after carrying our luggage through dozen others. These compartments were dimly lit and had four beds with no sheets or mattresses on them. I put my stuff away, took a deep breath, and let myself fall on one of the lower beds. My mouth was dry, my legs shaking and I could smell my own sweat every time I moved. We were now on our own without tickets, money or any knowledge of the language. It was almost nine o'clock by the time we had settled in, and made sure everybody was on board. Tired, hungry and dirty, we looked for anything to nibble on before making accommodations to go to sleep. I reached into my bags and got some of my grandma's fried peanuts out. My roommates also pulled out their meager resources and we all ate. Not knowing what surprise was next, I kept my shoes on in case of any possible rushed exit, because none of us knew our arrival time in Kishinev, nor the number of stops before our final destination. I barely slept, waking up every time the train slowed down or stopped. There were many of them, even in the heart of the forests, or in little towns or villages. Later on, I learned that those frequent stops were needed for a number of reasons: refueling, taking on or dropping off passengers or giving way to an oncoming train. Other stops were timed to avoid passing through some sensitive areas during daylight time, the government did not want foreigners to see.

Early in the morning the next day, we all met in the corridor one by one, most likely awakened by a dire hunger. After sharing night stories, we decided to look for something to eat and to find out more about our journey.

Now the dilemma was that we did not speak any Russian, and only carried the precious foreign currencies our dear parents had put aside for us. But, we could not use these notes on the train anyway; our French francs or dollars were just like paper, unusable. It was only at a bank or in specialized stores that one could use foreign currency, as Fidel had told us few days earlier.

We headed to the restaurant and started to make our case to the waitress, unsuccessfully. We all tried to get through to her, but she just laughed, making some signs and saying things I had never heard. We gave up talking to her, and sat down in the restaurant looking for other ways to satisfy our howling stomachs.

In that limbo, we spotted a foreigner seated at a table not far from us who seemed unworried. We approached him, and one of us said hello in French. He replied with a little smile as if he knew that we were newcomers in trouble. It turned out that he was a student from Mali going to Kiev, the city my acquaintance David back home, escaped from. He told us that this would be his third year there, that the next stop was in half an hour, and that Kiev was about halfway between Moscow and Kishinev. He gave us some rubles and taught us few basic words in Russian like "tchai" for tea, a very widely served commodity on the train. Our savior also asked why we did not have any money left for the trip, since everybody was supposed to receive three rubles in Moscow. We all looked at him with dropped jaws. "Did you not get three rubles each for the trip, from the girl that informed you about your destination?" he asked. "Well, she is filthy rich by now. The SOB just pocketed 100 rubles richer, a whole monthly salary for an engineer". He give us some more rubles before getting off in Kiev.

The stress and anxiety made the trip longer. The landscapes were all alike, and so were the people getting on and off at every station. Their stares, malicious smiles, suspicious whispers and laughs became unbearable as we neared Kishinev. It would be an understatement to say that we felt unwelcome, and peeved by what we had gone through so far in the USSR. We knew, however, that there was no going back, especially for many of us whose options were limited. I came to the conclusion that I was starting what could psychologically be a long and painful six-year stay in the communist paradise. Now all I had to do was to load up with more patience, courage and determination.

As we approached Kishinev, we started to pull out our belongings to avoid being caught by surprise again, as night had already fallen. Finally, the train slowed down and came to a stop. We walked through the dark towards the only lit building between the rails. Halfway to the station, we met a Malian student with someone we assumed was a Russian teacher. They quickly greeted us and led us to the minivan that was waiting in the parking lot. The teacher introduced herself in English as Natasha, and told us that there was another van for the rest of the group, so we split. They left for the dorms of the university as we headed to the Agriculture institute.

b. Dorm Life

The ride was very quiet as everybody was busy looking out the windows, to get a glimpse of our new foster-city Kishinev. It took about fifteen minutes to get to the dorms, which were in a big yard with almost all the windows opened and lit. We got our bags out of the van and followed Natasha. She instructed us to queue up, to either get our keys or go straight to the room and find our Soviet roommate(s).

I was in the second category. She indicated that mine was number 55 and on the third floor. I walked upstairs with my belongings through freshly painted hallways and wet floors covered with newspapers. To my surprise, I could not find my room. Suddenly, I saw a tall guy coming toward me with a big smile. "Are you from Mali, and just got here?" he asked. "Yes, and I cannot find my room on this third floor," I replied. He laughed and told me that this was not the third, but the fourth floor, because the Soviets count the lobby as first, so our first is their second floor. I shook my head and followed him one floor down.

He was a student from Mali, too, who had gotten there a week or two before us. I managed this time to find my room, few doors away from the big common kitchen. I knocked at the door and dragged my luggage in. There were two young Soviet students, each laying in a single bed, separated by two wooden night stands, with their books and hair brushes. I put

45

my stuff on the remaining bed right by the door, and said hello in French to my roommates. They got up, shook my hand, and told me their names by pointing at themselves: Sasha and Tolea. I did the same and pointed at the cupboard, the third bookshelf and at myself, enquiring if they belonged to me. They explained that the shelf was mine, but the cupboard was for all of us, and they moved some of their bottled food to make room. I got my soccer cleats out, and asked if there was a place to use them. They both pointed outside the window to a field that I would explore the next day. While I was unpacking, they were all over my old Sony tape player as if it were from another planet. Then they both left, certainly to notify their friends about their new roommate. When I got done putting my things away, I did the same and found other Malians introducing themselves to their Soviet roommates. After a brief tour of the dorm, I came back to my room to reflect on my very first days in the Soviet Union. I put my suitcase under my bed with the $600 I was given when I left home. I did not know where else to put my fortune, and was very worried about losing it. I then hung some pictures on the decorative piece of carpet, protecting the wall by each bed.

After hanging up my familiar items, I went on to see the bathroom. Three doors down the hallway, was a very low-ceilinged double room with just a doorway between them. The first one with a sink, and the second one with five toilet seats next to each other without separating walls. The windows were open, letting in an early fall breeze, cold enough to make you shiver. The water was running in the stained toilet bowls, constantly flushing them. I looked around in shock and disbelief, as my mind refused to process the fact that this most private place was rendered so public. Before Kishinev, I had never encountered such a set-up for bathroom, not even in the world's poorest regions. I have seen holes in the ground, bushes or fields used as bathrooms, but even in those cases, privacy was always paramount. And here I was supposedly in Europe, looking at the worst toilets yet. All of a sudden, one of my mom's numerous sayings rang in my head: "You do not know that you got it good until you get it bad." Once again, the Soviets had surprised me with something I could not even

46

imagine in my wildest dreams.

The kitchen was a big room with a large table in the middle and two stoves for the entire third floor. It had just been remodeled for the occasion, and stunk fresh paint like every other place in the dorm, for that matter. The wooden floor, painted in dark brown, was still tacky. The garbage bins were hidden under the table and half empty. I stood there and reluctantly imagined myself cooking, or fixing a meal of some sort, to be exact. That would be quite a challenge for someone who had never stepped in a kitchen, thanks to my mom, sisters and countless invisible maids who still help in an average Malian family. After that brief tour of the two most important places on the floor, I returned to my room and put more things away. Later, I needed to go to the bathroom, but once there I heard people talking, so I went back to my room. A few minutes later, I went again, hoping to have the room to myself. I met other foreign students in the hallway, probably looking for the same privacy I was after. Once in the bathroom, I saw two Soviets squatting side by side over the toilet bowls and chatting out loud to overcome the noise of the running water. I ran back to my room again, frustrated and unable to break that cultural barrier. I postponed my trip to the bathroom again, hoping to be alone in there at a later hour.

My roommates were already in bed and reading their newspapers before going to sleep. I kept busy again for another half hour before deciding to go, no matter what. This time the room was empty, and I heaved a sigh of relief. But, a few minutes later, a foreign student came rushing in. He promptly stopped when he saw me, but proceeded anyway. He was also uncomfortable, but evidently had no choice. I imagine this was also his first time sharing this most private moment. I will never forget that first night in the communal toilet, Soviet style.

When I finally got in bed, I tossed around for hours. The events in my new life where unfolding in front of my eyes and kept my mind busy. My single bed was not the greatest either; the springs were so loose that my back almost touched my suitcase under the bed, every time I turned over. Physically, I was sore from my 36-hour trip, and here I was bowed in a bed

47

that was probably as old as the dorm. The noise of people walking on the wooden floor in the hallway did not help, either. That first night, I questioned everything about the trip.

The next morning, we went to our language school across the soccer field to receive our first 80-ruble monthly stipend. We also met the dean of the language school, who many said was a KGB member ordered to monitor all of us. I think we all started then to develop some paranoia or a KGB-phobia that never left us. Even if we were all innocents at that time and had nothing to hide, we all dreaded the unknown, a faceless enemy living among us.

We got called one after the other into the accountant's room to sign our names and receive 77 rubbles instead of 80, because of the three rubles we supposedly got in Moscow for the train trip. We were also briefed that the next day, one of our elder compatriot would accompany us to the polyclinic for our first complete medical visit, and that we should all bring urine and stool samples along.

One senior named Moses was to lead us there. He told us to meet him in the yard right outside of our dorms, around seven o'clock the next morning. He explained that we would be given containers at the polyclinic for urine samples, but that we all should collect the stool samples in an empty matchbox that night or first thing in the morning. That was our first homework ever.

I went back to the dorm, and while observing my new place and talking with my roommates, a group of three Soviets entered our room without knocking. They made us stand up, and proceeded with a short introduction. The older one said his name, and stressed that he was the "commandant," or head, of the dorm. The second one, a body builder with strong arms and wide shoulders, was the head of the third floor and a freshman in college. The last one was just a friend of theirs, who was visiting my roommates. I understood that we should refer to them with any question or problem, and that we should also stand up any time they entered our room. That last comment made my blood boil, and the language barrier made matters worse. I started to rattle in the languages I knew, that I would not put up with that rule of subordination to simple fellow students. They mumbled back to me something in Russian, and we all went our ways. That was my very first confrontation.

Getting up the next morning was as hard as falling asleep. Somehow, everybody made it on time, and Moses led us to a nearby public restaurant for breakfast, then to the bus station right behind the language school. However, we soon learned from one student that he could not find his matchbox, left in the bush by the entrance of the restaurant. Moses himself was perplexed, and did not have anything to add. We started to speculate about all kinds of scenarios. Some suggested that the KGB got hold of it and planned to frame somebody with it. Others said that kids took it, thinking that it was a real matchbox. Anyway, to this day I am still scratching my head over that. Fortunately, somebody promised to make an extra stool sample for him once at the clinic.

Moses got tickets for all of us, and we rode the trolley bus for about five stops. All the way to the clinic, the locals looked at us like we were Martians and kept pointing at us to friends and families. Once there, we waited again in the hall while Moses went in to talk to the doctor. I understood that he successfully bypassed the long queue and had the doctor take care of us right away.

The nurse handed out bottles for urine samples and they began calling us one by one into the office. Each student came out with a little smile from the corner of the mouth, without exactly saying what went on inside the room. Some said to wait our own turn if we really wanted to know, while others indicated that doctor and crew will be playing with us.

Finally, I got called in and the nurse started to fill out a form with my name on it, as a male doctor sat alone near the entrance. I sat in the chair next to him after handing my samples to the nurse. He checked my tongue, my teeth, and my ears before ordering me to take my shirt off so he could check my lungs, heart, armpit and skin, etc. Then he ordered me to stand up, drop my pants and spread my legs. So I did. He grabbed my penis, turned it anyway he pleased and checked my testicles by squeezing them in his palm before ordering me to dress and leave.

I left the room and proceeded as indicated with a string

49

of X-rays, which took until the afternoon. The day was long, unforgettable and the trip back to the dorms, very quiet. I suppose all of us, without exception, had just gone through something we never expected to experience. We later learned that at the university, where the other half of us went from the rail station, one Cuban student provided both urine and stool samples for all the rest of his community, as they unanimously refused to submit their own samples. What would have happened, had he tested positive for something? How could the hospital miss that?

After that ordeal, we had another consultation scheduled with another doctor who would eventually come to check us right on the first floor of our school. We were told to go to a designated room that day in the afternoon for a checkup. The same scenario like at the clinic was unfolding again. We were called in to see a doctor, not having the slightest clue about the nature of the visit. Students went in and out pretty steadily, but silently disappeared down the long hallway after doing their best to avoid eye contact.

When I entered the room, I saw a very skinny woman sitting on a rotating chair, ready to prey on me just like her colleagues did few days earlier. She had her long hair held together with a plastic band partially covered with a colorful hat. Her big eyes and long bony chin and nose gave her a sinister look in the poorly-lit room. I felt like visiting a witch doctor. Her spinning chair and a desk were the only furniture in the room with a strong hospital smell. She asked for my name and pulled out what would be my medical file for the rest of my student years. She started by checking my temperature, mouth, lungs etc. and then ordered me to drop my pants. I obeyed like a little boy listening to his mom at the doctor's. She too carefully examined my genitals and asked me to turn around, slightly bend over, spread my legs and hold my derriere opened in her face. She checked, then indicated to me that she was done. I dressed and waited for her findings. She gave me some big purple tablets to swallow right there. I too exited silently, but waited around for some friends to take their turns.

I did not know what to think or what to say about this

50

humiliating experience. I was speechless and worried about any future test. There was never a word about these very intrusive checkups from our diplomats, nor from the Soviets prior to our departure, nor from former students for that matter. Why nobody, officially or not, mentioned them to all newcomers?

Meantime, my friend's brother was trying to entertain me with some stories. He caught my attention when he started to laugh out loud as he shared a funny episode that had happened just after my exam. He said that his buddy from Ghana, having learned about the protocols of the examination from a fellow Ghanaian, went to the bathroom and never cleaned himself before seeing the lady doctor. He went in and followed all the steps until she told him to undress, turn around and hold his butt cheeks. He obeyed, took few steps back and shoved his smelly derriere right in her face. "Enough, enough!" she yelled at him, covering her nose with one hand and waving the other one up and down as to induce some air movement. For a moment I forgot my shocking episode and could not wait to see my other friends to break the news to them.

When we asked about the results of all the tests we had taken, we were told to not worry, because we would be contacted personally about any positive result. This was exactly the opposite of what we knew in our humble countries, where at least you got the documented results of any test you happened to undergo.

A few days later, some rumors started to go around that one of our Malian students had a disease called bilharziasis (when a parasite takes up residence in the urinary tract and makes the urine bloody). The Malian community was notified that the Soviets had decided to send him back home. The general secretary of the Malian community then asked if there were any possibility of getting some medicine from my doctor brother-in-law in France. The idea of seeing this student go home because of a very curable disease was unsettling.

We contacted the authorities to ask for some time to get the appropriate pills through one of the seniors (nicknamed ancients), on his way back from vacation in Paris. I called my brother-in-law in Lyon-France, to get at least a name of a prescription suitable for the case. Our general secretary then forwarded the name of the drug to the returning ancient, who brought the "lifesaving" drug. Without that, the Soviets would have contacted our embassy in Moscow to make arrangements and would have sent the poor guy home because of a curable disease.

In a related case, we heard about some of our compatriots being quarantined in Krasnodar (the Russian Federation) because of diarrhea. The Soviets there locked them up in a separate wing of the dorm without visitation, while they were dosing them up. Fortunately, they all recovered and resumed their language classes.

Another ancient warned us about getting sick in this country. "You set yourself up as a guinea pig for their uncontrolled experiments," he said.

These initial real-life incidents didn't help the mosaic picture we were forming about our hosts. Fortunately, the ancients were around to cheer us up and keep the morale if not high, at least at a decent level.

After these unpromising and demoralizing events, we met with the school staff and eventually started Russian language classes.

During the first official meeting, we were introduced to all the staff of the school, from the dean to the concierge of this old three story-building. We received information about the school year, which would begin with an intensive program enhanced with tapes and specialized teaching techniques. Then, three months later, we would start specialty Russian regarding the vocabulary of our specific fields: biology, math, physics etc.

We were also briefed about a general alarm in the dorm that would ring on every floor at six o'clock, every day except weekends. On top of that, there was a yellow AM radio in every room, without an on/off button, that was set on Radio Moscow and played the Soviet anthem every morning at six o'clock. That yellow AM radio, hanging on the wall right by the door, was a main source of news and music for our Soviet roommates.

In Kishinev, as in every town or city with Malian

students, there was an association called the Association of Malian Students in the USSR, with its headquarters in Moscow. The association organized a meeting right after our arrival in Kishinev to welcome and introduce us to all. Many of them came to visit and share some information about our future in Kishinev and beyond. I met some students, and heard of many more who were still on vacation. I gathered that everybody traveled outside the country when on vacation. Our ancients warned us to be strong in the face of disturbing and provocative situations we may face, especially with the limited Russian we spoke.

We enjoyed the close proximity of the classes, the stores, and the fact that many other Malians were at the veterinary school just next door. The soccer field in the middle was a godsend for many of us who saw an opportunity to get away right at home. Our elders encouraged us to visit them and each other as a cure for the monotony and inhospitality that would certainly mar our lives. Visits and sports became our favorite pastimes before they turn into perpetual unpleasant challenges.

Day to day life in the dorms was a little different from what we expected. There were some sets of rules that everybody had to abide by, but that did not always make sense. Every foreign student lived in a dorm, with or without a Soviet roommate, except the ones married to a native who could rent an apartment. No foreigner could rent or buy an apartment or a house, period. Since there were dorms across the campus that did not house foreigners, the dorms we lived in stood out and were known to all. In Kishinev, we revolved around only four main compounds where foreigners lived. Two locations were managed by the university and two others by the Agriculture Institute, with separate dorms for freshmen and "ancients" (sophomores, juniors and seniors). All the dorms, with or without foreigners, were built alike and under the same strict rules and regulations. Each was headed by a commandant in charge of the day-to-day management and repairs. Each floor also had a leader called 'starosta' or Resident Assistant in charge of the cleaning schedule. There was another schedule involving every student living in the dorm, for front desk duties along the concierge between 5 and 10 p.m. Everybody got to do that at least once a year. The students also elected their internal leaders and secretaries. Among all of the posts, the secretary of exit and admittance came to be the most significant of them all, and coveted by foreign students. We will see why.

Life inside the dorms was quite an experience, and getting in and out of them was dreadful. The internal regulations were read to us, and each of us received a copy of the brochure detailing them to the core.

A weekday, generally Wednesday, was set aside for cleaning. We were supposed to clean our rooms inside out. Those on duty according to the schedule, were to clean the bathrooms, the kitchen and take all the garbage out. In other dorms some of the rules were somewhat different. At the university the commandant of the dorm would shut off the electricity at bed time. All our friends there had a stock of candles in order to study later in the night. Noise was also prohibited, and any trespassing was reported to the secretary of foreign students in the dean's office. No alcohol, no guests before five o'clock or after 10 p.m. and no sleep overs. To get into any dorm, a strict registration protocol had to be followed. Guests had to deposit a photo ID card with the concierge or the student on duty at the front desk. The admittance and exit time, the room and person to be visited and the data from the ID were all recorded in a registry that subsequently went to the militia for review. The Soviets were required to show their student ID or driver license or their internal passports; foreigners only had to show a student ID. Trespassing could damage one's reputation in the dean's eyes or those of the secretary of foreign students, who could further cut some of the already limited rights. As we matured and got some counseling from the ancients, relations turned both testy and profitable. Testy because we learned each other's true colors over time and profitable, because we needed each other to satisfy some of our own hidden guilty pleasures. The Soviet authorities, on one hand, could give us permission to travel, have a late night party, pick our roommates or even dodge the cleaning schedule. We, on the other hand, could help them by bringing cheap goods from abroad they dreamed of all their lives. That symbiotic relation between foreign students and their wardens tainted each and every situation.

The front desk was the place where the friction would manifest itself the most, leading to some unpredictable conflicts. Our only sanctuary was the dorm, where we spent ninety-five percent of our time after classes. By visiting each other all the time, we were always confronted by the tough rules of the front desks, whether as hosts or as guests. When we first arrived, before getting our IDs, every visit turned into confrontational negotiations either to get in or to stay beyond ten or even overnight. Most of the time, we had to send somebody to get the ancient we wanted to visit, to come and negotiate with the concierge. Most of the ancients had their favorite one they had bribed before and could always reach a deal with. Sometimes, they stayed at the front desk late to retrieve our documents when everybody was away, especially the commandant. In those cases, even going to the bathroom was a cat and mouse game. We would first check in the hallway before stepping out, because the commandant always made a final round before joining his family in the basement.

There were also the nightmarish concierges, the ones that never compromised and would call the commandant or the militia to enforce their will. Sometimes we would run past the front desk and disappear in the dorms, and occasionally they would find us and call the commandant. After negotiations they would leave us in. Sometimes after passing the concierge, the commandant would stop us by misfortune when going to the kitchen or from room to room, later in the night. Some wicked commandants would send us home; some others would negotiate the leaving time. It was a hide-and-seek game we learned to enjoy because of the adrenaline rush it provided.

That strident regime at the front desks led to all kinds of unfortunate situations. Early on, anticipating and mitigating them, occupied more than one mind.

Inside, our roommates and fellow Soviet students were very interested in our lives, by curiosity and on behalf of the authorities to whom they reported every little event. My two Soviet roommates, Tolea and Sacha, welcomed me with open arms. Because of them, my Russian excelled in a very short period of time compared to my colleagues without Soviet roommates. We went from sign language to full conversation in three months. They were very friendly. Sacha seldom went home because of the long distance to his village, but Tolea did almost every weekend except during finals. Both always brought back bags of cooked food and huge bottles of home-made fruit drinks that they gladly shared with me. They introduced me to a lot of the Soviet cuisine made with meat and cabbage, and also homemade fruit beverages and bakery. Food was plentiful, cheap, and a bit strange in some cases. I could not remember the specific names of the dishes and all the different flavors of the drinks. But thanks to them, I put on almost twenty pounds by spring. We always had many of those big green bottles of drinks under the table that anybody could reach for at any given time.

To my surprise, they were fascinated by my old Sony tape player that was also my radio, clock and alarm clock. Sasha always had me set it for his special needs. According to my friends who came looking for me, Sacha and Tolea used my Sony all the time in my absence. They could not keep their hands off of it, and would call all their friends to our room around it, and play tape after tape while I was gone. They would put it back where it was, sitting the way I left it, thinking that I would not know. To verify the rumors, I zeroed the counter of the tape player as I left the room couple times. Sure enough, the counter would show that they had been using it. When I talked to Sacha about it, he did not deny it, and thought that it was OK since we were roommates and friends. I said that it was OK, as long as he asked first, and despite his insistence, I refused to tell him how I knew that they were using it behind my back.

Our relationship was pretty good, and they always helped me with my Russian homework. What they could not help with though, was my daily frustration over not being able to listen to the BBC or Radio France Internationale. Some afternoons I would be in tears trying to listen to the European soccer games I used to religiously follow from Mali. The Soviet authorities would jam the broadcast, especially at news time.

Since we almost all had Soviet roommates, it was not uncommon to share with other Malians, stories from day to day life with them. I can say without a doubt, that it was the case for our Soviet colleagues too. The majority of them had never met a foreigner before, much less live with a black or brown one in the same room. Cultural differences led to some pretty interesting situations, nobody could ever foresee. One day a Malian colleague told us that his roommate squeezed some of his toothpaste on a piece of bread for lunch. The poor guy later said that he thought it was a tube of mayonnaise, and decided to have a little snack. The nicely designed tube of the paste looked too appealing not to be edible.

On the other side, a Soviet colleague on the fifth floor pranked his Malian roommate for months about saluting the Soviet national anthem each and every morning as it played. Every day before bed, students would turn the volume of the yellow radio up in order to be woken up the next morning at 6 AM to the anthem of the country. So, a Soviet colleague told my countryman to respect the rules and had him get up every morning, put his hand on his heart and stand stock-still until the anthem was over. One day, after months of subordination, he innocently asked another Malian how he was coping with the cold morning salutes. When he found out that he was the only one duped into doing them, he was not very happy.

The female Soviet students and the front desk ladies had a particular take on how we dressed in the dorms. They could not stand seeing us in shorts in the hallways, either visiting each other or going downstairs to shower. Every encounter was a shouting match. They would go on a rant for minutes even though there was no way we could catch all that they were trying to convey. Then we fired back in our broken Russian mixed with French and Bambara, the Malian official and native languages. They would get furious because they could not understand what we were "mumbling" either.

We were incensed by one notion that kept coming back. "Nee Kulturna" was that dagger in the heart that nobody could tolerate. To us the words meant "without a culture" if you translated them literally word-for-word. Anybody who has spent some time in Mali or with Malian citizens would recognize their

57

exceptionally high and misplaced sense of pride. That sentiment is so prevalent that it makes them act sometimes against their own best interests. So, to tell us that we did not have a culture was unbearable. We could not stand to be called names, especially for wearing designer shorts like Adidas and Puma. We were very proud to show them off, knowing damn well that our male Soviet colleagues would die to possess them. That friction continued throughout my language year, and it would be an understatement to say that feelings were deeply hurt.

After numerous skirmishes, some enquiries, and with a few months of Russian under our belts, the light came on. The fact was, the Soviets saw our shorts as underwear (the natives wore shorts as underwear), and therefore were complaining about us walking around in our undergarments for everybody to see. The term they were dishing out at every turn actually meant: inappropriate, rude or indecent; not lack of culture as first assumed. What a cultural mix-up!!!

On the soccer field, we were taken by surprise by another deep cultural difference. When we played soccer, it was mostly us foreigners against them, the native Soviets. Looking back at it today, I wish we had mixed the teams up and played just for fun. Unfortunately the game was played as an international event between two legendary rivals. We played as though we were defending our honor, and on top of that, we teased without mercy like we did back home.

What we refer to as teasing in Mali would be defined as fanaticism or poor sportsmanship elsewhere. This phenomenon of teasing or making fun of cousins or a losing team was part of growing up. So, during those games, we would vociferously tease our opponents almost to tears. The same rivalry was displayed every time a Soviet team played a foreign one on TV.

In the basement, there was just one big bicameral room that served as bathroom for the entire dorm and for both genders. The two small rooms were without windows or air vents. The first was kind of a waiting room where you could hang your clothes before entering the real bathroom, per se. Its use was on a first-come-first-served basis. It could not accommodate all of us and would sometimes lack hot water. Coming from Mali, a shower with cold water in the fall was like pulling teeth. Many times some of us would resort to heating water on the two stoves in the collective kitchen. After soccer, you would hang around your room while waiting for the water to heat up in the kitchen. That would sometimes create a conflict with people trying to cook their evening meals. They would remove the water containers from the stove, rightly so, to make dinner, which again would delay our shower time late into the night. We would sometimes end up taking our shower in the toilet/laundry room to the dismay of fellow students getting ready for bed. There was one at every floor with many sinks and mirrors for washing hands, brushing teeth and doing laundry.

It was always best to check the situation in front of the shower beforehand if you had plans, because you could not take a shower whenever you felt like it. Needless to come down if women were in, with others waiting in line. Same case for women if men were in, as others queued up. Postponing shower time also resulted in more traffic late in the night. When we complained to our Soviet roommates, their response always was, "You do not need to take a shower every day, even the doctor advises not to." They were pretty content with the only situation they had known all their lives, not us.

In some other dorms, the week was divided: Monday, Wednesday, and Friday for men, and Tuesday, Thursday, and Saturday for women, with Sunday set aside for cleaning. One late night during my first year at the institute, I went down to the basement to take my shower, thinking that there would not be many people in line. Luckily enough, that was the case, because only one couple from another dorm was there waiting in the hallway. I asked about the situation in the bathroom, only to be told that some women were in there and that, as a couple they were waiting for them to finish so that they could get in and shower together. I gently told them that I would not wait that long. I suggested that the girl gets in now and showers with the other girls, and that I would get in with the boyfriend afterward. They said no, and insisted that it was their turn and they would not give it up. I tried again, explaining that a one-room shower is not made for couples to keep everybody else out while they monopolize the room. They refused to compromise, even though a growing number of male students were coming to line up. I finally told them that I would not wait for the women to finish and then wait for the two of them, too. The man replied that they would get in no matter what I thought. Soon enough, the ladies finished and exited. As I proceeded to enter, he pushed me away to allow his lady to get in. I held up the door so that he could not lock it from the inside. We pulled back and forth for a while, and then he let go to join her. I opened the door, got in and took off my pants (not my underwear) in front of them in that dimly-lit room. She screamed at the top of her lungs, yelled some unkind words and dashed outside at the speed of light. He was left to follow her or take a shower with me, and he chose the former. I then undressed completely and took my shower. The other cowards in the hallway, who never said a word as I argued with the couple, happily came in and started to condemn them for their selfish plan. By the time I got out, they were gone.

Another night, a different couple (also not from our dorm) was keen to pull the same trick. I told them to leave, because I was not going to wait twice. The man aggressively came in my face. I kept my composure and explained to him again what was on my mind. He brushed that away, saying we will see who gets to take showers first. When the ladies got out, we both rushed in. He pulled me by the shirt and I grabbed his collar. We argued pulling each other back and forth on that dirty, slippery bathroom floor, while his partner waited to see what would transpire. We finally exchanged few punches, he then ran outside, grabbed her hand and left.

Sometimes after a soccer game, we would get access to the showers in the middle of the night, and by then the hot water would be finished. Some other days, we would check and find the room empty and would rush upstairs to get our stuff, only to find that there was no hot water at all, hence the empty room. That shower business became so frustrating that I didn't even bother to check anymore, instead would just heat my water and take my shower right in the little laundry room on

60

my floor. This situation was the same in most of the dorms, not only in Kishinev but around the country. We could not leave our stuff in the first room either, without keeping an eye on it. If by misfortune you forgot something there, it was pointless to go back for it because it just would not be there. From toothbrushes and toothpastes to towels, underwear, socks or soaps, anything was good to steal as long as it did not come from the Soviet Union.

Socially, there were not many activities available to us, and the ancients advised not to wander around late at night to avoid being attacked. This was something we knew from our history classes and the media, happened only in apartheid South Africa and the KKK-infested southern US. We took the warning seriously, and started to build shields against the verbal assaults and frequent laughter we heard in the streets. The ancients themselves cautiously roamed from room to room or dorm to dorm always mindful of their level of exposure.

Since there were more than thirty of us, we reinvigorated the Malian soccer and basketball teams. We played as often as possible either in our dooryard against a Soviet team or among ourselves. We soon started to practice for the cultural show the Malian community put on every year to celebrate the country's independence. Faculty and staff along with friends from other communities got all invited. Those activities in the fall, plus the soccer practices, were our distractions until the first snowfall. After these few months, we all had a pretty good idea of what we had gotten ourselves into and how important it was to stay strong in order to make it out of there in six long years, still sane.

The Malian community, in spite of its internal divisions, was the unifying and nurturing fabric in this cold and condescending society. I tried very hard through them to change my major, but without success. We wrote a letter to the embassy in Moscow as required, and I never got an answer. I placed several phone calls to push my application through, but felt like I was talking to a wall. They never made the change, and they never wrote back. I stayed the course, passed all the exams with prospective agronomy students, hoping to later be with the veterinarians. It never happened. After a trip to the

61

embassy the following summer, I found out firsthand about their mediocrity and careless attitudes. At best, our diplomats were a bunch of incompetent and irresponsible oddities, lacking the slightest sense of duty.

Since I and my institute never got a word from them, I got oriented to Kharkov (a Ukrainian town at the Northeastern border with the Russian Federation) for my remaining education in agronomy. I lobbied hard with an ancient to talk the dean of foreign students into letting me stay in Kishinev. The dean could allow me to stay, but not change my major, which could be done only in Moscow between my embassy and the Soviet Department of Education. Once again, by chance or destiny, I stayed in Kishinev and in agronomy, instead of the vet school I yearned for.

My fate was Kishinev, the capitol city of the then Republic of Moldavia, one of the fifteen that formed the Union of the Soviet Socialist Republics (USSR). That first summer the small capitol city, felt just right. It was not too big and busy, not too small and lifeless. It kind of felt like home in the sense that I was not pleasantly surprised by anything, nothing took my breath away, and there were no must-see places, unlike Moscow, Timbuktu or Cairo.

The night life for us outside of the dorms was dead at best; there was nowhere to go without being provoked, ridiculed, or laughed at. That pushed black students to constantly visit and entertain each other within the walls of our dorms. That first year we did not have much to do besides school and soccer, therefore constantly trying to occupy ourselves. This led to drinking groups, improvised parties, and trespassing Soviets getting thrown out by the dorm commandant. The nights were very quiet since everybody was forced to sleep by 10:30 p.m. Many natives, including our roommates, avoided night life en masse. They did not hang out late in bars, movie theaters, or restaurants, leaving the deserted cold streets to the patrolling militia. They preferred drinking vodka at home or at their friends', thus avoiding troubles with the militia while waddling drunk in the streets. During the day, the same streets became overcrowded with consumers looking for bargains in the huge government stores.

Since the government alone produced, sold, and planned outputs, it would often miss its targets for many items or produces. People would sometimes queue up for household goods, produce, and the imported items that briefly and rarely showed up in stores. Sometimes people would get in line without knowing what was being sold up ahead, only to say after a long wait, "Oh, I do not need this," once they reached the store. Also, as a rule of fairness, nobody was allowed to buy multiples of some articles, so that everybody could get a shot at them. To circumvent that, we would hire each other in order to get several of the same item. Sometimes we would also stand in line many times over, ignoring the calls or frowns of anxious clerks.

Often, stores would be overstocked with things that would not sell because of their jumbo size. For example, a shoe or clothing store would look adequately stocked at first glance, but, upon enquiring, one would find out that not only were the displayed items all alike, but they were all of extreme sizes. Either too little (toddler size) or too big (XXXL) for the majority of the population. Why? Because, the government made and distributed the same quantity of size nine in women's shoes, for example, as size thirteen to its numerous and gigantic stores. Obviously, all of the size nine would go before a fifth of the size thirteen would, leaving the store full of useless items.

Socially, life was morose, and we were our own cheer leaders if we wanted to survive. The Soviets, our classmates, and roommates lived in a state of fear and suspicion of each other and could not openly befriend us, reducing their world to their rooms, too. All sources of information were government-run, depriving the common citizen of unfiltered news. The few radio stations from the West that could be heard were constantly jammed. AC/DC, Bad Company, Pink Floyd, and Dire Strait tapes were confiscated at the border to "curtail outside influence." The government even decided who should live where, since it owned and distributed all apartments. Every foreigner living among them was "a potential capitalist, enemy of the people," to be spied on and not be embraced. These artificial parameters and guidelines pushed all natural human behaviors into the gutter, dumbing down our guests to ridiculousness, nonentity.

Those who had a Soviet girlfriend did not even know where she lived, much less pay her a visit. She came to the dorms, period. We could not work at all, not even on campus. Nobody had Soviet friends to visit at their residence, and by law, none of us could rent, buy or share an apartment, not even a single room in town.

Everything belonged to the people, to the government, and, therefore, to nobody in the end. No private ownership was allowed for anything: land, water, forest, sky, raw materials etc., all belonged to the Soviet people.

In school, we were getting to know our teachers and staff. They were dedicated to our wellbeing so much that I sometimes wondered if they had lives of their own. Besides teaching, they tended to all our needs outside of class without hesitation.

Slowly but surely, Lenin and his predecessors, Marks and Engels, were becoming part of our day-to-day curriculum. Everything started with Lenin and everything came back to him, regardless of the subject matter. Even physics and chemistry books started with some of his sayings and thoughts. You could not walk a block without seeing either his statue or one of his catch phrases plastered on the wall or on top of buildings. We were bombarded so much by his life, ideas, and achievements that we soon started to experience some Lenin overdose. The Soviets were compulsorily atheists but they deified Lenin; unfortunately for them, we foreigners knew a little more than what they were unsparingly trying to "feed" us.

Once we were settled in, the time came to get in touch with family and friends across the Soviet Union and abroad. There were two options for that: write a letter, invite or be invited to a phone conversation at the post office. Given my situation - too many friends and relatives scattered around the globe -- I had to use both options, but not as I wanted to. I could write to anyone, anywhere, sometimes with delays or sometimes not, but I could not directly call people any time I pleased. Stamps were very cheap, and I took advantage of that low-priced postal system to write tons of letters.

The ancients warned all of us to be careful about what we write, since the Soviets opened all letters without exception. That was why letters took ages to reach destinations abroad and weeks within the Union. The natives themselves knew what was going on with their letters and phone conversations in this atmosphere of secrecy and suspicion. A tiny number of them had friends abroad and were mindful of the surveillance whenever they called or wrote letters. Everybody was looking over his or her own shoulder, and over neighbors' and relatives' shoulders, too. The USSR embodied the notion of a land where "walls had eyes and ears." Informing the government was bred into the Soviets' DNA, and not even one mutation occurred along the way. So, a palpable climate of suspicion reigned and kept everybody on their toes.

The phone system was a different animal. Here again, local, domestic, and foreign calls were treated differently and separately. Since there were no phones in our dorm rooms, direct outgoing or incoming calls were out of the question. All of our huge and crowded dorms had one phone at the front desk and perhaps some public phones outside. Local calls could only be made at the front desk or at a public phone that only worked half of the time and was, by default, bugged by the State.

To call a colleague in another dorm, you had to either do it quickly and publicly at the front desk, or outside. One had to dial the front desk and ask the concierge or the student on duty to physically go and get your party while you held the line. More often than not, the call would be dropped either because of the long wait or because somebody hung up the phone at the other end. As a result, we started to use the front desk as a voice mail box. We would call and leave a message with the concierge for our party in this or that room, and hoped for the best.

Domestic calls could only be made from the post office. You could either have the post office connect you to a particular phone number, or set up a conference call, called a peregovor, between you and your party at a given date and time. Here is how:

To call domestically, one would go to the post office and

fill out a form. On it, you put down the names of the city of your party, the dorm address, and the number of minutes you would like to talk for. You would then stand in line to give the form to the clerk, pay the fees, and be told to take a seat. After about thirty to sixty minutes, an announcer would say, for example: "Chicago, booth number 5." You would then rush to the named booth, grab the receiver, and wait until you were connected to your party. The designated "connector" would sometimes talk to you and ask for guidance if she could not get through. She could try another number or give up and refund your money.

Another way to make domestic calls was a sort of a call-by-appointment set up by the post office. To do that, one would go there and fill out a form reserved for that purpose. You would put down the name of the city or town, the name of your party, the number of minutes, and, in this case, the day and the time of the call. An invitation would then be faxed to the front desk of your party's dorm. When the appointed day came, you and your party would go to your respective post office with the invitation and hand it to the clerk. Hopefully, after a little while both parties would get called into a booth to be connected.

The protocols for international calls were similar to those for a domestic call cited above, except that one provided a phone number or two. Occasionally, you would be prompted during your conversation to speak another language. Why? Because the "minder" listening to your overseas call could not understand the language you were speaking in. One could resume the call by switching to French, English, or other commonly-used languages your "minder" could understand. This never happened to me personally, but some colleagues confirmed it. At the end of the time allotted for the conversation, the clerk would simply disconnect the call without warning.

At the dorms, we all accepted the fact that the front desk was one of the most powerful and controversial features of students' lives. It had to be taken into account for every venture one contemplated. The Soviets themselves never questioned the draconian regulations that were imposed on them, and seemed pretty much content to obey them and stay out of trouble. The opposite was true for foreign students. Simply entering or exiting the dorms, including our own, was ground for frictions. We had to be mindful that all the guests would be registered upon entry, and that the authorities would thoroughly check the information for "dirt." The sense of privacy went out the window as soon as we were assigned a room, two or three roommates, and a student ID.

But, according to some elders, the surveillance actually started in Bamako as soon as we gave 15 pictures and a bunch of documents to the Soviet authorities.

The amalgam of information from ourselves, roommates, classmates, teachers, front desk, dorm commandants, girlfriends, and the post office was more than enough to paint a complete portrait of each and every one of us. In turn, blurring that mosaic portrait became an existential exercise that we all engaged in to evade scrutiny. I still wonder who got the most out of that cat and mouse game.

At first sight, Moscow and its great Cheremetyevo International Airport, resembled any other modern capital city until men in uniform started laughing at us. The hotel we transitioned in, was as normal as normal could be until we were told to show our passports between floors. The train ride from Moscow to Kishinev seemed fine until we became the laughingstock of other passengers, who in some cases refused to share compartments with black students. These first and sour ordeals temporarily overwhelmed me with mixed feelings, overtaking my initial inquiring emotions as I settled in Kishinev that fall. However, the anticipation of new experiences, the presence of other students, and the dread of returning home as a quitter, kept me going. The reception by the Malian community and the tenderness of our Soviet teachers also calmed a lot of raw nerves. Without realizing it, I was embarking on a consequential journey that would shape the rest of my life.

c. Nationalism

Since 1917, when Lenin overthrew the tsar in the Bolshevik Revolution, a regime of body, mind and spirit control prospered. Seventy years later, as I was nearing my first year in the Soviet Union, its social damage was palpably overwhelming. Religion and freedoms were banned or driven underground. With no compass, no basic freedoms to think, enquire or express themselves, the average Soviet citizens could not rationally ponder. They simply "were". Contemplating a serious conversation about life, politics, philosophy, education or even jobs was a frivolous endeavor. Education, health care, apartments, dorms and jobs were all guaranteed by the government, even for underachievers. The entire society was like a flock of mindless beings without an ounce of motivation to excel. Salaries were not performance-based which led to careless attitudes in every sphere of the society. Everything was taken care of by the communist party, including how to think about the Soviet Union and the rest of the world if it ever registered on their radar. Ninety-nine per cent of the population thought the USSR was the best place on earth, especially while talking to foreigners in front of other Soviets. Of those, ten percent felt a chill go down their spine every time they somehow remembered, without even talking to anybody, that they did not subscribe to the cant. Talk to any Soviet, he or she would tell you what we were taught in class "We have everything and in great quantity". If and when an outdated foreign movie showed at the movie theaters, they would all congregate to see it. But when asked, they would tell you that the stores, cars, clothes, and houses in the movie were only props, and that in reality those items were rarities in the West. When the young German Mathias Rust landed in the heart of Red Square in May of 1987 with his small plane, I heard it first on the International French Radio (RFI) and informed my Soviet roommates. Their reply was typical - Why was such a huge deal not in the newspapers? This must be another made-up story from Europe, they replied. A few days later after seeing it on TV and in Pravda (the government newspaper) it became "true" to them. So, instead of debating the meanings and implications of such a serious event, you find yourself quarreling about its veracity right off the bat. Needless to say that such a conversation is never pleasant nor fruitful, and did not get you anywhere. Intellectually, it was not challenging at all to engage a serious and intelligent conversation with the average Soviet. To the contrary it was mind-numbing.

Morality outside their borders was another topic the Soviets liked to bring up with an unparalleled sense of supremacy. The talking point was that women were not respected in the West, and were instead treated as sexual objects to be bought and then disposed of. A professor of history of the Communist party even said that he was told by a friend that people overseas wore T-shirts with the word "sex" written on them. I still wonder if I should have cried for the poor guy instead of laughing at him. They maintained that Western societies were rotten to the core due to rampant prostitution that led to overwhelming numbers of rapes and Sexually Transmitted Diseases. As a consequence, many Soviet women did not want to travel to Europe and be raped or sold into prostitution. This alibi was more like a self-fulfilling prophecy, or an appeasement stratagem since at that time they could not travel by law even if they wanted to. While the society as a whole was feeding on these kinds of accepted wisdoms, Soviet girls were for sale right behind Red Square in the heart of Moscow. The rate of STDs was among the highest in Europe, even considering the numbers released by the government. On top of that, the average Soviet woman was typically referred to as "bitch" by her male peers, who raped her and beat her more often than they would admit. In that male-dominated society, like many others in the world, women were scared to death to deny sex or to defy their boyfriends or drunken husbands. Giving in and keeping their mouths shut was the best way to avoid the "fist," as these men described their actions. These deeds were so much a part of relationships and the Soviet psyche, that few, if any, were reported or even considered as crimes.

In such an environment, alcohol was the match box among fuel barrels. Moldavia, a mostly agricultural republic, was the Champagne of the union, with alcohol as its main export. It was cheap, strong, unregulated, and part of life. It flowed at each gathering without limit. When some of us declined to drink, the Soviets always replied, "What kind of man does not drink?" Typically, we could sense the disappointment and near-anger of our hosts anytime someone refused the offer of a drink. In the same way that they did not understand why someone would not drink at all, it was hard for me to understand why they would be offended by our refusal to get drunk with them, and why anybody would drink so much.

Such a strong sense of competition and machismo was built around drinking that it became, by far, the favorite pastime for too many Soviets, and unfortunately foreign students, too. Out-drink each other and brag about it the next day, was the name of the game. Countless productive hours were wasted by workers and missed by students all across the country with no end in sight.

If getting drunk was OK for the Soviets, foreign students paid a huge price by joining the dance, especially those who never drank in their native countries. That first year, many skipped classes, others were sent back home without graduating. Something had to be done at both the federal and the individual level to protect the lives and productivity being despoiled by alcohol.

Everyone worked for the government, since no private enterprise was allowed. Physical labor paid better than intellectual work because of its hardiness and the physical strain on workers. "A woodcutter makes more than a doctor, and should," argued one of our teachers. They (teachers) earned a miserable salary, but at least the government took care of all their basic needs. Food and transportation were very cheap (prices were fixed by the government) and education, healthcare, and housing were also guaranteed by the government. With no extra income, the measly salary the teachers made was enough to survive and drink on, but not to enjoy life. Even if they had any money left over, they could not do much with it. They could not travel abroad or buy anything of any quality because none was available, whereas foreign students traveled to the west twice a year, dressed better and had Japanese TVs, tapes and video players in their rooms. On top of that, we could illegally sell them a single pair of jeans for more than 120 rubles. This kind of trafficking allowed us to afford anything we wanted, and more than any Soviet could dream of in their own country. We sold toothpaste, chewing gum, instant teas, coffee cans, and even plastic grocery bags from Europe. You name it; foreign students could bring it from overseas for a lot of rubles.

Many of our teachers were trapped between what they were told to teach us, and the reality of their own lives. Our monthly stipend of 80 rubles was close to their salaries of 100 to 120 rubles. The more they got to know us, the worse they felt about themselves. We all supposedly came from the poorest countries of the world on a 6-year scholarship entirely paid for by the Soviet government. But it was obvious to them that each one of us was better off than any Soviet citizen, from doctors, scientists, teachers and deans to professors, state mall managers, mechanics and architects.

As they touted the superiority of communism and bashed the West in class, many secretly envied poor foreign students. Something was amiss; the narrative did not match reality. Suppressed frustration was their daily companion as they tried to convince themselves they were living in the best country in the world, while not believing in it. Worst yet, they did not have a say when it came to influencing the course of their lives. Internally many had given up hope that it would change anytime soon. No wonder alcohol was revered.

Then, came Gorbachev. He became that glimmer of hope for many Soviets and us foreigners - everything that the Soviet Union could be.

Politically, we were supposed to stay out of the internal affairs of the Soviet Union as guest students. But the Soviet government itself was engaged in the most aggressive political indoctrination known to mankind. No resources were spared in their enduring mission to convince us to embrace their politico-economic system and philosophy. The propaganda machine was everywhere, constantly trying to condition us to see the good side of socialism and the repulsive side of the west and its capitalistic system. Schools, movies, television programs, books, newspapers, posters, organized visits, roommates, impostors, were all part and parcel of the steamrolling Soviet persuasion to subtly induct us into the communist fold.

They wanted us to blindly accept whatever they fed us, with no questions asked. They did not understand how hopelessly unrealistic and inadequate that strategy was. They ignored our backgrounds and seemed to be completely oblivious to what everyday life in the union was doing to us. The whole Soviet apparatus had been tone-deaf to our grievances and those of the ancients before us, for decades. It was like having two construction teams on a site, one building the house and the other destroying it almost at the same pace. The situation reminded me of the saying of the late dictator of Guinea, Ahmed Sekou Toure. He thought that if you wanted people to become capitalists, you should send them to the Soviet Union, and if you want them to become communists, then send them to the United States of America. Why? Because they would learn to hate the system while living in it, and discovering all its flaws. They would subsequently yearn for the "other system", the one they know the least.

After only three months of Russian language, we started to take classes in political economy, learning about the history of the Communist Party, Socialism, Marks, Engels and Lenin. They wanted us to know from start how great the country was, especially when compared to the US and the West. Comparing and contrasting Socialism and Capitalism, Communism and Imperialism (the highest and final stages of the two systems, according to Marks and Engels) never let up. We, as well as the Soviets themselves, were constantly bombarded with all kinds of off-putting aspects of life in the West and attractive ones about the Soviet Union. The classic one we heard over and over again from just about every Soviet was the "absence" of exploitation of men by men in the "classless" Soviet society, and its unbridled presence in Western societies. I could see why the Soviets would hammer home that notion, given the widening gap between rich and poor in the West. Or, how the deck is set for the rich, famous and influential people and companies, and against the rest of us. I would give them that.

But in this Socialist "paradise," it did not take long for us to sense the same widening gap between the party officials and the rest of the society. The two classes had pretended for decades that they were equals, while the former not only subjugated the latter, but also manipulated it to keep the status quo. The party phonies had special stores filled with imported goods, or the best Soviet-made items. Their doctors and pharmacies were separate from those of the average comrade, and they never stood in line to buy cars or get apartments. With their membership cards, they could get on any fully-booked train, plane, or bus to go anywhere in the Union.

On top of these privileges, they started to abuse their position by taking bribes and getting cars and other special items for friends, families, and those willing to pay top rubles. They all had a Datcha (villa) in the countryside on top of the government-provided apartment, while two or three generations of average Soviets lived together in one apartment, while waiting in line. One of our teachers (an outspoken communist) privately acknowledged to a student that, he was ashamed to invite foreign students to his apartment as some others did. He did not want us to see the conditions he lived in, and report that back to our home countries. I said too late, because we detected that, light years earlier than he came to that conclusion.

Racism, murder, rape, and bank robbery statistics in the West, were often used to woo numb domestic brains and our young, impressionable minds. We were mindful of the fact that these rates were inflated and were not so nightmarish, by any stretch of the imagination. Fortunately, unlike the domestic audience, we could compare and contrast just because of where we came from and what we knew about the rest of the world. When you come from a developing country, you learn a great deal about the developed ones; again by design. I guarantee you that, in high school, we knew more about the history, economy, and political systems of Europe and the US, than many of their own citizens. This general world knowledge was in the DNA of foreign students; it shielded them all along from a lot of bull crap, and the Soviet authorities ignored it at their own peril. Not only did it keep all of us grounded in the face of the well-oiled Soviet propaganda machine, but it also singlehandedly defeated it. Knowledge once again proved to be the most potent weapon of them all.

It is precisely that ignorance of, or condescension toward others, that imperils many powers too. Afghanistan, Algeria, Cuba, Iraq, Lebanon, Palestine, Somalia, and Vietnam are some of the sore reminders of the dangers of such hubris. The Soviets also fell victim to it, as almost all its targeted foreign students despised Socialism by graduation time.

On the issue of freedoms, we were taught that the Soviet constitution guaranteed freedom of speech, press, association, movement, and religion. The reality was that we all came with our facts and prejudices and did not need anything else but our Soviet experience to shape our opinions. Every minute counted, and the clock was ticking as soon as we filled out our entry forms to the Soviet Union at the Cheremetyevo International Airport. Some of us questioned just about every line coming from the Soviet authorities, or the ditto heads in our classes or dorms. Others went along just to avoid subtle retaliatory measures that could sour an already rough stay.

Yes, these freedoms were mentioned in the constitution, but the average Soviet could not travel outside of the country. Those restrictions were also extended to students coming from other socialist countries like Afghanistan, Angola, Bolivia, Cuba, Ethiopia, Laos, Mongolia, North Korea, Nicaragua, El Salvador, Vietnam etc. When confronted, all we heard was, "I do not need to travel. What have I lost over there?" Some teachers even said that with their membership card as war veterans, they could take a discounted trip from Moscow all the way to East Germany, but that they just didn't need to travel, having everything right here at home ! To that, I would say bull crap of unprecedented proportion. They simply could not admit to foreigners that the mighty Soviet government would not even allow its own citizens to travel, fearful of losing them all. A perfect example of this was Louba, one of our Russian language teachers, who was denied permission to join her husband in Argentina unless she dropped her Soviet citizenship and right to return. Really, Mighty USSR, what were you afraid of?

In terms of freedom of movement, the average Soviet could not simply move from one city to another without the government's permission. Every citizen was registered in a specific town at a specific address, and that information was in their internal passports, which they took everywhere. For example, if one went from New York to Milwaukee, one could not get an apartment there with a New York registration in the passport without official paperwork from the government. This pushed people to marry in order to get a new registration and settle in a different town.

Now, when traveling from another city or state, you were allowed to get a room at a hotel by showing your out-of-city or out-of-state registration. However, that also meant that you could not get a hotel room in your own city, because you were already registered at a specific address there, and could not possibly need a hotel room. When probed, our hosts maintained that the government knew how many people were needed in a given town etc., so it knew better how to control population and resources. Privately though, they showed frustration and resentment.

In terms of freedoms of association and speech in the constitution, the average Soviet made a distinction between theory and practice. Yes, the constitution had all the right words, but in reality the Soviets had little or no choice at all. The youth organization KOMSOMOL (Counsel of Young

Communists) was ubiquitous. There was not a way to escape it as one grew up anywhere in the Union, and it was the only one. Nobody could ever create any other political organization, much less one that opposed KOMSOMOL; only the government could create and run such associations. Every leader the Soviet Union ever had, without exception, started with the KOMSOMOL. Additionally, there were government unions at every workplace with 100% membership, and here again there was no possibility of opting-out.

There was not a single organization that was not set up or overseen by the government. Everybody had his or her card, everybody took part in the numerous meetings, and everybody envied the leaders who got showered with praises and privileges. Nobody dared challenge them for fear of life-altering consequences. So, you could associate with anyone you liked, as long as it was in a group founded and run by the government.

Print and the rest of the mass media were all government-run. There simply were no dissenting voices to challenge the communist party's line.

Free speech was another one of those decorative concepts in the Soviet constitution. That freedom never materialized, since those who spoke their minds ended up jailed or ostracized by friends and family. Since everybody spied on everybody, freedom of speech could be exercised only in very tight circles or nowhere at all. Our young, smart, and controversial teacher of political economy, found that out the hard way during our first year. We foreign students loved him because of his candidness. He told us that the Soviet Union was not a socialist country, and that all the votes at the first communist party meetings, under Lenin himself, were not all unanimous. There were dissenting votes, contrary to what is in the history books, he claimed. Needless to say, he did not last, but at least he spoke his mind as it had never been done before.

In Kishinev, we also witnessed Russians publicly yelling at the natives to speak Russian. If Moldavians could not even speak their language on the buses, in the streets, or at the post office in Moldavia, then where could they? Statute 34 of the constitution says: "All citizens of the Soviet Union are equals in front of the law regardless of origin, social standing, race or nationality, gender, education, language, religion, occupation, neighborhood and other circumstances." Yeah, Right.

For six years we faced that permanent attempt by the Soviet government to brain wash us to embrace the communist system. That same system in return was making our lives a living hell. As outsiders, we also witnessed it lying to, jailing and brutalizing its own population, in order to postpone a revolution that was bound to come. Shake our heads was what we were left to do, powerless in front of a scary but doomed paper tiger

II
Два

B. EDUCATION

In September 1986, when we started school, the USSR and its educational system were at a crossroad. The socialist system was at its pinnacle, while Gorbachev was only a year and a half into his term with his accelerated attempts to transform the Union. The mood of change throughout the country was obvious, as was the uncertainty that came along with it. Our teachers and faculty were all going with the flow and started to teach us some of the differences since the onset of Gorbachev's perestroika or restructuring.

School was the only reason for our presence in the Soviet Union. Aside from the diplomats from different embassies, the only others allowed to be there legally were the foreign students. We came by the thousands from all over the world on different kinds of scholarships. The reputation of the Soviet education faced tougher scrutiny with each succeeding generation of foreign students. Back home, some looked down on it while others swore by it. My best friend's father wanted him to study architecture only in Kiev, Ukraine; over any other place on earth. But in the end, his dual citizenship and his mother tipped the balance toward France.

A few months into my language year, I exchanged some ideas about the subject with one ancient from the university. We were discussing the perception of the Soviet educational system by people in the USSR and back home. It was obviously too early for me to judge, but my counterpart was in his third year there, therefore had some credibility. We both tended to agree that the Soviet Union could not have been first in space or a military super power, and have a substandard educational system. So, only time could tell.

During our first year every language teacher would come on duty in the dorms, according to a rigorous timetable. He or she would help the concierge at the front desk with guests, calls, messages or any other issue that came up. He or she would also go from room to room to see the foreign students in their own environment, help them with questions they might have, and gather a maximum of personal information. They would ask all kinds of questions and demand to see pictures or crafts from home.

These frequent one-on-one meetings were great opportunities for us to ask questions we were shy to ask otherwise. That close monitoring also helped them assess our character and behavior in a very innocent way. The teachers were also mandated to have open hours every afternoon to assist any student with questions. Those free hours were called consultations, prompting me to come without books the first time. I thought that we were going for another round of those Godforsaken tests at the clinic.

Due to the close proximity, the teachers would also look for late or missing students, right in the dorms. A teacher was also assigned to each foreign community as its administrator. The one for the Malian community was a KGB field officer, according to some seniors. His role was to guide, entertain and advise us about excursions, trips, and other social activities.

My teacher was Olga Grigorievna Nocik, a very nice and articulate lady from Odessa, a port city in the republic of Ukraine. She was a very professional, demanding and serious single lady in her late twenties. "She never married because she dated a foreign student from Burkina Faso," said one senior. It would take us more time and experience to fully understand and cope with that strange fact. We were divided in small size classes (eight students) and mingled with students from all over the world. I was with the only Malian girl, two Afghans, two Ethiopians, and one student from Burundi. Later on, a girl from Congo, also named Olga, joined us.

The first day our teacher asked us to say a few Russian words, we might have learned back home. My Malian classmate, who had Russian as a second language in high school, got us going. I, proud of the vocabulary I had learned with some friends in Bamako, followed with the few words I could remember. My teacher was pretty happy about that, until I said a word that made her blush and scream my last name. She managed to keep a smile while explaining that I had just said "your ass, or butt" to her, thinking I was saying "you lied" as my friends so maliciously taught me. I was very embarrassed by that incident, and from then on, checked with my colleague first, anytime we were asked to say new words.

Later on, when I found out that the consultations were not compulsory but up to us, I deserted. The timing was very badly chosen, right after lunch when everybody would like to digest in peace or nap. Being pretty good with languages, I did not have any difficulty learning Russian, and the practice I was having with my two Soviet roommates kept me on top of things.

At the cafeteria below our dorms, all of our teachers would stand in line with us and would refuse to step forward anytime we offered. They always replied, "We are all equal here in this country." I personally was amazed by that, until they stopped coming there a trimester later.

Before we knew it, we were being steamrolled by the Soviet propaganda machine. The hallways at school were full of pictures of U.S. Marines invading Grenada, or in training camps wearing black hoods, or police dogs attacking African-Americans in the U.S. during demonstrations. There were also pictures of the American south, with signs saying "white only". Many books or brochures with similar content were displayed here and there in hallways, lecture rooms and especially in the lobby of our dorms, or anywhere we would sit either to watch TV or wait to see a teacher or a staff member. Talk about product placement, just like at the supermarket.

I still remember my first Soviet History teacher, who persuasively contrasted the West and the Soviet systems side by side. She was the one who introduced us to V.I. Lenin, the founder of the Soviet Union and mastermind of the Great Russian Revolution of 1917. "He is the person I respect the most in my life," she said, pointing to one of Lenin's numerous pictures.

Every book, without exception, started with a citation by Lenin, and some had his picture right on the first page. From architecture to nuclear physics or even microbiology, he had something to add. The man was everywhere.

We would learn poems about him by heart and recite them on stage at the culture club, in front of the faculty and fellow students. I hated every minute of those moments because I felt like caving in to the indoctrination many talked about, even if deep inside I knew that my mind was not that simple and up for grabs. I just could not stand these poems about somebody so remote from me, especially when I sensed the unmistakable scheme of brain washing.

I also still remember a famous sentence from one of the numerous poems about the Russian language that said, "I study Russian only because Lenin spoke it." There was another poem dedicated to the Russian language, which by the way was beautifully written and went like this:

Russian Language
Language of Languages
Language of Peace
Language of Vladimir Ilitch Lenin.

Many other times we watched movies about him and even went to the club just to listen to Beethoven, Bach, Tchaikovsky, etc., because they were Lenin's favorites. We would gather at the culture club next to the dorms for many painful and torturous hours, while one of the teachers played disc after disc of Lenin's favorite classical compositions on an old gramophone. The scratchy speakers set on each side of the empty stage, drove me crazy and resentful. Everything about the man was blown out of proportion and was becoming unbearable. His wife, too, was a superhero, and subject of a lesser adulation than him, but still big enough to choke on. We watched many movies about her alone and the two of them together.

One day in the queue to the cafeteria, my teacher Olga approached me about a movie devoted to Lenin's mother being shown at the club right after lunch. By then I had had enough and in a very deterring tone, I told her that I was not going anywhere. I stressed that I could understand watching long exhausting films about Lenin himself, but not his mom. What is her merit here besides giving birth to Lenin, I asked? On the verge of tears, she vanished without answering my question.

Olga was also very knowledgeable about Karl Marx, Engels, and Lenin's doctrine and philosophy, especially with reference to the exploitation of the labor class by the rich bourgeois and the alternative socialist "classless society" they pretended to have. One time, we were to stage a play at the culture club in which I was a policeman. I showed up in my military fatigues and Olga categorically rejected my outfit and sent me home to wear something other than a Western army fatigue. I was very surprised by that.

Another time we got in a big, ferocious argument after she asked, if we agree that, the bourgeoisie could be defeated and a classless society could rise from the ashes of a capitalistic society. I said that there was no way to defeat the bourgeoisie, one can only adapt. She was miserable and could not cope with the fact that I was not lining up with something as obvious as the "future demise" of the Capitalistic System. An "inevitable" demise, due to the fierce antagonism between the classes of haves and have nots within it. Per the Soviets' "dreams".

When we touched the arms race question, she told us that the Soviet Union was building weapons just because the US was doing so. She said that they did not need very many, and as a matter of fact, the manufacturing of all their weapons was costless, because the labor was provided by volunteers. "Our citizens put these hours for free, for the protection of our motherland against foreign invasion" Olga proudly said.

Once we got further with our Russian, and could go grocery shopping without an interpreter, we started to take

82

Soviet history classes and got more involved in discussions. This was also one year and a half into perestroika, Gorbachev's brainchild and the new doctrine of radical change of the seventy-year-old Soviet system.

We had a very young and enthusiastic Soviet history teacher name Sergei, whom we all enjoyed because of his unbelievable pedagogy skills and straightforwardness. He would openly criticize facts in the books and in daily life, something many others would die before they did. He also pointed out that the Soviets were not the only players in the defeat of the Nazis in 1945 and that it took the Allies to come from the Western front too, to free Berlin. Because Soviet history books downplayed the role of the allies in the victory against Germany, he felt compelled to point out the reality. Equally this is the case as well in the West, where the Soviets' role in Hitler's demise is softened. He touched on the limited freedoms people had, and Gorbachev's efforts to improve civil rights since his arrival in March 1985.

The other history teacher, an old lady named Marina, was Sergei's exact opposite and taught the other group. I believe she was in love with Lenin, by the way she would listen to the poems dedicated to him at the culture club. She appeared transfixed when students recited poems about Lenin on stage. She could not hear or acknowledge anybody or anything around her, and did not even blink while the poems went on. She was a different breed of Lenin's fanatics. I still wonder what happened to her after the fall of the berlin wall.

Unfortunately, Sergei was fired just as his classes were becoming more and more interesting. He was precocious, far ahead of his colleagues and his time. Then Marina took over both groups to everybody's displeasure. One day, she asked, "What was at the core of the Soviets' victory during the great patriotic war (a.k.a World War II)?" A disgruntled student answered, "General Snow, the Germans could not even fire their guns because of the cold and their convoys were getting stuck in the snow and mud." This very insulting piece of propaganda suggested that, extreme cold temperatures were at the core of Germany's defeat, not the bravery and sacrifices of the Red Army. Marina had tears in her eyes and her voice was shaking, while she tried to explain the different tactics of the undeniably courageous Red Army. She could not process such a slap in the face of the Soviet Army.

Later on during a lesson on Soviet help to developing countries, she asked the class to talk about all the good things the Soviet Union was doing for the third world. When nobody volunteered, she turned toward the Ethiopian students and lashed out at them, "Shame on you! Why do you not say a word about all what we did when your whole country was dying of hunger?" She was very upset, desperately trying to convince us about the Soviets' good heart and soul.

The school also organized excursions to some of the best plants in the area. We went to the circus, museums and parks free of charge. We got to see a group named "jok", perform. The best folklore dance ensemble of Moldavia, well known in the Union and abroad. We also visited the best grade schools, and answered pupils' questions. The accompanying teacher explained in depth how schools were free and well-funded by the Soviet government. At that time we were studying the communist system, its founders and its meaning for the world, expected to "turn communist one country at a time," according to Lenin. One chapter from our history notebook put it this way:

"At the end of World War II, the international situation completely changed towards forces of democracy, progress and socialism. As the result of the defeat of fascist Germany, the peoples of Albania, Bulgaria, Hungary, Poland, Romania, Czechoslovakia and Yugoslavia, led by the Communist party, started to build socialism. In 1949, the German Democratic Republic was created. In these countries, the dictatorship of the proletariat won in the form of social democracy. The Social revolution in these countries happened peacefully through debates. In some imperialistic countries, social democrats came to power, and in France, Italy and Austria, even some communists were in the government. The crushing defeat of Japan allowed a socialist development in China, northern Korea, Vietnam and later Laos. In 1959, the peoples' democratic

84

revolution won in Cuba. The Soviet Union helped greatly those countries. In ten years, from 1945 to1955, the help of the Soviet Union reached 21 billion rubles. It helped build about 400 huge plants and factories. The Union for Mutual Economic Assistance (SEV) was created in 1949 and already in 1979 the industrial output in those countries rose 17 times. In 1955 the Warsaw Pact was created as an answer to NATO." [13]

Schools never missed an opportunity to compare their system with the West, from their point of view. We learned all about their great history, the socialist system and its place in the world. For the celebration of labor day (on May 1), they rounded all the foreign students up in front of the school, gave us big signs to hold up and take part in the huge parade the whole town attended every year. These remarkable signs said things that we did not know the meaning of at times, or had not much to do with the celebration in question. I remember one of my pictures taken on Labor Day with signs saying, "A nuclear-free world: demand of all peoples." Some other signs were drawings of weapons broken in the middle as a call for disarmament, or saying "stop the arm race now". Those powerful pictures of foreign students marching with signs demanding peace, independence and equality can still be found in books or brochures. We naively just came out and unknowingly participated in their PR campaigns for the first few years before realizing their subtle goals.

After learning Russian the first year, we were ready for our freshmen year in college. Everybody moved into a different dorm, made new friends and met new classmates and roommates. Our Agriculture Institute was located high up on an isolated mountaintop, where students and teachers were the only inhabitants. I moved into a ten-story Soviet-style dorm among many others, with two roommates. All the freshmen in agronomy, Soviets and foreigners, were divided in six groups of about twenty-five to thirty students. In some specific classes, we were divided into groups of either Soviets or foreign

---

[13] *A Paragraph from my own History Notebook from our History class, November 1986.*

students. Each side had its own head of students called starosta to deal with questions regarding the group. We also took some classes all together in big amphitheaters, where the front rows were always occupied by foreign students. I still do not have an explanation for that, but we always occupied the first two or three rows, no matter how late we came in.

Classroom walls were covered with pictures of great Soviet leaders, scientists, poets, composers, and writers such as Lenin, Mendeleev, Pavlov, Pushkin, and Tchaikovsky. Honor students also had their pictures behind a glass wall in the hallway for everybody to see.

The first few weeks were quite challenging for us as we tried to locate our classes and keep up with the Soviets, who were on their own turf and studying in their mother tongue. Ninety percent of them came from rural communities, so while dazzled by city life, they were very familiar with the agricultural practices and machinery we were learning about. Classes on the History of the Soviet Union and History of the Communist Party were among their favorites, since they knew so much about Lenin and communism from birth.

For us, it was the opposite. We were a bunch of city boys and girls fresh out of high school, who barely saw a tractor and by now were learning to hate Lenin for being EVERYWHERE. From the onset, we felt we were at a distinct disadvantage and were a little bit intimidated. But not for long, by the end of the observation month, we began to find our way and became more confident.

From 1986, when we landed in the country, until the fall of the Berlin Wall in 1989, it was a true learner's paradise. Anybody whose aim was to study hard, learn as much as possible, get his or her hands on just about anything to conduct experiments, the USSR was the place to be. The communist government poured a lot of money into the academic system. Education was free for everybody, from kindergarten all the way to the PhD level for those who wanted to go that far. By law, the government was also required to hire each and every graduate. The libraries were spacious and full of books for anybody who wanted to use them. There were no computers but we always found all the books we needed. They only cost pennies for those who wanted to possess their own. Each and every dorm also had a study hall called "Lenin's room" full of reading and yes, propaganda materials. At the universities or institutes themselves, classes, books, slides and other educational resources abounded. The laboratories were well-equipped, and I do not recall a single time when teaching materials were lacking. Special language labs were also well equipped with tapes, books and earphones for a thorough learning experience. We had everything we needed and only had to want it bad in order to succeed. In the dorms, noise was prohibited after certain hours of the night. The teachers were obliged to stay and explain to students anything they had trouble with, until satisfied. What more could a focused and dedicated student ask for? It was really up to the students, native or foreign, to work hard and graduate.

On its face, the Soviet system was a dream-come true for any studious and conscientious student. The string of renowned scientists, discoveries and Nobel prizes that came out of the Soviet Union speak loudly. Faculty came to the dorms to enquire about delinquent students and assess their issues in order to bring them back into the fold. Parallel to all that effort, there also was a network of advisors who did their utmost to mentor both gifted and struggling students. That extra effort to educate all students came at no extra cost to the school or the state.

Any developed country would have wanted a system like that for its people. We had all we needed to succeed if that were our goal and had only ourselves to blame if we failed. Anybody who wanted to get a great education and graduate among the best did so. Those who wanted to wing it and just get a diploma also did so. Others who decided not to even try to graduate also had their wish fulfilled.

Beneath this layer of near-perfect educational system, was one of the most potent propaganda arms of the government. The communist party wanted to kill two birds at once: fully indoctrinate all students (indigenous and foreign) to assure a bright future for the communist system and still groom world-class scholars. Over time, the former not only jeopardized the latter but eventually supplanted it, as more and more hours were allocated to party curricula. The philosophical and idealistic aspects of the party curricula made them attractive to anyone with any imagination, therefore more attractive to average students. Good grades in communist-based classes and strong voluntarism in community activities were very prized. We foreign students were doubly targeted in school by the teachers, and at home by our roommates or floor mates. By the third year and as college sophomores, we all deserted their indoctrination parades. Now more fluent in Russian, they aggressively started to teach us more and more unrelated or unnecessary classes at the Institute. Overall we took countless hours of ideologically slanted credits. As future agronomists, we took 570 hours of heavily tainted and coercive Russian language, 120 hours of Soviet History (20 would have been enough), 140 hours of Marxism-based Political Economy, 90 hours of philosophy, 80 hours of Scientific Socialism and 28 hours on the Basis of Scientific Atheism. Over a thousand hours squandered on an unsuccessful brain-washing campaign, which only drove us away from a dreadful system that turned our day-to-day life into hell. I would rather have had more hours of Selection of Tropical and Subtropical Crops (20 Hrs.), Environmental Protection (20 Hrs.) or Information Technology (40 Hrs.) etc. Instead, we were overloaded with useless credits.

In history, philosophy and Russian classes we studied nothing but Marx, Engels and Lenin, plus their theories about communism's bright future and the demise of the West as a political system, down the road. We got introduced very early on to the heroes of the Union, especially Yuri Gagarin, the first man in space, and Valentina Tereshkova, the first woman in space. We gladly watched movies about their breathtaking achievements with envy. Pictures of other science heroes covered the class walls, always with Lenin's on top over the chalk board.

The teachers of communism-related classes were having the time of their lives, enjoying great respect and instilling fear in all enemies. But as we started to stand up for ourselves, the discussions in class grew more interesting. In our sophomore year, we had a history teacher named Mavrody who always compared the Soviet Union and the West and shared condescending comments about the third world. One day, after one of his comments about the prowess of the Soviet medical system and their close friendship with third-world leaders, a colleague from Guinea Bissau butted in: "Why do you think President Sekou Toure of Guinea (a raving anti-Western dictator) went for treatment in the U.S. and consequently died in Cleveland, and not in the USSR? He was your guy and you brag about your medical achievements?" We could hear a pin drop in class, and the first things out of Mavrody's mouth were, "Where are you from? What is your name?" We realized that our colleague had just hit the nail on the head, and could be in trouble without our support. So, other students started to talk back to Mavrody in the heated commotion that ensued. Someone asked, "What does that have to do with the question asked?" others demanded he answered instead of cross-examining the student. The class went nuts; he turned pale, gave some phony arguments to a class that was no longer paying attention, and tried to continue with his lesson. But he clearly was not OK with a simple question that cast a doubt on the great Soviet medical system. He never forgot the incident and gave a "C" to our colleague at the final exam.

Mavrody was also the one who conducted a weekly hour-long class called the "information hour." It started at 7 a.m. and only foreign students were required to attend. It was designed to discuss the latest news with foreign students from the Soviets' perspective. Mavrody took great advantage of that hour by telling everybody to attend it or face retaliation when the time to sign students' exam books comes around. Since every foreign student was required to pass all exams in order to be allowed to travel overseas, many teachers abused more often than not, the power of their pens. With that power, Mavrody blackmailed many students who would not show up otherwise at these party-line sessions. We all hated the hour, but attended it for the sake of getting his signature and our travel visas. This early risers' hour was the perfect setting for Mavrody to take apart capitalism without restraint and hype the goodness of socialism to a sleepy foreign audience.

Matsarin, a math teacher, also used his signature power to denigrate students. One day a friend from Mali came late to his class, when he knocked at the door, Matsarin lashed out: "You foreign students travel abroad and bring jeans and other items for sale to our youth with my permission. But you cannot get up early as I do every morning, to come on time to my class. Next time I will not let you in, nor will I sign your exam book, grounding you to stay here for your vacations." He was a very good math teacher but bitter, jealous and revengeful. Our perceived material wealth did not sit well with him, especially when contrasted with his own. The poor guy, as a college math teacher, had just few clothes and one pair of genuine Soviet high-heeled leather boots, for the entire school year. At the end of classes he would wrestle every day to hop on a rush-hour bus. He was among the few teachers who openly took out their misery on foreign students.

Another overly powerful philosophy teacher named Brouma had us, and the Soviet students, under her control as she took attendance at the beginning of each of her well-attended classes. The Soviet students disliked her more than we did, because of her irrationality and blind love for the motherland. To us foreigners, she was just another ridiculous performer for the system but necessary to have on your side. We knew both sides of any issue she could possibly bring up, and we would feed our ideas to any Soviet colleague, brave enough to converse with a foreign student.

One day, she said that the manufactured products from Soviet factories were of higher quality than anything in the West. That triggered an uproar in the class, and she did not know where to hide. We told her that she could not possibly compare, since she has not been abroad and had never bought a foreign product. (We all also knew that she did buy Western items like many Soviets, but could not admit it in front of the Soviet students.) Since each and every one of them had bought something, mostly tape players made in Japan, they started to pepper her with questions. One of them asked, "Which one would you choose - a Japanese 'Sharp' or a Soviet 'Maiak' cassette player?" She stood her ridiculous ground and dared say, "I would pick my Soviet brand." The whole class burst into loud and raucous laughter. She went crazy, raising her voice in desperate damage-control mode. I could read a strong defiance in her eyes, betrayed by a much more telling body language of frustration. Right there, she lost credibility and standing in her students' eyes, the worst kind of sobering feeling for a teacher. She was the kind of patriot who would enjoy their Western-made products in the privacy of their homes but never outside, just to appear to keep the faith in a system they secretly and internally resisted.

Another time, while justifiably talking about inequality and racism in the West, Brouma cited a friend who visited France. According to her, there were places in France with signs saying "white only" and "forbidden to non-whites." This was in 1988, and many of us had been in France many times before, but had never seen anything like that. No one ever read or heard lately about such blatant racism in France. Yes, even as we speak there is still racism in the West, but not as Brouma described it. We told her about our own experiences, but she would not listen. Once again, she stuck her head in the sand and defended the testimony of her friend. Knowing her, my own belief is that she made up this story to back up her misguided concept of the world, while trying to indoctrinate others to hate the West.

In Political Economy, we had two teachers from different eras, one was an old guard in his sixties, and the other was a young teaching assistant on his way to a PhD in the same subject, but in Saint Petersburg. Once again, our group landed with the young and aggressive one, Mr. Golavatiouk.

The very first day of classes, he told us that the Soviet Union was not a socialist country and should not be called as such. We were flabbergasted by a statement that could have landed anybody in the Gulags few years earlier. We foreign students loved that as much as our Soviet colleagues hated it. We found in him somebody who spoke like us and had the authority not only to put it to an audience, but also in a better Russian.

The Soviet students always argued with him in a very tense atmosphere. One day, a student asked him what he was doing here if he hated the system so much. He replied that hatred of the system was not the case, but criticism of it was the issue. Golavatiouk even challenged Marxist theories of economics, to the chagrin of many native classmates. He questioned everything in the book of political economy and backed his own arguments up with specific, pertinent examples. I never missed his classes and always looked forward to them. I learned something new every time, and, most importantly, how to counter or debate an indoctrinated teacher, colleague or stranger. He simply inspired and empowered me. A few months later, word got out about this young teacher who was challenging the very essence of the Soviet society. He heard the rumors and the threats, but never gave in to the building pressure. To the contrary, he enjoyed being at the center of the new growing controversy about his teaching, which made our classes far more interesting. Some Soviet students started to desert, while others chose to fight him head on in class.

Unfortunately, he was ahead of his time and alone in his struggle to change opaque minds. Before long, he was fired and the old guard took over. He then made sure he rectified the "damage" done to the soul of the student body by bringing down Mr. Golavatiouk before resuming his agonizing lectures. According to him, the Soviet economic system was better than any other because of the planning, the lack of class and absence of exploitation of the workers by a rich class owning all the means of production.

We studied economic cooperation among the Eastern bloc countries in detail, especially the SEV (the Council of Mutual Economic Assistance) between members of the Warsaw pact. This economic marvel allowed member countries to trade by exchanging, not buying and selling, goods and products based on their monetary values. For example, Romania would exchange ten tons of wine worth "X" rubles against truck parts from Poland, worth the same "X" rubles. We continued to slave over that economic brainchild and passed exams on it even long after its disappearance. I still wonder why that was. One day, Mr. Aleksey, while touting the communist system, told us that he, as a war veteran, could have a huge discount on train tickets going anywhere he pleased to visit. We asked him why he had not been abroad yet for all this years. He replied that he had everything he needed here, and did not see the necessity to travel. We insisted that a train trip to France through Poland, Germany and Belgium would give him a different perspective of the world. He replied, "I do not want to visit countries where rape and bank robberies are frequent". We laughed, shook our heads, and gave up on him. We knew very well his situation of poverty, despair and frustration that betrayed him at the bus station, when he let his guard down to run after the bus that came once every two hours. His clothes, shoes and even hat were overused to their limits. Collective patriotism kept him and people like him, supporting a dying way of life. Students knew his weak point and used it to their advantage. Vague talks about the system and a few sweet comments about Marxism-Leninism made him generous with his grades. The "beautiful pictures" that some designated teachers always painted about their country, slowly drove us into permanent hangover status. The further we got, the more repugnant it became to sit through one-sided narratives about a system that was not living up to its basic promises. Our innocent Soviet classmates, who never traveled and only had one government news outlet, had not the slightest idea of what was really happening to them. These propaganda classes were melody to their ears, but also an opportunity to earn "easy" grades. To us foreign students, it was painfully frustrating to know the world better than the teachers and the entire student body, and not be able to show them the light. I always felt like trading places, hearts, minds or souls for a minute with all of them, just to save them from themselves.

An added aggravation was the impossibility of skipping any of those communist-oriented classes because of the certain retribution from the teachers during finals. A few missed hours here and there could cost anywhere from repeated classes to failed exams, to summer and/or winter travel restrictions - a dreadful outcome for any freedom lover.

Teachers who would die before questioning anything about the communist system ruled, but with perestroika that seemed to have reached its climax. With transparency, openness and an infant democracy, their days were numbered. It was like looking at a storm coming, either you get out of the way or you get swept. Many hang on and hoped for a reversal of fortunes, as fighting the inevitable was easier for them than change their minds or even go with the flow. Some of our very dedicated teachers began to slowly transition without abruptly cutting the cord with the old system. They were still focused on us and would do anything to help academically. From small size classes to one-on-one tutoring, through in-dorm visits, we had it all.

The average Soviet university teacher was shockingly poor. Teaching was more of a means to survive than a planned or chosen career path for most. None of them would openly admit their hopeless conditions and low morale, but it showed in their daily tasks at school. They had a very low salary and would only grumble privately to a good friend. Their pay was around 120-150 rubles, about the price of a pair of blue jeans that foreigners sold left and right. They had no cars or decent apartments, due to the long queue they needed to stand in to get one. They were very uncomfortable having students over, and always arranged to meet at school.

In the Union, all the tests and exams were conducted the same way, as students bought flowers for the occasion. Yes, the starosta (head of students) would collect money from everybody in order to buy a bouquet or two. He would then place them on the table at which the teacher sat for surveillance and to listen to students' answers. All the questions were on tickets we drew before sitting down to work on them. Once ready, a student would come up to the table and orally answer the questions from his or her ticket. Afterwards, the teacher wrote the grade and signed in a small book, called an exam book. It had our picture, name and major in it. Different departments had different colors, but they held all our grades since freshman year. There was a five-point grading system in place that later became a ten-point system. Five was the highest, and three the minimum passing grade. Two was a failing grade, automatically prompting a do-over. On the other end, the system also allowed students to retake a test or an exam if they were not pleased with their grades. This was called "otrabotka", and it literally meant to work at it again, with the goal of enhancing one's grade and level of understanding of a particular subject matter. I had a colleague from Uganda who took advantage of that, and "repaired" all his grades into fives. He wanted to finish with honor or to have a "red diploma" according to the Soviet system. He was very smart and outperformed all of us, foreign and Soviet students combined. But he thought that a few fours among his fives did not look good enough, so he retook them and had only fives in his exam book.

After November 1989, when the Berlin Wall fell, the situation turned into chaos. A new dynamic was born from the debris of the wall that would literally change everything. Each of the fifteen republics that formed the Soviet Union issued its own rules and regulations regarding education. The triangular relationship between the republics, the teachers, and the students (foreign or native) entered a new uncertain era. All of a sudden, the main department of education in Moscow was not in control anymore. Tens of thousands of foreign students lost the safety net that protected them all over the Union.

At first, the republics immediately demanded thousands of dollars from the central government in Moscow to help pay for the education of the remaining foreign students in their schools. Against its will, the Russian Federation, in the blink of an eye, became the de facto guarantor of all foreign students. Since it was wide spread that foreign countries paid Moscow in goods and services for our education, each one of the republics was now claiming its due share. The Baltic republics took Malian students out of school and sent them to Moscow to either ask for compensation or to find another institution. Many republics in Asia warned foreign students to get in touch with their embassies in Moscow and discuss their financial situation in order to continue their course of study.

In Moscow itself, teachers threw foreigners out of their classes for not paying in dollars for an education that had been free just a few weeks earlier. Everybody, every republic, saw the foreigners as an opportunity to get rich quick.

Embassies then entered a gut-wrenching negotiation with the Russian authorities, the only credible inheritor of all the problems that the Union faced in the days immediately after November 1989. Some suggested to send all of us home, others proposed to shorten our program, issue diplomas and send us home. Finally, after an upsetting period of uncertainty and hopelessness, an unclear compromise was reached. Some students left the Baltic republics and central Asia for Moscow, and others transferred to the West, but most of us stayed exactly where we were.

In that insecure environment, the irresponsible Malian government still continued to send new students to the Soviet Union. This was a way to justify their own presence at the embassy and delay a dreaded end to their diplomatic careers.

In Moldavia itself, our best and brightest teachers were pressured to leave the Institute and make room for the "native sons" who spoke the local language. They were harassed or attacked in their apartments just because they were of Russian, Ukrainian or "other" descent. Our Soviet and now Moldavian colleagues spoke exclusively in their native tongue (the same as Romanian, on the other side of the border). The tension grew by the minute in class between the native students and the few Russian students and teachers among us. Every morning, as teachers took attendance; the students would greet and answer in Moldavian. Many times, they would undertake a conversation in Moldavian with a native teacher in the presence of Russian colleagues and us foreign students. This intimidating behavior, added drop by drop to the long-repressed hatred and jealousy toward the "condescending Russian occupiers", and by default to other nationalities like Ukrainians, Byelorussians or Georgians. One morning, a student responded in Moldavian to our geodesy teacher from Ukraine. The teacher got angry and said, "What you just said sounds like Chinese or Japanese to me, two languages I do not speak, so you'd better answer in Russian." That incident only emboldened the students to press on with their native language. Before we knew it, native teachers were offering their classes in Moldavian, which led to the splitting of the whole junior class of Agronomy, into Russian and Moldavian groups. Good teachers all over the state, were leaving one after another, replaced by less prepared natives. Unfortunately,

96

there were not enough books or decent materials in Moldavian. Many of the new teachers were not up to the task yet either, but got thrust into serious positions. The Russian and other non-Moldavian teachers always maintained that their parents and grandparents were sent to develop and educate Moldavia after it joined (or got annexed, depending on who you talked to) the Soviet Union in August 1940. They did not have deep roots anywhere else but Moldavia, and would have to start all over again, were they to leave. The hardship was unimaginable and daunting for these middle-class intellectuals who had literally helped pull Moldavia out of backwardness.

In this turmoil, some teachers saw their bargaining power with students, strengthened. This time, they started to demand what they wanted or how much they wanted. The after-class practice or one-on-one consultations of the Soviet era became history. Now everything was for sale, including teachers' time. They never missed an opportunity to extort dollars from unprepared students. Some, deliberately made students fail their tests or exams in order to ask for money or gifts.

Education went from tough to unbelievably tough with the fall of the Berlin wall. Some dishonest teachers justified their unscrupulous behavior by alluding to a wide-spread tale about the West, and especially the US. It stated that in the US, the failure of the students benefited the teachers, because the students would pay a lot of dollars again to repeat a class or a semester. The story circulated year after year, and many faculty members repeated it and acted accordingly. Subsequently, a female advisor of an acquaintance from Sri Lanka, asked for a specific set of jewelry in order to have her thesis reviewed. The poor student had to relinquish the silver earrings, necklace and bracelet given by her mother when she was leaving Sri Lanka for the Soviet Union. She had nowhere to go and had no choice but to give in.

During our 17-week training at one of the government's huge farms (Sovkhoz), we witnessed more erosion linked to the monumental changes taking place in Eastern Europe and the Soviet Union. Fertilizers were now stored in the open, insecticides and other toxic products were not under key anymore, and used without proper protection. Laboratory chemicals for field experiments, started to disappear because workers sold or traded them for vodka bottles. The milking cows would stand knee deep in manure in order to eat, as nobody cared. An entomology PhD student with plots in Georgia (Stalin's home republic), lost almost a year because of the chemical applicator of the research center. After selling the prescribed insecticide, he sprayed the citrus plots with water. Needless to say that the poor PhD candidate lost his plots that year. Other Sovkhoz employees only cultivated or sprayed the headlines of designated fields in order to work less hours and sell the rest of the chemicals. Sometimes, they would dump the remainder of their chemical mixes in the nearby river or waterways. Carelessness spread to unimaginable levels and corners of the society in search of its footing. The abrupt political changes in Eastern Europe following the fall of the Berlin wall, negatively affected the dynamic in every aspect of life included education.

III
Tpu

C. THE TEMPTATIONS

As foreigners studying in the USSR, our day-to-day life was clearly defined, predictable and mostly spent indoors. The indoors meant either your own dorm, or some friend's dorm and nowhere else. After classes, we would sometimes go out together as a group, not venturing far from familiar places. Restaurants, movies, bars and nightclubs were everywhere, as well as outdoor parks, stadiums and beaches. Unfortunately they were not outlets for fun and entertainment, but guaranteed sources of serious confrontations. As a very visible minority group susceptible to the worst kinds of prejudice, we were not welcome in public places. That hostile atmosphere outside of the dorms pushed black foreign students deep into their rooms. We all learned by necessity to sell imported items, study and have a little fun, away from the battle lines in town. Consequently, each and every one of us, had to strike a personal balance among these activities. All the conditions were ripe to wholeheartedly embrace some or all of them. However, it was obviously impossible to study hard, party hard, drink heavily and constantly travel to the West, to import and sell Western goods. Our Individual make-up and deep-rooted family backgrounds made the difference when it came time to prioritize among the tantalizing pulls.

1. Contraband

Before leaving Mali for the former USSR, I heard here and there about students' commercial activities. Six years prior to my departure, I had a conversation with friends that all came back to me once I landed in Moscow. That particular day, under a scorching sun, a bunch of us were walking to a soccer game. Spread out in one of the many unpaved streets that led to the stadium, and talking very loudly to each other, somebody brought up the shocking profits foreign students made, selling jeans to the Soviets. Thinking of all the pairs of jeans I had just brought home from Paris, I said, "Man, if I were there now, I would be a millionaire", without thinking that it might sound like bragging. Fortunately, nobody took offense; to the contrary, they all agreed with me on the matter and voiced their disbelief about this Soviet paradox.

So, in August 1986, during our brief stay in Moscow, I connected many dots regarding the subject. From the colleague with the shiny fabric, whom got searched at the airport, to that Soviet teen who wanted to buy Barry's leather jacket by the Kremlin, to the fact that all our visitors at the hotel were just returning from Berlin, Paris or London. When we got to Kishinev the scenario was not any different, as most students either just got back or were still in Europe

After just a few days in town, we all got the scoop from the ancients about the illegal but lucrative activities every one of them engaged in. They were already talking about their next trip during the winter break, five to six months away. As newcomers, the image of the colleagues' luggage, full of fresh pictures from Europe and foreign goods, made our brains "salivate" with wishful thinking. We wanted to be like them, without seriously questioning what it took and why they were doing what they were doing.

With time, we clearly understood that this illegal activity of selling imported stuff to the blind-folded Soviets was too important to overlook, and a direct competitor to students' education. The activity was so widespread and time-consuming that many pushed aside their studies in order to focus on it. Paradoxically, the same "mosquito had bitten" our diplomats in Moscow, who could travel any time and as often as their irresponsible minds allowed them to. Specifically, I am speaking about third-world diplomats who saw their appointment in Moscow as a retirement plan. These shameless diplomats got so crazy about buying and selling stuff that they forgot why they were in Moscow in the first place. Doing so, they compromised themselves so much, that they were afraid to take students' problems to the Soviet authorities.

In September 1986, a little over a year after Gorbachev came to power, the Soviet population had what they needed to be happy, and at the cheapest price possible. The system worked in spite of some grave underlying problems. Sure, they had to stand in line for hours for some goods and for years for apartments or cars, but still they could get what they wanted overtime. Since the borders were closed and state TV and radio were constantly brain-washing them, the majority could not compare their situation to anybody else's and be depressed. In short, they did not know better. However, an "economic army", represented by the foreign students and diplomats, was slowly but surely chipping away at the aging economy.

Since all their goods were domestically made, they could not compete against the smuggled ones from the West. Foreign goods were therefore rustled into the country by students and diplomats, to the delight of the exponentially-growing-by-the-minute, indigenous customers. This demand for

102

foreign goods that the Soviets could not legally get for themselves, gave foreigners the motivation to import more and more stuff, ignoring the serious risks involved with trafficking.

Not only were the Soviets bared from travelling abroad, the special stores carrying foreign goods and sold in foreign currencies, were also off-limits for them. Additionally, by law they could not hold foreign currencies, since everything was sold in rubles. So, to them, having a foreign currency was like having a bikini at the North Pole.

Foreign students in turn could legally travel twice a year, after passing all exams and a thorough medical checkup, including HIV AIDS tests. The only exceptions were students coming from hardcore socialist countries of the communist bloc. Students from Afghanistan, Cuba, Ethiopia, Somalia, Laos, Cambodia, Vietnam and North Korea were also banned from traveling abroad. We wondered why, until we were told that a huge number of them defected to the West, while on vacation. The Soviet authorities then completely forbade them from travelling.

Diplomats from every foreign embassy in Moscow, however, could travel any time and as often as they pleased. Over the years, these aberrant rules pushed the Soviets to an irrational yearning for foreign goods. The result was a huge demand that neither the Soviet government nor the foreign guests, could satisfy.

The third-world diplomatic corps and students were in a position to make a fortune, to the extent that they almost forgot about their main mission. You basically had an army of foreign students and diplomats, trying to satisfy the gigantic appetite of 280 million Soviets, by smuggling in Western items. From chewing gum to underwear, tape players, plastic bags, denim jeans or even toothpaste, you name it and the Soviets wanted it. They would spend as much as their monthly salary, or more, as long as the items came from abroad. This phenomenon that started as a benign import activity by foreign students to make ends meet, evolved into an out-of-control lucrative trade. The colossal Soviet demand created a whole black market, run by foreign students and unscrupulous diplomats.

Almost every foreign student who landed in Moscow

took part in this wild activity to a certain degree. It was clear to all that it was illegal and sometime dangerous, but very lucrative if neatly conducted. The rule was simple enough: bring some popular items, or almost anything from outside of the Soviet Union, and sell them to the indigenous population. Then, exchange the profit from rubles to dollars or Francs in the black market, and smuggle out that money to buy more items in the West. The profit margins were head-spinning, and thus outweighed the risks associated with the activity.

There were three main routes for every student to exploit, without really competing with fellow students: The Soviet Union itself, Europe and the Third World. For obvious reasons, the nature of the trade items we imported or exported varied significantly with the need and sophistication of the targeted population.

The Alpha and Omega of the whole system were travel documents and foreign currencies. At first, you could not operate with one without the other, but over time the dynamic evolved and took different shapes and forms. However, the Soviet authorities had clear rules on the books regarding these two components. First year students could travel only once, and only after passing all their final exams and medical checkups. The ancients could travel twice a year also after finals and medical exams. The secretary of the dean of foreign students would then issue our exit and reentry visas, after verifying our signed exam books. As far as the foreign currencies were concerned, we had to document every cent of them, meaning that we had to have proof of ownership of any currency, or be dispossessed at the borders. These draconian rules pushed students, faculty, and diplomats toward unorthodox techniques in order to circumvent them and operate at will.

At first, everybody respected these rules of conduct, and things ran smoothly at the dean's office as far as our visa applications were concerned. Nobody could have his or her documents without finishing with the finals, period. Nobody could apply for a travel permit outside of summer and winter terms, period. This gave the faculty tremendous bargaining power over students, because they knew that traveling abroad was our lifeline. Without openly acknowledging it, theirs too.

Then, at some point, a corrupt relationship took root between students and faculty members. The secretaries, the deans themselves, and the teachers, all started to bend rules and ask for something in return for delivering travel visas to the students. The doctors at the clinic who signed the medical checkup papers, started to abuse their power too. Students, by the same token, engaged in bribing right and left to get their travel visas without finishing with all their exams, or in the middle of the school year, or even multiple times a year.

The situation with foreign currencies required a little more sophisticated maneuvering, and had major hurdles with dire consequences. It was clear that the indigenous population did not have, and did not need, foreign currency. They could not travel abroad or shop in special stores selling items in dollars. So, the only legal tender for the Soviets and foreigners was the ruble. The regular ruble was commonly named the "wooden ruble," as opposed to the diplomatic one, used to pay Soviet diplomats posted abroad. The latter was reportedly strong against the dollar in government-run papers, giving a false sense of pride to the average Soviet citizen.

For trafficking purposes, we needed foreign currencies in order to buy Western items, and import them into the Soviet Union. But once inside, the Soviets paid only in rubles that we could not take abroad to buy more stuff to bring back. In turn, banks could not sell foreign currencies, especially to students, because we did not need them inside the country and because they themselves needed them for some of their own transactions with foreign banks. So it was imperative to locate some foreign currencies inside the country, and find a way to smuggle the money out in order to be able to buy more stuff abroad.

Another way of procuring foreign currency was to buy Soviet-made items and sell them abroad, then turn around and buy foreign items to bring into the Union for sale again in rubles. However, the demand for these Soviet items depended on the location. Our European clients had little or no interest in big-ticket items from USSR but craved church icons, caviar, or cameras, which were extremely expensive and hard to find. On the other hand, the third world could not get enough of cheap Soviet items.

In order to keep their isolated economy in check, the Soviets had flawed and frustrating measures in place regarding foreign currencies. Anybody entering the former Soviet Union had to declare all of his or her belongings, especially foreign currencies. The issued declaration form then became as precious as the items listed on it, and was not to be lost or replaced under any circumstances. It needed to be presented to custom agents when exiting the country. At that point, you could have less foreign currency than you declared when you entered the country, but not more. Any excess foreign currency that had not been documented would be confiscated by custom agents, because it could have been obtain only illegally. A receipt from an embassy as proof of annual scholarship payments, or a bank statement for scholarship money disbursed through a local bank, were the only legal ways to document one's extra foreign currency.

This tough and exasperating rule, just like all the other controlling measures in the country, pushed people to come up with unorthodox alternatives. From our first days in the Union, the ancients taught us many of the tricks they used to deceive the border guards. With this great number of travelers, the guards in turn had seen it all too.

On the train, some would hide their excess money in a cooked chicken or a half-consumed sausage intentionally left on the table. Others would wrap it in a plastic sheet and drop it in a half-full bottle of rotten milk, purposely left behind in the bathroom. Sometimes though, the bottle got thrown away by the conductor in charge of the car. Others would try shoe soles, pants' hems, dirty baby diapers or underwear, etc. Tens of thousands travelers per year, tens of thousands tricks to deceive border agents and save one's fortune.

Many others came to the borders with fake declaration forms they had secured inland, months before embarking for the trip. Some students specialized in counterfeiting and selling declaration forms by using boiled eggs to remove the stamp, the original amount it was made out for, or the name of the holder. These specialists could make a genuine declaration for any amount of foreign currency, for anybody that needed one. Also, students who had spent their money and did not need the relevant declarations anymore, would sell them to the highest bidder.

The simplest approach was to bribe the custom agent trying to seize the undocumented currency by giving him a fraction of it. Students would sometimes give their undocumented currency to the conductor managing the train car they were traveling in for a fee, and then recuperate it on the other side of the border.

We, the new comers, could not wait to visit or be invited by those elders still trickling from Europe. These visits were our learning classes, as far as trade was concerned. We would ask all kinds of questions and contemplate the eye-catching merchandise they had just brought from overseas. The new goodies from the West, littering their tiny rooms "mentally transported us" forward to our own trips whenever those were to be. By November, we all knew what it took to travel to the heart of Western Europe, and, most importantly, what to bring back to the Soviet Union for sale.

It was around this time, that the ancients started to ask us about the declarations we had filled out at the border when we came into the Union. They pretended to explain to us how the whole declaration thing worked, while in reality, they were busy figuring out how much money each of us had. Once they had an idea about our fortunes in foreign currencies, they would visit us privately and ask us to lend them the currencies for their winter break trip to Europe. A close friend of mine did just that. He asked to lend him my foreign currencies for the winter, and pledged to give them back as soon as possible after his return. I gave him a fourth of what I had, just in case something happened. A few weeks later, another ancient approached me with the same request. I told him that I had just given my savings to another friend. About a month later, yet another ancient jokingly brought up the question of French francs and wanted to know if mine were in a secure location. I told him that they were already in Europe. I am pretty sure that almost all of us got probed by the ancients for our foreign currencies, which literally fueled the trade.

In December, we accompanied ancient after ancient to the airport or the train station with envy. Every time, we would imagine ourselves in their shoes the following year. We could not wait to pass our finals in the summer and take our maiden trip to Europe.

In the meantime, we considered alternative ideas, on how to make a buck or two before the summer. Some said that a telegram from abroad or the embassy in Moscow, requesting an immediate trip home, could convince the authorities to issue travel visas. I contemplated the idea of getting one, but did not act on it. However, I did act on another money-making scheme, based on a little known perk that the Soviets authorized. It turned out that we were allowed to receive a parcel from home that first year, but only once. Many elders bragged about getting and selling jeans from home, when they first came. I dared try that one, even though I risked not getting anything at all, coming all the way from Mali through the Soviet post office. I wrote to my mom asking for two pairs of jeans with zippers everywhere, called "Bananas" by an indigenous youth ready to die for one. Soon enough, my dear mom told me to look for a package with two pairs of jeans in it, the maximum the Soviets would allow. A month later, I recovered my package from the post office and opened it in front of my roommates. I decided to wear one myself, and try out my selling talents with the other. It became a matter of proving to myself that I could sell too, without an ancient holding my hand. I therefore declined to ask for help, or to give it to the numerous ancients interested in selling it for me. I decided to take my time while enquiring about price range and safe exchange precautions.

In early spring, shortly after the trees and flowers began to bloom, young natives started to parade in our yard. Armed with a pint of courage, but frightened to death, they would wander around our dorms looking for something to buy. In general, a young Soviet buyer would approach any foreigner passing by before loudly whispering, "Do you have this or that for sale?" During that quick and tense dialogue in the open, both parties would watch for potential militia presence, since the whole thing was illegal. Others more daring and experienced, would deposit their passports with the concierge and give a random room number. Once inside, they would go from floor to floor asking any foreigner they met, if they knew anybody with stuff to sell. Other regulars simply had contacts among us with whom they placed orders twice a year. They would come to buy their items in the dorms at their convenience and in a secure and safer manner.

We learned to recognize a potential customer from the average Peter in the streets or near the dorms. With hands in their pockets and an empty black duffle bag on one shoulder, our clients were always on edge, looking right and left for the common enemy -- the Soviet militia. During the season, you could not miss them.

After enquiring for a while and being probed many times by numerous customers that spring, I decided to go ahead with my sale. I was now open to those brief dialogues I had rejected for some time. One day, I talked to one of the street clients interested in buying a banana. I told him that I had one pair for sale upstairs, if he wished to see it. He nodded, and started to ask all kinds of questions regarding my roommates, the commandant of the dorm, and my own friends. I told him that he should give my room number to the concierge and pretend to visit my Soviet roommates, Sacha and Tolea, who were away, I thought. I went up to my room first, only to find my two roommates there. Minutes later, he knocked at the door and I let him in. My roommates stared at him like an alien, but he kept his cool, stood his ground, and gave me a very questioning look which seemed to say, "Oh man, you said that we would be alone. Now get the stuff out, and let's get on with it!" I pulled my suitcase from underneath my bed, and reached in it for the banana jeans. My heart was pounding out of my chest, while his eyes were scanning around like a thief. My roommates, like jurors in court, sat silently to witness the entire transaction. I handed him the pair of jeans and he took it from my hands like a parent would a newborn, with deliberate care. He held it up to himself not only to measure up the length, but more importantly to verify the intricacies and design patterns of the zippered pockets - a crucial criterion. After dissecting the brand-new banana and imagining himself in it, he finally asked for the price. I replied "200 rubles", almost double the monthly salary of a teacher at the time. He pondered for a while, clearly under the pressure of the dead silence that took over the room, and the intense stares of my two roommates. Then offered 180 rubles, more than twice my own monthly stipend. I jumped and clapped my feet in the air, in my head and said "davai" or, OK, give the money. He pulled out a stack of bills from his pocket, counted 180 rubles and handed them to me. I proudly recounted them before handing back the pants. He neatly laid them in his duffle bag, made his last eye contact, and said good-bye.

That was the last time I saw him, and I swear that I could not point him out in a crowd a month later, the sign of a very fast transaction. My roommates never asked me a single question about the whole situation, but I am sure that they reported it first thing the next morning to the appropriate authority, as they were required to. I proudly went to spread the news to all my friends in the dorm like a little hero.

That was my first sale ever. Summer could not come soon enough for me and tens of thousands of foreign students desperately looking forward to try out. We were all making plans and figuring out profit margins, knowing that we would make at least ten trips during our six-year stay. A missed trip was a fortune lost, we were constantly reminded by some elders.

a. From Europe to the Soviet Union

The challenge was to reach Western Europe, just past Poland, in West Berlin and in the former German Democratic Republic. Strategically situated in the heart of Europe and at the crossroads to the major capitals, West Berlin was THE destination for the cheap items that fueled the trafficking. We all had different vacation destinations throughout Europe, but we all met in West Berlin for a final stop, on our way back to the Soviet Union. French speaking students would fight to get to Paris or Brussels, English speakers to London, and Portuguese speakers to Lisbon, but everybody stopped in Berlin to pick up hot items to sell back in the Soviet Union. Others would just come to Berlin early in the morning, buy their merchandise, and catch the late afternoon train bound for Moscow through Warsaw.

In the mid-80s to the early 90s, foreign students were well aware of the tastes of their Soviet consumers regarding big and small items from the West. The hottest small items were:

Clothing:
90% of the outfit foreign students brought to the Union for sale, were from Berlin, and the rest either from Paris or London. In Berlin, stores like Bilka and C&A, were conveniently located right next to the Zoologische Garten train and Metro stations. We loaded up with mostly cheap female clothing, from sweat

111

pants, underwear, stockings, T-shirts and dresses to skirts, scarves, jackets, Banana jeans and sweaters. The cheaper the better, because the Soviets did not know the difference, and had nothing to compare them with. In Paris, the favorite store was Tati, where we found the cheapest items in all France, much like Wal-Mart in the USA, only cheaper. We all loved their very deep, sturdy and colorful bag with their logo on it. We would keep our merchandise in these during the long trip across Europe to Moscow.

Shoes:

Any kind did the trick as long as they came from the West. Soviet females were mostly targeted for shoes because the men were mostly crazy about jeans, but bought all kinds of outfits and shoes for their girlfriends or wives. Women's summer sandals, and even winter boots, were sometimes sold out already in Moscow before students even reached their respective towns and cities.

Cosmetics:

These were very convenient to pack and sold faster than any other items. Soviet girls loved the neat cosmetic boxes with a wide variety of colors, and stored them in secret places to keep them safe from jealous roommates. They would often show off as they dressed among peers. These items made them feel privileged, and more beautiful because of where they came from. Sometimes, our female colleagues would help us choose cheap and popular items from the huge array of choices we faced in Western stores.

Body lotions and perfumes:

These were other hot items everybody bought by default in Berlin, Paris or London. Cocoa Butter and Avon were well-known in female circles in the Soviet Union, hence their popularity. Many girls would specifically order them for friends and family. We loaded up on perfumes without trying them, since the design of the bottles and the look of the boxes were more important than the scent. Size did not matter here, either, which made them incredibly popular among all foreign traffickers.

Walkman cassette players:

These were very popular among young indigenous males. We would usually buy them for our own use, but always ended up selling them after few months. They cost peanuts, but sold for a lot more right in the dorms to our colleagues and roommates.

These small-ticket items were the bread and butter of the average foreign student and diplomat in the Soviet Union. They were cheap to buy, easy to handle, sold like hotcakes and, most importantly, brought great profits. Faculty, students, cab drivers and factory workers, would flood the dorms or literally harass foreigners while hunting for these Western goodies. They would pay a fortune compared to both the price we paid for, and the income of the average Soviet at the time. With these items, an average foreign student could illegally make as much as ten to 20 times the monthly salary of a university professor in one trip abroad. Yet, tens of thousands of students imported an incalculable quantity of Western goods twice every year, and always sold everything out.

Along with these poor man's goods, other bigger items were literally dragged between trains from the West to Moscow.

Sharp 939 double tape player/recorder:

To many, a trip to the West without bringing back a Sharp, was a worthless one. We all bought these in Berlin from a tiny shop next to the Zoogarten station called "Tony Shop." The manager made millions from foreign students studying in the Soviet Union alone. He would pack and hold on to them, while students shopped all day downtown Berlin. The business grew so big that he would even deliver the Sharps right to the train station, moments before departure. Since the orders were all the same - the Sharp 939, Tony Shop would bring a boatload of them to the rail station, and deliver one to anybody with a receipt. His employees spoke Russian just to accommodate those of us coming from the Soviet Union, not fluent in German but bought the biggest share of his supply. They then cost about 300 Marks each and sold for 2000 rubles cash, duty-free.

Television sets:

Many student-tycoons would import TV sets for the more

sophisticated or better-off Soviets. Their favorite was the Sony Black-Trinitron 55-centimeter screen. The Soviets could not take their eyes off of it; some even asked how in the world the Japanese made such things. It was the jewel of deans, army officers and crooks with mounds of rubles under their beds. JVC's 202, 210, 140 ME 55-cm models, or Sanyo 51-cm models were also sought after. Again, Berlin and Tony Shop were THE places to buy them for up to 1000 marks, and we sold them for double or triple that amount in the Soviet Union.

Purple fabric:

This was one of the most profitable items brought to the Union from Berlin or France, but it was also a very tricky one. You needed to know exactly the right type to avoid bankruptcy, because buyers were very finicky and would not buy a centimeter of a slightly dissimilar fabric. According to some ancients, it was adored in the central Asian Islamic republics for weddings and special events. Nobody really saw what they did with it there, and nobody really cared. I have never seen it in use, and still do not know anybody who has. We just imported it, and southerners always bought a ton of it before heading back. This silky fabric with golden embroidery and stripes, came in different shades of purple. The two popular kinds had either three stripes or four. Students bought it in Paris from a shop named La Goutte d'Or, which belonged to a short guy named Joel. Without leaving France, he knew exactly what was hot in central Asia, just by dealing with foreign students who bought thousands of yards. Just like Tony Shop in Berlin, Joel would take the money and give a receipt to buyers who would go do other errands, before recovering their wrapped fabrics later in the day. After a while, students started to complain that he cheated on the length of the wrapped fabrics. Many complained that their fabric started to be a meter or two shy of the 150 or 200 they usually bought. Unfortunately they could not do anything about it thousands miles away. Joel was obviously making a killing, given the fact that he sold thousands of meters on a good summer day.

Other students bought their fabrics in Berlin from Asian stores. This was exactly the kind of fabric a friend was carrying, when he got stopped and searched at the airport as we all flew into Moscow for the very first time. The demand for the fabric was never even close to be met, guaranteeing astronomical profits.

Computers and copy machines:

In the late 80's and early 90's, computers and copy machines were the biggest items foreign students smuggled into the Soviet Union. They were rare as water in the desert, but a huge underground market was in the making. Only a selected few students could afford to buy them in the West and successfully bring them into the country. Scientists were very interested in them, and students loved them for the different games they came with. Selling a computer or a copy machine, said a lot about a student's wealth and trading skills. It was a big deal to handle an expensive IBM from Berlin to the dorms in Moscow. They sold for tens of thousands of rubles. Selling them was also very dangerous due to the huge amount of money involved. Besides that, the Soviet authorities were wary about the misuse of computers, in writing and distributing antagonistic leaflets on a massive scale. Just like copiers and type writers were forbidden after the revolution of 1917, they were still seen as potentially dangerous to the communist establishment. Still some ancient tycoons imported and sold many of them to the few natives who were evidently living years ahead of the communist government and their fellow citizens.

For us, getting these items in the West was just a small part of the whole ordeal, smuggling them into the Union and selling them safely presented another set of challenges. Once in possession of these items, most of us took the train straight from Berlin to Moscow or Kiev, through Poland. Flying was more expensive (tickets and extra pounds) and prone to more scrutiny from the numerous agents at Cheremetyevo International Airport in Moscow. Corruption was potentially less likely due to the presence of numerous cameras, agents, and superior officers.

The main border towns between the Soviet Union and Poland were Lvov in Ukraine, and Brest in Belarus. In Brest, everybody was subject to a scrutiny that sometimes turned sour at the hands of border guards. The rules of importation were blurred at best, and subject to interpretation or corrupt practices on the spot. Needless to say, Brest and Lvov evoked both fear and triumph, since it was at these frontiers that fortunes were made or broken. Sneakiness, tricks, the ability to think on your feet and negotiate, were some prerequisite skills for anybody looking to excel.

The general consensus was that the import of some specific items (Sharp 939, Walkman, computers, copiers) was limited to one per student per trip. Two hundred to five hundred feet of the fabric, were also okay to import. All the rest of the items were subject to the mood of the custom agents and every student's negotiation skills, or the level of corruption at the border on that particular day. To this day, I have yet to be informed by anyone with authority as to what or how much of anything could be lawfully brought into the country. The tens of thousands of foreign students crossing the borders at least twice a year, studied the mindset of the border guards, trip after trip.

It was not at all uncommon for students to buy a few cheap items, specifically for the potentially opportunistic custom agent. Some students would wait until they got to the borders to decide what to give away, depending on the appetite of the agents. Some of them would accept money; others would take a handful of cosmetics products or scarves, out of the hundreds or thousands a particular student was trying to bring in. At other times, students in the same train compartment would pitch in and give a considerable amount of money, or a substantial gift to the agents, in exchange for clemency. We would also divide items up among ourselves, so nobody would have a lot of one specific kind and thereby draw attention.

However, as in any business, there were days when nothing worked, and important items got confiscated. When that happened, students were given a receipt in order to collect their items the next time they exited through the same border.

Sometimes, unhappy students would smash or destroy their confiscated items right there at the border, rather than trying to come back for them. That way no border agent gets a second chance at asking for a bribe or get away with thievery.

Now let us talk about the numerous diplomats, who were supposed to represent their respective countries and fellow citizens in the former Soviet Union. Name a country in central and Latin America, Africa, Asia or Eastern Europe, chances are it had thousands of students in the Soviet Union, therefore a diplomatic mission in Moscow. Before I left Bamako, I heard that a distant cousin of mine was sent to work at the Mali embassy in Moscow, in order to "prepare his retirement." That sentence stuck with me and only made sense once I witnessed in person what kinds of activities African diplomats led. Unlike the students, our representatives could travel in and out of the Soviet Union at will. They did not have exams to pass, nor restrictions on the number of trips they could take per year. They were not subjects either, to intrusive searches at the borders because of their diplomatic passports. Foreign students could only dream of such privilege in a country relying more and more on a growing and fruitful black market.

Diplomats from third-world countries could not ask for more. Just like many students, the majority of them forgot about their mission in Moscow and dedicated their time, energy and focus to the lucrative trafficking between the USSR and the outside world. Representing students became secondary; as embassies were turned into storage units. The Malian embassy was later nicknamed "the Mall", due to the business that took place there. Diplomats enthusiastically put their privilege to work for themselves, regardless of the potential damage to their reputation. They unscrupulously "milked that sacred cow" dry, with every ounce of their being.

Ambassadors, their coworkers, wives, drivers and cooks, led the way in this once-in-a-lifetime opportunity. Many of them traveled to Berlin weekly and brought back tons of merchandise. I saw boxes upon boxes of body lotions, cosmetics, clothes, cassette players, computers and copiers at the residence of many Malian and third-world diplomats. Ironically, many embassies, among them the Malian one, did not have computers in their offices, while diplomats sold them weekly to the Soviets. Sometimes diplomats would travel by plane with some items and ship others, especially TV's, video players, and computers, in order to maximize their profit per trip.

In the long run, being able to travel at will and bring in anything they wished, was no longer enough. Greed took over. Not content with this glut, diplomats started to use students for their unquenchable thirst for wealth. Just like any other illegal trafficker, they began to put their minds to work on different and more efficient ways to increase their already-swollen profit margins. Some diplomats illegally gave diplomatic passports to regular students, to make their travels smoother and more frequent. They did not want to wait for summer or winter, to send their protégés on a quick trip to the West. Since Berlin was less than 48 hours from Moscow, you can imagine the traffic jam at the ticket counter of the railroad stations.

As if all that was not enough, Malian diplomats in particular, started to use students' yearly stipend of 2400 French francs for their own trafficking purposes. At the embassy, these disingenuous diplomats would hold onto the stipends of thousands of students, claiming that the money had not yet come from Mali. Meantime, they would use the money to go buy more merchandise in Berlin. After selling the goods, they would exchange the rubles into French francs in the black market, to finally pay the students. They also took advantage of a ruling of the sole political party at the time (Democratic Union of the Malian People), that required every student to have a membership card in order to get his or her stipend. Just imagine US students needing a membership card from the Democratic or the Republican parties, in order to receive their scholarships. At times, students found themselves in Moscow without their cards, unable to collect their dues from worthless representatives. Meantime, those temporarily unclaimed monies, would finance some diplomats' trips to Berlin. It took a lots of complaints, and a coup d'état in Mali in 1991, to reverse some of the prevailing goddamn policies.

b. From the Soviet Union to Europe

Students and diplomats also smuggled countless Soviet items into Western Europe. There was a considerable market for Soviet-made household items, as well as high-priced and dangerous ones. We poor students had our niche in Berlin, London and the French suburbs, among low-income and middle-class migrants. Diplomats and other well-established students, handled other objects with their shady connections in the West.

Between trips abroad, we were always on the lookout for possible merchandise that would sell in the West. The profits brought much-needed foreign currencies that would finance the trip back to the Soviet Union. So, every summer and winter, the immigrant population looked forward to foreign students bringing affordable household goods from Moscow.

In general, students sold their items to their hosts or their hosts' friends and neighbors. They were very aware of the limited time we had, before heading back to Moscow. As a matter of fact, they would ask about our return dates for better payment coordination, they pretended. In fact, it was a powerful inside information that our hosts and clients used to their advantage. Sometimes in a pinch, we reluctantly worked out long and interest-free loans until our next trip.

We did not have a stand or a store per se in London, Paris or Berlin, but had clients who knew that we had inexpensive Soviet items for sale. In that direction (USSR to Western Europe), the profit margins were also huge, because we bought our articles with a much-deflated ruble and sold them in Deutsch marks, French francs or British pounds.

Let us start with the small, light and inconspicuous items.

In France, one of the hottest items from USSR, was the crock pot. They sold like cakes in all the low-income immigrant areas in and around Paris, as well as in big cities. Some French storekeepers also bought our items and resold them with a double margin. We did too, when not in a hurry.

Students jammed the small train compartments with crock pots or other household items, unfairly squeezing fellow passengers against each other. At times, I could see the pain in regular passengers' eyes. It sometimes felt like traveling in a loaded compartment of a cargo plane.

Photo cameras and slide projectors were almost as hot as the pots, but were not a necessity for struggling families in Europe. We just had to know how many to take and where, especially when we had verbal orders from the previous trip. People really liked the brands "Kiev" and "Zenith;" those were the best ones, and our favorites too. Sometimes we sold the accompanying flash devices, lenses, and filters to semiprofessionals at ten to twenty times their worth back in the Union.

Porcelain tea sets, called china, were in huge demand. The Soviets made some of the most beautiful ones in the world, in quality probably second only to China. The average foreign student carried two to three sets, or one very nice set of twenty-four pieces. People bought these and saved them for special occasions.

On the same order, Russian teakettles called samovars of up to five-liter capacity, brought a lot of foreign currency, too. Soviet silverware neatly arranged in black corduroy boxes also dazzled many in Europe.

Some students specialized in Soviet oil and canvas paintings depicting nature and people for tiny living rooms in the West. Special red comforters from the central Asian republics of the Union with complicated embroidery patterns, were also in huge demand in France. They sold in the blink of an eye. In the beginning, we would buy them in Soviet government malls without difficulty. When they became rarer and rarer, Soviet "businessmen" would bring them to foreign students, right in the dorms. They seemed to be imported from China to the southern Asian republics, then on to the rest of the Soviet Union.

Soviet-made rugs also made ends meet for many of us. In the West, people used them on their living room walls. Decorative wooden eagles, porcelain dogs, giraffes, elephants, and cats were also in huge demand going West, as well as Soviet watches, bracelets, necklaces and earrings (silver and gold).

In the music department, we exported mostly amplifiers, synthesizers, and a lot of huge 90-watt speakers. These were really reliable and sounded perfect. Students in France used to crank them up at their parties.

The profit margin on the above items was mind-boggling, given the exchange rate on the black market. That phenomenon only encouraged and emboldened students to drag more and more stuff across Europe to their faithful customers.

Items that were bigger and more dangerous to export, were mostly smuggled by diplomats and a few well connected students transitioning to a bigger circle. These people pushed their luck and risked their lives to make a fortune. To the best of everybody's knowledge, they were under KGB surveillance, due to the magnitude of their deals and the importance of their contraband items.

The most dangerous items smuggled out of the former Soviet Union toward Western Europe, were church icons. These priceless religious sculptures came from Russian churches, operating underground or very passively at the time. Diplomats and student-tycoons procured them through shady middlemen or trusted partners. Sometimes the icons came wrapped in plain cloth under the deliveryman's armpit. Smuggling them out by train or plane was very dangerous, but diplomats did not mind the risk, given the reward on the other side of the border. I never found out specifically which icon came from which church, but our representatives seemed to have pretty good luck with the delivery of this highly-charged merchandise.

Berlin was the first destination where buyers and sellers met, and from there the icons found their way around Europe and beyond for a fortune. One small twelve-by-ten inch icon would bring tens of thousands of Deutsch marks, or hundreds of thousands of rubles, something many of us never dreamed of making. Some diplomats and daring students smuggled at least one per year. It was a common belief that the KGB knew for fact, who dealt with these sensitive items, and was even at the receiving end in the West. One diplomat swore to have smuggled the exact same icon twice. How did he know that? He said that the first time he bought it, it fell and a small piece got chipped away from one of the corners of the icon. Later on he bought and smuggled to Berlin, the same icon, suggesting that the KGB would buy and return them to the Soviet Union, and back into the circuit again. Why? For surveillance purposes, many colleagues thought.

The next big item for Western Europe was caviar. A limited quantity of about a pound, was allowed to export per passenger. These delicious and exceptional fish eggs came mostly in two-, five-, or ten-pound cans. Our diplomats and other experienced students managed to always get them and in the quantities they wanted. Some supplied restaurants in Berlin; as others hid theirs all the way to Paris.

Winter trips were favored for caviar smuggling, given the cold temperature that helped preserve the eggs during the long trip across Europe. Because of the high risk of contamination and food poisoning, clients in the West were very careful about whom to buy from. Dealers from the Union had their specific customers who trusted them. Smuggling caviar out of the Union was only half of the burden, because at destination, the buyers opened and tested them for freshness in back rooms. I did not know the penalties for being caught illegally with a significant amount, but presumed them to be severe. The one and only time I dealt with caviar was in the winter of 1988. I bought about five pounds from a friend, who decided to stay and not travel to the West that winter. So, I took over and

122

asked as many questions as possible, before heading for Brest, the border town with Poland. Hiding such a bulky can became my next daunting task. After mentally going through thousands of scenarios, I decided to use my big woolly winter coat as a last resort. Because of a hole in the right pocket, I pushed the can beyond the depth of the pocket itself, and between the insulating layers. Then I hung the coat on a hook in my compartment, among other passengers' clothes. Once at the border, one customs agent ordered all of us to exit and wait in the hallway. He checked under mattresses and beds, in the overhead area full of suitcases, and finally swung our hanging clothes left and right to make sure there was nothing behind them. As his hand stretched toward our coats, my heart rate doubled and my whole student life flashed in front of my eyes. Fortunately, he did not thoroughly check the coats, and ordered us back in. I breathed a big sigh of relieve as soon as we left the Soviet side of the border.

Once in Paris, I went to see Joel, the fabric retailer, who contacted a restaurant owner not far from his shop. The latter soon showed up, opened the can, smelled and tasted the shiny black eggs. He liked it and paid cash, about four times what I invested in the can back in Moscow. It was a good deal, but I never carried caviar again. I still cannot imagine how some diplomats and students made many trips with more and bigger cans.

Cuban cigars, Soviet champagne, and vodka were also part of the arsenal for Western consumption. The Cuban cigars and genuine Russian vodka sold fast in Berlin and cheaper than what the local market offered, but expensive enough to finance subsequent trips.

With time and the implosion of the Soviet Union, foreign students lost their market share as the Soviets themselves started to travel. With that turn of events, the average and small student-traffickers died out, while the old guard and diplomats held their ground

Already by 1989 and the fall of the Berlin wall, foreign embassies in Moscow saw more Soviets applying for visas for than foreign students. The dynamic was shifting rapidly in favor of the natives, who just few months earlier could not point at any foreign embassy, much less foreign country on the map. Suddenly, any Soviet could travel anywhere in the world after being 'jailed' for seven decades. They started by visiting foreign countries first, then smuggled out items just like foreign students did. Soon enough with import permits; they opened shops after shops just about everywhere. We then started to lose our commercial edge to the Soviets, now crowding us out.

Diplomats saw some of their privileges reduced overnight. At the borders, diplomatic passports now, brought more problems than they solved. The Soviets even arranged special rooms just to search those with diplomatic passports.

In that commotion, the average student's life got worse. People started to sell their private items, or items for export, right back into the Soviet market in order to eat. Some sold alcohol right from their dorm rooms, for a marginal profit. Schools started to demand foreign currencies from students and embassies.

As we entered the nineties, the situation became so dire that students started to hold embassies up (Congo, Mali, Sri Lanka, etc.) to complain about late and insufficient stipends during this inflationary period. Students asked for help from home and from international organizations.

Some clever and still-affluent students from India, Pakistan, Sri Lanka, and Nigeria, seized the moment and played the middlemen between Soviet universities and potential foreign students. The universities were now requesting tuition fees up front from graduates overseas, who were desperate to get out at any cost to study abroad. Since money was king, universities started to collect dollars directly from anybody without consulting with the Soviet authorities.

That business of bringing in students and fellow countrymen, evolved into an illegal smuggling venue to the West. Potential students would pay tuition fees, get accepted at Soviet universities and then come. After a year of study, they would then apply for a student tourist visa to Germany, UK and France, never to return. In the early to mid-nineties, Moscow thus became one of the biggest people-smuggling points between the third world and Western Europe.

With the opening of the country, ill-intentioned and
124

creative Soviets, came up with new plans with lightning speed. Only this time, the merchandise was desperate women and vulnerable girls. After the fall of the Berlin wall and travel possibilities for Soviet citizens, sex trafficking began to reach the shores of the former Soviet Union and its satellites. In the late eighties and early nineties, unscrupulous travel agencies started to finance trips to Ankara, Turkey for women and girls. They would work the streets for a couple of weeks and use the proceeds to pay off their patrons, then buy some stuff for themselves. The concept spread like a bad rash from neighborhood to neighborhood, then from city to city.

Soon enough, gangs and organized crime stepped in. They started to claim all the profit and forced the girls to work more than they were willing to. From that point on, the whole thing turned into a huge international sex slavery ring, bringing unimaginable profits. In subsequent cases, the girls were promised jobs in the West or even in Romania, Bulgaria etc., only to find themselves forced to sell their bodies once on the ground, without any kind of support or protection. As years passed, these activities grew into what we know today as the sex trade. A phenomenon that is still gnawing at the countries from the former Soviet bloc, destroying families and marriages.

c. From the Soviet Union to the Third World

Third world students and diplomats made up to 95% of the foreign body, residing in the Union in any given year. Different students from different countries had a wide range of preferences when it came to export items.

The two main directions were Africa and Asia. Most students from Latin America did not travel home frequently, given the great distance separating the two continents. Most of my Latino colleagues stayed behind, while other students travelled twice or more a year, outside of the Union. I knew only one Peruvian couple, who travelled to the West every year. On the other hand, African and Asian students and diplomats could not have enough to export.

African diplomats, with their buying power and status, specialized in exporting big items in huge quantities to their home countries. They preferred power generators, water pumps, freezers, refrigerators, air conditioners, entertainment centers, furniture, welders, motor bikes, etc. You name it, they exported it in bulk. Being in Moscow, where all the flights originated, gave them more opportunities to gain the system and abuse the loopholes in the regulations. Aeroflot, the only Soviet airline at the time, required a ticket with confirmed dates and time for any fret shipment. Cargo shipments toward African countries were also depended on graduation or proof of returning home for good. Only one shipment per return ticket and one entity of any item could be sent, not multiples. Those days, Aeroflot flew once a week, to just about every African capital. To keep up with their insatiable appetite, many diplomats bought a ticket every week just to send items home. Then they would simply return the ticket and paid an insignificant fine. Aeroflot eventually closed that loophole and refused to take back unused tickets, even for a fee.

In order to overcome regulations and still ship their favorite items every week, diplomats resorted to "shopping" for travelling or returning graduates. Every week, they hunted down students and convinced them to take some of their items along. At the same time, they sought out graduating students about to ship their containers. Because they were constantly on the prowl for shipping opportunities, our diplomats had big items on stand buy. They started by storing freezers, air conditioners, water pumps and other huge power generators in their apartments and storage rooms at the diplomatic compounds. When they ran out of room there, they started storing in rented places in town. Then, when they ran out of room there, or were too greedy to pay the rent, they started to store in the basements and storage rooms of the embassies. That pitted them against the ambassadors themselves, their families and staff. That competition for space pushed them to take over the hallways, back and front yards of numerous embassies in Moscow. The Malian ambassador's residency on the second floor, was like a storage itself. Big boxes and huge items lined the corridors and corners, waiting to be shipped. The ambassador's wife traveled to Berlin all the time during the school year to load up on body lotions and other women's products. Their cook and his young wife knew Berlin, street by street and store by store. Her passport pages were full of tracking codes scribbled by border agents, after each crossing with her diplomatic passport. The ambassador's personal secretary, who handled passports and stamps, also went to Berlin like to the grocery store. Cornered once in Bilka (a superstore in Berlin) by a traveling student, he said to have come to buy water for the president's ailing son in Moscow. Bottled water from Berlin to Moscow? Wow.

The head of the diplomatic corps, a distant relative of

127

mine, was sent to Moscow "to prepare his retirement." He did not spare any effort to do so. Both of his wives came along to Moscow and, did they "milk" that retirement cow? On a weekly basis, they would hand 5 kg plastic jugs filled with eggs, to passengers going to Mali. Thus, his extended family's breakfast eggs, came all the way from Moscow every Thursday.

The consul's wife, who herself worked at the embassy, was quiet but efficient. Her apartment at the diplomatic compound almost spilled over with merchandise destined for Mali. One day, when visiting her with a friend, we waited so long for the elevator that we decided to use the stairs. Once down, we saw two Soviet deliverymen blocking the doors of the elevator. They were in fact unloading hundreds if not thousands of kettles for a Nigerian diplomat living in the same building.

The Malian cultural counselor was said to be a greedy bastard, who used to ship some of his items not only with traveling students, but also with the tickets of returning bodies of deceased students. What a disgrace.

Often than not, diplomats would also place orders with students for different kinds of items not available in Moscow itself. I personally accompanied a friend who sent water pumps from Kishinev to one of the shameless diplomats in Moscow. They had access to the entire Soviet Union, through a network of students. They made sure they could reach every corner with their tentacles, since different regions specialized in producing different items.

In 1990, the first lady visiting her ailing son in Moscow was said to be gone on a shopping spree. According to Malian students in Moscow, she went into a store for kitchen utensils, bought everything inside, and had the clerks close the doors and turn the Soviet customers away. "The wife of the president of Mali just bought every item inside. Sorry, we cannot let you in," they were told. Really?

The hallways of the embassy of Guinea were also packed with all kinds of merchandise, from washing machines to refrigerators or dryers. God knows what was in the basement, the backyard, or even the offices. They would store anything anywhere without blinking, as long as the item could be sent home for sale, the bigger the better. During my only visit, as I was waiting to interview the consul for this book, I read the following note posted on the wall: "On the 17th of November 1991, 990 cans of caviar, valued at 198,000 rubles, (average teacher's salary being 120 rubles) and two church icons were seized from Mr. and Ms. Barry in Ukraine, diplomatic passport number 3994." My jaw dropped as I tried to wrap my mind around the part of merchandize that did not get seized from that couple alone, much less from everybody else. That was just the tip of the iceberg.

Diplomats' activities stood between them and taking care of students' business the proper way. They spent most of their time looking for items to send, or at the airports or ports sending them, or even finding a place to store them. They came to work late and left early; that is why embassies never reached full staff on a given day, especially when you needed help. Their focus was always on where to get the next big items, and how to send them home. Anyone who visited the African embassies in Moscow must have asked themselves a few questions about the big items littering the alleyways and court yards.

As far as African students were concerned, we had our own system, but certainly on a smaller scale with less significant items. We did not have diplomatic passports, and we could not travel at will because of our obligations at school. So, we focused on two trips (winter and summer) abroad to make ends meet.

Malian students focused mostly on cabinets, refrigerators, freezers, air conditioners, generators, and water pumps. These items brought at least five hundred to eight hundred percent profit, and we never paid taxes on them given our student status. Regarding small items, imaginations ran wild from ear rings to soccer balls, shoes, whistles, watches, pots, pans, carpets, bolts, nails, wallpaper, etc. To make money off such small items, one had to send a ton of them, making us easy targets at airports, where bribes always saved the day.

Some students went as far as selling black pepper or

even the official stamps used in Malian passports. Given the exchange rate between the ruble and the French franc at the time, it made perfect financial sense to export pounds of black pepper from the Soviet Union to Malian retailers. Others, with the complicity of diplomats, would buy a bunch of Malian official stamps in rubles, take them back to Mali, and sell them for a nice profit margin.

Students from Guinea favored watches, earrings, and pots. According to a PhD student, Guinean students and diplomats flooded the markets with these Soviet items. Rumors had it that one woman put over a thousand watches in her checked luggage. She bribed the Soviet custom agents, who let her through, but when she reached her destination in Conakry, Guinea, she claimed only empty suitcases. She reportedly fainted and needed medical attention.

Students from the Democratic Republic of Congo adored kitchen utensils, and shipped them ceaselessly. Those from Senegal specialized in exporting linen fabrics, curtains, and bed sheets. Nigerians and Ghanaians targeted pianos, speakers, amplifiers for orchestras, and generators.

In Asia, students from Sri Lanka dealt in German shepherds and bulldogs. Every flight to Colombo carried at least a dog or two, bought for pennies in the Union. This traffic was so prevalent that people nicknamed Aeroflot, the Soviet airline, "the dog airline." Students from Vietnam and Laos were masters at packing and shipping articles to their countries. They did not deal with big items in general but specialized in small goods. They were the most discreet, organized and disciplined community. This export bounty was, for a time, the backbone of their economies. Just like foreign students and diplomats flooded the Soviet market with articles, they saturated their countries with small Soviet-made items. Since they could not travel outside of the Union, they concentrated their efforts toward domestic markets.

Gathering items from the Soviet market was an art itself, since not all merchandise was available in the needed quantity all the time. The Vietnamese students would take turns buying the same items to reach their needed quantity. They were also very good at notifying each other about the availability of some given goods in a particular store, without alerting other foreign students.

From the Union, they exported, among other things: Toothbrushes and paste, children's school bags, metals like aluminum and copper, two-burner gas stoves, pills, police uniforms, shorts, hats, socks, shoes, spoons, forks, knives, soaps, wallpaper, light switches, light bulbs, outlets, extension cords, watches, bracelets, rugs, curtains etc., and all those in huge quantities. After the breakup of the Soviet Union, they opened their own stores there and sold clothes and women's items, this time imported from Vietnam.

These activities required a high degree of trust, guts and caution. Since all trafficking was illegal, both parties (buyers and sellers) tried very hard to hide or disguise their deals. You always tried to avoid doing business in your own room. Some did business in the back of a taxi, others in their rooms with Soviet clients they knew and trusted, and some did it at the client's home. Average students, often gave their items to one of the ancients and recovered the money a few weeks later with no hassle. These extra precautions were necessary to prevent unpleasant surprises.

When I sold my first merchandise, a pair of blue jeans my mom sent me, I innocently took a great risk by doing it in my bedroom and in front of my roommates. Today, I could swear that they reported the fact the next morning to the dean, or their leader, to whom they had to reveal anything deemed valuable to the interest of the motherland. I also didn't consider the fact that my client could have come the next day or week, with a bunch of friends to threaten or beat me up and take away all my possessions. This happened to too many imprudent students, or to innocent ones who were at the wrong place and at the wrong time. A fellow Malian got beaten in the summer of 1992 by two Soviets who maintained in court that they were after a video player and a boom box they thought were in his room. He was taken to the hospital with severe head injuries. The perpetrators said that his room was targeted after they counted windows from the street. In their bag, they had a knife, a rope, gloves, and a roll of tape. On the spot, one got arrested and the other escaped, only to be brought to the militia later. They both got away with probation.

In the winter of 1989, as I was visiting a friend from Burkina Faso, a Soviet guy with short, dark hair knocked at the door. He said that he was looking to buy a Sharp double cassette player. By chance, a lady friend had just come from her winter break in Berlin with a Sharp 939. My acquaintance told me in French that he was willing to sell the boom box for her if I would help with the deal. When I acquiesced, he proceeded to bargain with the stranger, who wanted to see the item before any deal. My friend got the boom box, all covered in a bed sheet. After a short bargaining exchange, they settled on two thousand rubles, ten times the average salary of university professors. The client reached in his back pocket and handed us an envelope filled with cash in big banknotes. My acquaintance ordered him to count it first, then handed it to him to count, and then to me. I counted the cash last and handed it back to the client. They then agreed to go outside, get a taxi and exchange the envelope and the box at the last minute to avoid being caught by the militia. We wrapped the box with the same bed sheet and headed out to catch a taxi in the street. Once outside the dorms, and a few yards from the taxi station, we decided to do the exchange and part. The client reached once again into his back pocket and handed the same envelope to my acquaintance, who gave him the boom box. The exchange went as planned, he walked toward the taxi station, and we proudly rushed back to the dorms with a big smile. When we reached the room, we recounted the money one last time in order to put it away for the owner, only to find that eighteen one-ruble notes were sandwiched between two hundred-ruble bills. We realized that we had just sold the damned thing for two hundred eighteen rubles, instead of two thousand. The SOB duped us by handing a different stack of money that we never saw and never counted. We did not know what to think and felt stupid, dumb, and worthless. I did not know what to offer to lessen his anger, or more likely his fear of confronting our lady friend. I hung around for a while hoping to comfort my buddy. We later learned that many people had fallen victim to this kind of trick just about everywhere in the Union.

132

People later explained that the con men carried two envelopes, and have their prey count the correct one while inside, then switched envelopes during the exchange outside and in a hurry. Others said that these con men with dark hair coming from the south of the Union have some black magic power to change the monetary denomination when they touch it the second time. Go figure.

Another friend named Joseph, a biology student at the university, bought two color TVs from men whose description fit that of Soviets from central Asia. They used the same tactic of quick exchange of money and merchandise in the street, only this time a foreign student was the buyer. Joseph discovered later, that both TVs he just bought, were full of rocks instead of wires and circuit boards. What a trick.

In 1990, I went along with a fellow Malian and a classmate from Chad, to find a guy who had conned him few hours earlier, the same way we were duped. He had sold the man his brand new Sharp 939 only to find himself with100 rubles instead of over two thousand. He thought he might have seen the guy around a downtown hotel called Intourist, where only foreigners and out of state visitors (with proof) could lodge. We scouted around the place without any luck. Today, I still ask myself what we would have attempted to do, had we spotted him downtown. Calling the militia was not an option, since trafficking was illegal, and physically confronting him was not wise either because they always hung out with armed and dangerous friends. Looking back today, I am glad that we did not find him.

In this jungle of phantom sellers and buyers, some made millions and returned home with less knowledge for skipping so many classes, but five to ten years ahead of their peers, financially. Others went with the flow, struck the right balance, and did just fine in school and in business. Some others were not that lucky, and lost hard-earned property or got killed or injured, with no legal recourse.

There are many stories of KGB involvement in some students' deaths, supposedly because of the frequency and the scope of their activities. Two specific cases about two rich Malian students come to mind.

133

The first case involved Mr. Carmichael in Moscow. He was known to be the richest student alive, at least to the Malian community. He was the poster child for those who wanted to do business and make a crazy amount of money, before going home with or without a diploma. Everybody knew his name, but few could point him out in a crowd. He had unbelievable success in importing and exporting tons of sought-after items. He had a network of students who worked on his behalf, and rich Soviets who had more ill-gotten money than they could spend. He had to go big to make big, but also had to stay discreet and elusive to a KGB at the top of its game, and the "Soviet Mafiosi" he dealt with underground.

One day, news of his disappearance filled the rumor mills of the foreign student groups all around the Soviet Union. There was a sense of shock among the little guys, but to the big trafficking community, it was a grim warning. The tragedy was too close for comfort for many students who had crossed paths with him in the shadows, or those who knew him personally as a student or a friend. It was clear that this was a serious game-changer, as the Embassy and the Soviet authorities worked together to locate him. Everybody had an open opinion and an inner suspicion about what might have happened to him. About a week later, his body was found half-buried in a cemetery outside of Moscow. I still do not know the official cause of his death as per the Soviet death certificate, and the nervous embassy personnel refused to give me access to the files. The official rumor was that the KGB killed him because of his highly controversial dealings. End of story.

The second high-profile case was that of Mr Vanhise, whose brother lived in Kishinev for a year. He was considered to be the biggest and richest of all time, but with the lowest profile among his peers. When I visited his brother, I briefly met a tall, quiet, soft-spoken and handsome gentleman who projected confidence and perfection. With his demeanor, attire, and business skills, he belonged in the high-rise corporate board rooms of the world's financial capitals like New York, Tokyo, or Dubai. According to insiders, his room in Moscow was very simple, and he, his wife, and his siblings were completely down-to-earth, in spite of his overwhelming wealth.

134

Every kid wanted to be like him, without taking into consideration the danger that surrounded businessmen like him. He was thought to deal in computers, copiers, church paintings and icons, pianos and fabrics. These were the most conspicuous, risky, and expensive items of them all. But, he managed to trade them with perfection, and for a very long time.

One day in the summer of 1990, word came that he had died unexpectedly during a trip, from unknown causes. A classmate close to the family, said that he was traveling by train to Paris and had not complained about anything, until he convulsed with a stomachache after eating lunch. A piece of chicken he had just bought, like any typical passenger would. According to that family friend, the common feeling was that he was somehow poisoned through that chicken by the KGB. What a huge loss for the Malian community and his family. Our diplomats again, shaking in their boots, did not push to shed light on this case, either.

God knows why the KGB would kill students involved in illegal trade between the Soviet Union and the West, instead of seriously spooking them away, or sending them home. We will never find out, unless someone comes forward these many years later.

2. Boulafs

Ever since my name appeared on the list of scholarship recipients going to the USSR, my mom's mind has been working overtime. She was trying to come to terms with my departure for a society known in Mali for its secrecy where, as rumored, women try to escape their "jail-country." So, as I was getting ready to leave, Mom used the opportunity to point out some of the differences between my conservative society and the "promiscuous" one I was about to enter. She lost no time singling out some nearby examples as warnings. Right next to our home, was a three-story apartment block that housed foreigners and in some cases with their Malian husbands. Among them, a mixed couple with two children who had just returned from Moscow, and going through a bitter divorce. The unfortunate process clearly traumatized the kids, and all of us following the undoing of the marriage as reluctant witnesses. The wife was said to be seen coming home during work hours with other men, or not sleeping at home some nights. She had a noisy Volkswagen beetle that betrayed her just about every night, as she went out around dinner time and back in the wee hours. One day, her Malian husband left their apartment, never to be seen again. The kids were left by themselves in the evenings as their mom went out to hit as many clubs as she could. At that time, our society looked at divorced and single moms behaving like her as the personification of Satan himself.

136

In a traditional society where family is not only mom and dad, but everybody from both sides, seeing a divorced mother struggling with her children was unspeakable.

Mom spoke of a friend, also leaving for the Soviet Union, whose brother watched helplessly as his Soviet wife left with another man without even taking the time to divorce. She just left with a stranger. Even my mom's dentist had a story. He too lived with his Soviet wife and their baby daughter in that apartment block. He often complained to my mom about how his wife did not like his relatives and displayed her displeasure when people visited them. A flaw, mostly tagged to any white woman from a mixed couple. He claimed that even his own mom could not come to see her granddaughter at will. He also nagged about the expensive plane tickets to Moscow, he was forced to buy every year for his wife and daughter from his meager salary. Stories like these just reinforced negative perceptions in a deeply suspicious society, particularly when they came from a disgruntled native son. Husbands were supposed to lead, feed, shelter and protect their families, not to be bossed around and disrespected by their spouses. An outspoken wife, foreign or native, with a strong mind of her own was seen as a chipping chisel to the men's authority, therefore to the stability of the marriage.

Another couple with three children in the same complex called it quits, and the Soviet mother took off with the children to Senegal. She was a nurse we all liked, and appreciated her determination to learn Bambara, the main language in Mali. When my sister-in-law learned about my departure, she too threw in her two cents and warned me about bringing a Soviet wife home. "They are not serious, my own cousin married one only to catch her in the street kissing a Soviet embassy employee right next to their house. Be careful in your choices of friends", she added. So, Mom used these examples in her never-ending series of advices, over and over again. We were a bit baffled by these anecdotal separations that unfortunately became part of the negative statistics about my future hosts.

I sensed a huge culture clash looming in my future before immersing in my adoptive society. Most of us, armed with foregone conclusions and stereotypes got slapped in the

137

face by a brutal reality on the ground. It turned out that the social context in which black foreigners lived was so screwed up, that simple human relations like friendship and dating were seen as evil. To our surprise, these innate relationships were made outrageously hard through two pressure points: on the one hand, their bigoted rejection by the society as a whole, and on the other hand, the plethora of road blocks set in motion by the communist government itself.

Casual gatherings with Soviet girls was an intriguing enterprise full of danger. I say gatherings with Soviet girls, and not men (as in any other normal society), because they could not even imagine dating foreign girls or openly befriend foreign males, especially non-white ones. Not in their wildest dreams. Befriending foreigners, particularly non-whites, could spell trouble, given the bigotry within the society and the twisted paranoia of the authorities over state secrets. Those state secrets could be anything the communist apparatus deemed them to be, in order to punish or imprison its enemies. Any Soviet male seen with a black foreigner was looked down and mentally excommunicated by his peers, but also hastily put on watch list by the government. We played soccer together, roomed together and attend classes together, but could not be friends. It took only few documented visits to the same foreigner by a Soviet, to raise the government red flags and be under suspicions. At that point, Soviet roommates and classmates enter the game to provide day to day information to the authorities. That constant state of fear and intimidation, drown any genuine desire to befriend black foreigners, despised by most Soviets. Therefore, tens of thousands non-white foreigners studied for six years in the Soviet Union without befriending one Soviet man. No one returned home with a Soviet's address in order to keep in touch, no one. Now, contrast that with the main purpose of our presence in the USSR - to sure up the future of communism around the world – then you get a slight peek at what twisted logic made the Soviets tick.

The picture was alarming when it came to Soviet girls.

In the Soviet social conscience, dating non-white foreigners was considered an abomination. It was one of those unwritten

138

guidelines that everybody knew but did not discuss. At least in the Jim Craw south in the US, interracial dating and marriages were forbidden by laws of the land, not only by the collective conscience. It was clear cut and written down for everybody to see and know. In the Soviet Union though, the situation was very complex and sometimes contradictory, given the nature of the Soviet's psyche. Our crash course was appalling right from the start.

To Malian students leaving for Moscow, the stereotype was that the Soviets were not the sharpest tools in the shed and were worse off, compared to other white foreigners in Mali. To realize from the get go, that those same Soviets called you "Nieggri" – Niggers in Russian, and hated your gut, was quite a tremor. Non-white foreign students were tolerated, envied at times, discriminated against, hated, battered and even murdered. To the general populace, dating and marrying outside the white soviet pool was considered an egregious transgression. But, we all also know that in any society, the more you forbid something, the more trespassers you invite to "eat the forbidden fruit". The known-to-all and unspoken judgment, was that the girls who dated non-white foreigners were "bitches". It was also assumed that they were only after the foreigners for their money, sex, cheap stuff from the West, or their aptitude to get them out of their jail-like-country. To the society at large, there could not have been any other reason for dating black students. So, those "bitches" who dared cross the social line did so at their own perils, and concealed it as much as possible. And those "niggers" who were involved with them also gambled with their lives. Under such hostile social pressure, it was virtually impossible to make friends in town, at school or the movies. So the only outlet for non-white foreigners to socialize with the locals, was in the dorms, which were themselves under severe scrutiny. Foreigners relied heavily on the local pioneers who braved the evil eyes and insults of the entire Soviet society to come to dorm, sometimes dragging along some reluctant friends. Government disinformation and punitive restrictions abounded in order to deter current and potential visitors. Rumors had it that foreigners would gang-rape any visiting Soviet girl. In addition,

139

the fact that the Soviet militia collected guests' personal information, dates and times of visits to the dorms, deterred many. That data would be forwarded to the local KGB (Soviet Secret Service) office and sometimes used to blackmail those visiting nonwhite foreigners. Sometimes the militia would even inform parents or employers about those visits, causing tremendous havoc between parents and daughters, bosses and employees.

Female visitors to our dorms were called names to their faces, and were threatened with beatings if they did not stop seeing "fucking niggers."

Under this draconian state of affairs, non-white students still found ways to make friends under house-arrest-like conditions. To evade scrutiny or muddy the waters, visitors would often conceal their destination and the identity of their hosts. By purposely writing down the wrong room number and hosts they came to see, the brave visitors repeatedly sent the government on a wild goose chase. This tactic destroyed many leads and patterns sought by the bigot "big Soviet brother". Others would bring fake IDs or those of friends that did not mind their names being in the registry. Once inside, simple things like going to the bathroom were an ordeal. Hallways needed to be cleared, especially of members of the student body, or worse, the commandant of the dorm. Many visitors got thrown out or shunned, after being spotted. Some concierges even got in the habit of verbally abusing guests in their faces: "Are you back for more, bitch? What do they give you when you visit, whore? What do you get with 'niggers' that your fellow countrymen cannot provide you with?" among other insults.

Upon arrival, we saw first-hand how the ancients struggled to get their Soviet girlfriends in and out of the dorms. In our own dorm even talking to our Soviet female colleagues was out of question. They would either ignore us or give a little smile or a wink when it was safe to do so, without anybody from the Soviet community seeing it. It was the same situation in schools, at the grocery store, on the bus, or in the streets. Add to that the shortage of foreign female students, and you have thousands of young, healthy and frustrated students yearning to date by any means necessary.

The first six months in the country were depressing as black foreigners, watched with envy their white and brown counterparts commingling with the native population. As we were struggling to make friends, we saw Afghan, East-European, and Arab students dating right on the same floor in the dorms. Their guests would come in the open, register to see them, and even go out together to the movies, parks or restaurants. Our seniors stressed that their almost weekly dorm parties would help break up the monotony, and improve our chances of making friends. Armed with stereotypes and conversations with different ancients, we started to have a pretty good idea about the appalling state of dating in the USSR. One thing was clear - meetings happened mostly indoors and relationships were entertained underground through unimaginable obstructions and conflicts. Black Foreigners, could not visit the locals in their apartments, without risking their lives and their friends' lives and reputations. No foreign student could rent or buy an apartment or house, because of the Soviet paranoia about spies. We all had to live in dorms supervised incessantly by the control freak that was the Soviet government. So, the sight of a black or brown foreigner anyplace away from campus was a glitch on the natives' radar screens. The news would spread so fast that the Dean in charge of foreign students' affairs would know about it before one even returned back to the dorms. On top of that, your hosts reputation would be tarnished right there and then, leading to an unspoken shame and to a potential loss of job.

This hostility fueled our despair. Normal human behaviors were pushed so far beyond reason that every non-white foreigner and their Soviet partners had to relentlessly improvise and create their own "normalcy". Without that right to a normal life and the freedom to socialize, every gathering, meeting or date was timed. To the bigot Soviet big brother, that had to be between 5 and 10 p.m. with its permission. To the bigoted Soviet society, that multicultural interaction was not to be, as long as one drop of blackness was involved, period.

The battle lines were drawn at four levels in order to

141

frustrate the "sinful" friendships, as much as possible. The first line was at the front desk of every dorm, where a guest inventory was kept under live monitoring of the commandant. The second battle line resided in the office of the Dean of foreign students' affairs, who frequently met with the commandant of the dorm. The third battle line was drawn in every Militia (Soviet police) post in every community. The fourth and creepiest one was at the desk of every KGB (Soviet Secret Services) field officer. The system not only stood between foreigners and their adulthood, but also between the Soviets and their right and desire to befriend their foreign guests. To better prepare us, generations of students before us, passed down their stories like oral history recounted by griots in West Africa. In the past, our predecessors' Soviet girlfriends could not even wear outside of the dorms, simple gifts like jeans and T-shirts. That way they avoided being harassed in the streets or taunted by the militia. These brave souls were labeled either as prostitutes for dating foreigners, or traitors for potentially giving away some deep secrets of the motherland.

By the time we settled in Kishinev, things had not changed much.

With dating foreigners being such a challenge, a subgroup of Soviet girls or women braving the system, came to light over the years. Their number grew as more foreigners came to the Union and as these women convinced more and more of their friends and relatives to not be afraid to befriend the "chimps" (another popular nickname for black foreigners after "Niggers"). They put everything on the line, and faced harsh consequences like pink slips from work, expulsion from schools and universities, repudiation by their families, or even beatings by jealous, racist youths.

So, you had a situation where a constant and growing number of trapped Soviet girls, socialized with a huge pool of marginalized black students, literally indoors. Students did not even know where their Soviet friends lived, because they could not visit them, making the dorms the only possible meeting point. If you wanted to know the true meaning of "once you go black you never go back," this was it. The two sides had each

142

other's back, creating an interdependent relationship full of intricacies, all under the scrutiny of the Soviet big Brother. Once these girls or women were known to be seeing non-white foreigners, they became socially ostracized. That is why they would hide as much as possible, their friendship with non-white foreigners.

Within the French-speaking foreign community, they were known as "boulafs". To this day, I do not know the origin of the word, nor who coined it. It meant any Soviet girl or woman who dated or married a black foreigner.

Staying sane in this artificial and secluded life in the dorms, required quick thinking and improvisation. Plotting to have your guest come to the dorm and stay beyond 10 p.m. or overnight, was like going to Mars. Many stars in the sky had to line up to pull off such a stunt, given the numerous stumbling blocks to overcome. Dating became so socially proscribed and so scrutinized by the Soviet authorities that you would think communism's entire future depended on it. Maybe it did in their mind.

Every visit by any Soviet girl or woman to the dorms was full of anticipation and worries. Could she come without the knowledge of her loved ones, coworkers or male relatives and acquaintances? Because, any of the aforementioned would disavow her, the minute they learn about her "immoral" relationship. That weighed heavily on her mind every time she left to go to the dorms. Once there, the question becomes - could she enter peacefully without confrontation at the front desk, and could the host bribe the concierge to let her in unregistered, or falsify her registration? For a negotiation to even start, the front desk had to be cleared of students, and it had to be the shift of the "right" concierge too. Once that was taken care of, then managing the entire situation inside the dorm took precedent. Meantime, host and guest would try to have as normal of a visit as humanly possible - dinner, games, TV shows, visit others in the dorm, etc., without anxiety. Then, the same exact worries are there to confront again, as she tries to leave the dorm for home. Sometimes she lies to friends about what she was doing so far away from home, or when acquaintances want to know why such a cute girl does not have a boyfriend. The pitfalls were unlimited in number, unpredictable and diverse in scope.

All these obstacles required a lot of attention, planning, and a good deal of luck, to be managed day in and day out. The intolerant attitude of the Soviet society pushed students to the drawing board every week, leading to some dramatic circumstances.

During our language year, we met Tanya, girlfriend and future wife of one of our ancients. They have been together for years and she seemed to always be in his room, to our surprise. We were then told that she was de facto living in the dorms since her parents kicked her out because of the color of her date. She lost her job and became unemployable for the same reason. There was a human being loving another one, being rejected by her family and banned from employment by her government. She spent all her days in the room, and would sometimes go visit a girlfriend in a distant village. We could not believe our ears, that a human being could be marked for life for befriending another one.

Few months after our arrival, a Malian Junior from the veterinary school, confessed to me about his love life. He has been dating indoors his Soviet girlfriend for almost three years, and did not even know where she lived and worked. Her mom has been enquiring about her relationship for a while, but she always told her to have not found the prince charming yet. Few months later, she confessed under pressure and told her mom that she was dating a foreigner. Her mom could not believe the story and demanded she ends the relationship immediately. Mother and daughter fought, cried and reconciled over it, then decided to set up and appointment to meet. Mom came from the village to town and waited for them in a friend's apartment. They joined her there to discuss the couple's future. Mom first and foremost, wanted to know where he would settle after graduation. Knowing that she would not let her only child go abroad, he said that he would stay and work at one of the big state owned farms. She politely told them that, that was not an option. "We all know that you guys (black foreigners) cannot live in this society, you will never be accepted here", she stressed. The two continued to date on and off after the

144

meeting but eventually split under pressure.

Obvious mixed relationships where to be hidden, which was impossible and clearly beside the point

Meantime on my floor, an Algerian and a Jordanian were having the time of their lives dating without even looking over their shoulders. The following year, as freshmen, we moved to a new dorm with the same draconian rules. At this point, many fake parties were taking place in our own dorm, we had mastered the Russian language, and shyness was rapidly fading from our fabric. The doors to more silly and bizarre situations opened wide.

When a couple of freshmen could not bribe the concierge of the day, to let their guest in before 5 p.m. they decided to pull her through the kitchen window. They tied a bunch of bed sheets end to end and dropped her the makeshift rope. Halfway during the pull, the commandant of the dorm showed up out of nowhere. The panicked, and let go off of the rope and disappeared in the dorm. What a tragedy!

To also circumvent the draconian rules at the front desk, a colleague from Togo gave his white lab coat to his girlfriend. She then tried to enter the dorm as a nurse without being registered. The concierge asked for proof of the credentials she was claiming to have, as my colleague watched anxiously from afar. The concierge then decided to call the commandant to resolve the heated argument that ensued. Unfortunately, she could not convince neither of them and got thrown out of the dorm.

Another time, a classmate from Benin and his girlfriend confronted the Militiamen called up by the commandant of the dorm. They simply would not let her stay pass visit hours. After a long and fruitless argument, the couple showed them the positive result of her pregnancy test, to demonstrate their commitment to each other. As a final effort, they wanted to humanely show that they were serious and would soon welcome a baby. To no avail.

Sometimes bribing the student on duty at the front desk, was the way to go. He would check one's guest out in the registry and steal the ID from the pile, when the concierge goes to the bathroom.

One night, a classmate came to our dorm with his girlfriend, since he could not negotiate her overnight stay in his own dorm next door. He had the key to a fellow countryman's room, and engaged the concierge with all the diplomatic skills, life in the USSR had taught him. For a mere three rubles, the concierge agreed to hold the passport and to later check her "out" in the registry. But, she insisted that the girl stays with her at the front desk until things quieted down. So, to kill time, our classmate went to visit other friends in the dorm. He made frequent trips to the front desk to check on the status of his guest. He would often find the two chatting, only to be told to come back again when things clear out. The next time he came down, he found the concierge alone at the front desk. Surprised and agitated, he asked about his guest's whereabouts. The concierge replied that she had handed the passport to her, so she could go upstairs to find him. He rushed upstairs, looked for her everywhere in the dorm without success. Furious, he raced downstairs to confront the concierge. At first, she stuck to her story and tried to scare him away with threats of calls to the militia or the commandant. He remained undeterred and told her that he would welcome the presence of any authority. She tried to retreat behind her desk, but he insisted that he either gets his three rubles back, or he would alert the commandant himself. Angry but defiant, she finally returned the three rubles. From then on, he became her number one enemy, and the two never cut a deal again.

Given the circumstances, every boulaf led a double life. One covert and lived exclusively in the dorms with a non-white foreigner. Another one unconcealed and away from the dorms, within the Soviet society proper. Being in the middle of these two worlds took an emotional and physical toll on these heroic and marginalized women. With time, as the pressure mounted, every one of them would be force to make a decision - "to be or not to be" part of the subgroup. "Not to be", meant to abruptly close the chapter, cut all ties with the dorm and all foreign contacts living in it. After letting all the pressure out, she would completely fall back into the Soviet society and pretend from then on to have never met a foreigner. Whereas, "to be" meant to come out and not hide anymore the "evil" relationship she was secretly having, despite all the difficulties ahead. Once any girl accepted that fate, she would gear up for upcoming verbal abuses and unnecessary road blocks, the racially prejudiced Soviet society had in store. From then on, she would work twice as hard on her relationship, hoping to follow her love out of the country to a better place. Since any place in the world was better in that regard, than the bigoted Soviet society, who would not want to leave? Unfortunately, that comes full circle to match the stereotype claiming that Soviet girls dated foreigners solely to get out of the country. The other side of the equation, namely the persecution of interracial couples or Soviet girls naturally falling in love with black foreigners, never gets mentioned. The urge to get out of the Soviet Union got even stronger when kids were involved, since they could never have a future there.

Life within this hostile society only pushed students to openly defy the blatant discriminations and unfair practices, sanctioned by the Soviet big brother itself

Needless to say that coping with this inhuman environment, took a serious tool on everybody and everything we were involved with.

.

3. Vodka

Last, but certainly not least, alcohol was another temptation that haunted foreign students in the former Soviet Union. The "bitter water," as it was sometimes referred to in Mali, was cheap and everywhere.

Unfortunately for us foreigners, especially those coming from Muslim countries, drinking was more than a national pastime for our hosts. It was a way of life in the isolated empire. As we settled in Kishinev, we learned more and more about its place within students' underground life, as well.

There were those who drank before landing in the Union and openly continued to do so, those who started there but were still in the closet, and finally those who did not drink at all. Mix these three groups in a society that drinks like a bottomless pit, and you have a recipe for more abuse and dependency. The first group was working overtime to get the second out of the closet and join it. The third or dry group was the target of the first two in order to widen the faction and legitimize their unholy activities.

"Alcohol helps you withstand the God forbidden winter", or "You look like THE MAN with a bottle", or even "a little bit is not going to kill you", were some of the selling points we heard across the country. But the best recruiters were the young Soviet girls who dared the new guys and questioned their manhood if they did not drink. And the best recruiting environments were the real and phony parties that served as a refuge from the racist, boring and dangerous Soviet society. The combination of all these factors weighed heavily in the balance, for those of us trying desperately to resist the temptation. The only "fun" places to go were those parties, which were also the only meeting and drinking places.

When I say drinking, I am not talking about couple cool ones here and there, or a few glasses of wine or champagne at a birthday party to have a good time. In the context of the Soviet Union, and within the students' community, drinking meant a whole lot more. Cases of booze under beds, vomiting, passing out, fights and hangovers were the name of the game. Every gathering was like a competition to see the last man standing, get in trouble with the authorities, and ridicule the "weak" ones afterwards. Year after year, new students were courted to join this or that group, depending on his lifestyle and character.

There was never a shortage of free drinks or company; to the contrary, offers abounded. Alcohol was forbidden in the dorms, but it was also dangerous for black students to go drink in town. So, students bribed the front desk to let them in with cases of alcohol. And, since rooms were randomly assigned at first, many dry students ended up rooming with drinkers. By the end of the first trimester, there was a clear attempt by students with similar habits to board together. That made it easier to entertain drinking buddies any night, without disturbing a dry roommate trying to study or sleep. In the streets, we would sometime witness drunken Soviets trying to stand up straight by hugging a tree, as a militia man passed by. As soon as the latter was out of the picture, he would call us all the names in the racist book.

It was gut-wrenching to see fellow students, close friends or even relatives, going down the self-destructive path. To the Soviets and to most of the addicted students, it was about being a man, enduring shameless consequences and ignoring the advice of well-meaning friends. This universal deafness to people who cared about their well-being, literally meant life or death for those who lost their footing to the bottle. In the case of Malian students, parallel to private advices, our

149

community decided to send our elders and leaders to talk to some of those going from bad to worse. Unfortunately, the overwhelming reaction to these preachers was, "Thanks for your concern, but this is my business. You did not bring me here, and as an adult I can make my own decisions." This false sense of adulthood and independence, cost many students their diplomas, their health, and sadly, their lives in many cases.

Take Ottman for example, a tall and handsome man from a neighboring family in Bamako. He was the athletic one playing very well both soccer and basketball. Their father was a diplomat in Moscow and they used to visit Bamako every year. All of a sudden, Ottman's behavior became very strange. He would silently sit apart, and sometimes strummed his guitar for hours without socializing. When we enquired about this sudden metamorphosis, we were told that the Soviets beat him to many times. He took a lot of blows to his head from young Soviets who found him drunk in the middle of the night. He was even left for dead in the snow and for hours, one time. He was "gone" forever due to head trauma inflicted by the bigoted Soviets. The story never left me.

As we arrived in Kishinev, I heard stories about other students before I even met them. Some I knew personally from Bamako, like Drew. He and my first cousins used to hang out all the time in a small community south of the capital. Everybody knew everybody, and people's night-time activities were not hidden secrets, either. In Bamako, Drew was charming, energetic, outgoing and popular; he embraced life to the fullest. He was always well-dressed, with a particular afro cut that made him shine among his friends. Nothing had changed when I met him again in Kishinev; his attire was still impeccable and his aura overwhelming. I often visiting him at the university, and he in turn would stop by my room every time he was in our dorm.

Since he was older than me, he hung out with friends of his own age and interests. He rarely traveled and was never part of the huge army of traffickers between the West and the Union, like most. He showed his soft side, when he cited the cold as the reason for not traveling to make some extra money.

He had everything going for him and potentially had a great life to look forward to.

Unfortunately, it became clear to me that he was part of a circle of friends who often drank and got in trouble. In his particular case, things were getting out of control. Friends from Mali and Guinea Bissau, who were known for their relentless drinking, were in his room almost every weekend. The front desk was getting fed up, since his guests left the dorm well past exit time, or tried to stay overnight. The dean and the foreign students' office finally got involved in trying to tone down the troubles caused by his guests. Add to that, the constant fights and shouting matches he was involved in, and you have an alarming situation that needed attention. The issue was brought up at some of the meetings of the Malian student association in Kishinev, and it was decided to send the general secretary and other wise members to talk to Drew. He did not like the helping hand stretched toward him by the community. He subsequently decided to reject the delegation's advices to stop drinking, stay out of trouble and do well in school. Instead, he thanked them for their concern, adding that nobody brought him here and what he did was nobody's business. So, he was left alone without any change in his activities and behavior. He was also openly dating a beautiful girl named Sveta, provoking the ire of the entire bigoted faculty and town.

In the summer of 1988, as I returned from London to Paris, a friend met me at the railroad station with the sad news that Drew had died back in Kishinev. Different causes of death were rumored: He either jumped from the fourth floor, or was pushed from his balcony, or was killed by the Soviets. I could not believe what I was hearing, and we did not have a way to verify any of the reasons given for his sudden death. I was shocked, confused and did not know what to make of this horrible news. We threw around our own theories, but could not make sense of the tragedy.

We heard all kinds of gossip about the man and his death all summer long, before we reached Kishinev in late August. Not surprisingly, Kishinev was also red-hot with conspiracy theories, and just about every dorm had its own.

151

When the dust settled, it became clear that at least two colleagues from Mali were there the night of the incident. From what I heard from witnesses, that infamous weekend was no different from any other. As usual, people began gathering in Drew's room in late afternoon for a good time. Music was playing and people were sipping their beer, visiting with each other, pacing between the narrow room and the small balcony. At one point in the evening, Drew went to the balcony with some buddies, including a Soviet chum. My colleague was adamant; nobody was drunk, including himself because it was too early in the night. Without any arguments, fights or discord of any kind, he maintained that the people from the balcony came into the room, yelling that Drew had fallen all the way down. They raced to call 911 and to attend to him on the ground, four stories below. He was rushed to the nearest hospital, where he was pronounced dead. When his girlfriend came to visit him very early the next morning, she was told that she could not see the corpse. One militia man even asked her why was she crying over his death, instead of rejoicing for being saved from HIV-AIDS. Drew's friends wanted to raise hell after such a comment from a guy in uniform, but decided to hold their tongues out of respect for Drew.

The Malian embassy got involved, and the Soviet authorities said that they would do an autopsy to determine the cause of his death. A few days later, they said that they did what they had to do and that they would not reveal any results, nor would they allow anyone to see the corpse. A delegation from the embassy in Moscow flew in to get the body and to hear the last words from the authorities. The Soviets did not reveal anything, and transferred the corpse to the Malian authorities bound for Moscow. There, they permanently sealed the casket, making it impossible for Drew's family to say good-bye to him in Bamako, we were told.

The secrecy around the Soviets, fueled more conspiracy theories regarding the cause of death and the state of the corpse at the time of the transfer. Some people still maintain that the Soviets killed him because of all the trouble he caused on campus, and that they harvested his organs and sealed the casket. Others said that he accidentally fell from the balcony to

152

his death from being drunk; others did not rule out suicide under the influence of alcohol. Nobody knows for sure what happened, despite the presence of some students and the Soviets authorities' enquiry. What a terrible loss.

William too, one of Drew's buddies, was a serious student and an older brother. I respected him for his intelligence, down-to-earth attitude, and especially his frankness. We clicked without a hitch, and I felt at ease during the numerous visits I paid him. He lived right on the first floor with a window on the street, ever since our arrival in town. A promising student with excellent grades, William had good standing at the university and in his dorm. Given his background, he was never drunk and was not known to misbehave or cause any trouble.

As time went by, things slowly but surely started to go awry for him. First, he lost his room on the first floor for bringing guests through the window. Then, he and the University stopped seeing eye-to-eye for dating his biology lab teacher. The Dean relentlessly tried to fire her without success. To make matters worse, he started drinking and fighting at parties and gatherings away from his dorm. Alcohol became his bête noire, as he got drunk very fast on very little, and would assault anybody in front of him for no reason. He would become very aggressive when drunk, kicking doors and windows. One time, he cut his vein after he punched through a glass window, following a dispute at a party.

As things unraveled for him, all of this started to take a toll on his health and education, leading him to consider a year off, called an academic break. Everybody, even his drinking partners, advised him to settle down and quit drinking. He was now on the radar of the authorities of the town, since reports were shared between the schools and militia posts. William decided to take a year off, to get his act together among family and loved ones in Bamako. This was welcome news in the community, and we all saw it as a unique opportunity for redemption, not to be missed.

When plans for the trip were finalized, I decided (against the conventional wisdom) to write William a private letter that he was to read only after leaving the Soviet Union on his way home. In it, I admitted that my letter was out of the ordinary since I did not know him before Kishinev, and was too young to counsel an elder. I made it clear that I cared about him, and that I thought he should use this opportunity to bury the past and come back a better person with a plethora of possibilities ahead of him.

When William returned to Kishinev a year later, he came to my room to thank me for the letter, and for being the only person to approach him this way. I became proud of him for trying to turn his life around, and very hopeful for the future. He resumed classes as planned and stayed away from alcohol, but not the environment. He was still seeing the same circle of friends but did his best to refrain from the "bitter water." A few months later, we started to see cracks in his resilience, and the same old issues slowly creeping back. Before the year was over, it all galloped back to him. William was at square one again, fighting at parties, skipping school, and getting drunk. Friends and others tried to intervene, without success.

Finally, he agreed to the idea of enrolling in another city with a clean slate away from his "drinking brothers". With the help of some friends and the university, he got accepted in Voronezh, a port city on the Caspian Sea, in Russia. We all felt better about his severance from Kishinev and his drinking circle, hoping it would give him a chance to make new friends in a new environment. So, he went to the university in Voronezh, to the relief of the Malian community.

This community that wanted so much for him to turn the page, quickly turned the page on him right after his departure. The feeling about the drinking problems was at its tipping point, so William's exit was felt as one less burden.

A few months later, to everybody's surprise, troubling news started to reach Kishinev. He was slipping back into the same mindset and attitudes - skipping classes, getting drunk, and fighting, just about everybody. Unfortunately, he was now out of the reach of all of us who wished him well. I do not doubt for a minute that the Malian community there, too, did its best to save him from himself. But, just like in Kishinev, the bond around the bottle was stronger than any other relationship he might have had with the "dry" members of the community.

Later on, he either dropped out or was let go by the authorities and ended up in Moscow. We heard that he was trying to solve some of his problems at the embassy or at the Soviet Department of Education, and was still drinking at night with some new "bottle buddies". He eventually hooked up with a driver from the embassy of Argentina, who took him under his wing and more or less helped him survive in Moscow for a while.

Then, out of nowhere, came the news that William was in the hospital with a broken leg, after falling or jumping from a building. I still do not know how he got injured or how long it took him to heal, get his stuff together and go home. From then on, he walked with a limp because one leg was shorter after the whole ordeal.

After wasting almost seven years, he ended up back home, hopping on one leg, without a diploma and or positive prospects for his life. All that, because of what was at this point an addiction. Back home, given the culture, a very different picture was painted regarding his misfortune. The fact that he could not free himself from the destructive path of drunkenness, was seen as a curse or a spell from his enemies. Nobody knows for sure what fed William's addiction, since he did not drink at all before landing in Kishinev. It simply destroyed his short term dreams.

Let's also look at the case of a young man from Mali named Ben. He joined us in Kishinev in 1988 and was a superb soccer player. He was soft-spoken and so shy he could not even make eye contact. He always looked down with a smile as he tried to have a conversation. He was so quiet and reserved that people would forget about his existence in town. His father held a very high position at the Malian Department of Education, which prompted the cultural consul of our embassy to visit and keep an eye on him. We always gave him a hard time during soccer games, for hiding in his room and not visiting with the rest of the members of the community. As a freshman, we saw less and less of him, even for the soccer games, which he loved.

Out of the blue, I learned that Ben had taken up drinking beer and could reportedly handle a lot for a beginner. Since he did not get out much, I never saw him even try a beer, hence my surprise. Next, came rumors about his vodka drinking with the "big boys". Just like them, the usual symptoms got hold of him, and little by little he spiraled out of control. This polite, shy, and baby-faced brother, became one of the biggest vodka consumers in town, and in record time. I am told that he would go out to buy bottles of it, and isolate himself in his room for days. His academic performance and social behavior went from bad to worse, to the bewilderment of everybody who knew him. As he continued to seclude himself and grow dangerous to his own health, word reached our cultural counselor at the embassy in Moscow, his godfather. He tried just about everything to straighten him out through third parties, letters, phone calls, and face-to-face talks, to no avail. Ben was becoming a huge embarrassment for everyone who was involved in bringing him to Kishinev, from his dad back home to the cultural counselor charged to oversee him. After numerous tries, Ben's dad threw in the towel and ordered the counselor to finally go pick his son up and send him home. Once again, another promising career was abruptly brought to a halt by alcohol.

There also was "old Steve," an acquaintance who came to the Union to attend a technical college, shortly after we arrived. He started to drink back in Bamako, before joining others in Krasnodar (a Russian port city) during his language year. He got in so much trouble there that the administration transferred him to Kishinev, hoping for the best. Once among us, he did not observe any transition period before hooking up with the "big boys." It soon became apparent to the community that he too, was going to be a very serious problem. Despite his long drinking history, Old Steve's alcohol tolerance and self-control were wanting. After only few glasses, he became particularly aggressive toward his companions, and could not be stopped. Before long, he picked up a couple of warnings, and then was seriously reprimanded for misconduct by the dean. Multiple fighting incidents, poor class attendance, and below-standard academic performance, once again got the better of an otherwise exceptionally smart fellow. He got in so many altercations that his own drinking buddies started to avoid him. Ultimately, he was also sent home without diploma. This was another waste of talent because of alcohol in a country that was, it seemed, almost always drunk.

Take also Sam, a friend of mine since middle school. Our families went a long way back, and we had mutual relatives and friends. He was daddy's boy among his siblings, because of his very good grades. His dad loved him and showered him with money and gifts, making him the envy of the other kids in the neighborhood. After graduation from high school, he was also offered a scholarship by the former Soviet Union and our government. He landed in Poltava, another one of the many godforsaken towns of the Union, for his language year, and subsequently to Kishinev for his master's in economics. We hooked up as best friends and relatives, and did just about everything together. To this day, I do not know if he drank prior to setting foot in Kishinev, where he started surreptitiously sipping a few glasses here and there. Before long, he came out of the closet and would occasionally drink at the dorm parties, where alcohol and enticing company were never in short supply. I tried my best to steer him away from alcohol and cigarettes, since he was also asthmatic. Eventually, my repeated words of advice started to sound hollow and unwelcome, especially in the toxic drinking environment that was Kishinev. He went from pitching in some rubles for the common good during gatherings, to bringing his own bottles of wine. Hanging out with him became less and less fun and more dangerous, because of the fights and flying glasses. Needless to say, our promising bonding was doomed, and it was only a matter of time before it would crumble. Sam was under the influence of something stronger than his will power.

Finally, vodka, the almost pure alcohol, became his favorite drink, like all his drinking buddies. The catastrophic damage inflicted by vodka on an empty stomach and too little sleep, were common knowledge. According to some consumers themselves, it fried your brains, a condition called "belaia gariatchaia", or the "white and hot one." Patients exhibit an emotionless glassy stare, some loss of memory, and strong antisocial tendencies. In short, it messes up your brain.

As he sank deeper and deeper into the vodka bottle, our relationship worsened to the point where we actually became enemies. I made every effort to avoid meeting him, and dreaded going places knowing that he might show up there and purposely try to pick a fight. My heart sank every time I saw him in this condition that did not have to be.

I would sometimes compare his high school days, riding his motor bike in Mali, with this self-destructive behavior in Kishinev under the influence of vodka. I could not understand why this dramatic change had occurred, nor could I point to a catalytic event that could have prompted this chain reaction to his breakdown. As with many others before him, the community wondered about what to do for him to secure his future. After a tumultuous time full of close calls and provocations, he also decided to take an academic break. Here again, I saw the year break as a way out of the polluted environment in Kishinev, and a healing time with his parents and dear ones back home. By the time he left we were not in speaking terms, but somewhere deep inside, I wished him well. A year later, he came back in a very good spirit and ready to resume his studies. He stayed strong and away from alcohol until my departure. I was glad to see someone beat the odds once.

Let us consider another unfortunate statistic named Raj, a bright, aggressive and jovial kid from the northeastern region of Mali. He lived in the dorm next to mine, and also attended our school. He always had a wide smile as he held your hand and frequently called you koro (elder in Bambara) throughout your entire encounter. We all loved him and teased him good-naturedly every time we met.

Because of his very fair complexion, he instantly became a sensation among Soviet girls, since he could pass for white, or at least not black. The population of the northern cities of Mali, like Timbuktu, has an Arab-like complexion dating back to the spread of Islam. To season his story a notch, Raj told everybody that his mother was Italian. All the girls wanted to be seen with him. He was the talk of the dorms, and attending parties became part of his routine.

Soon enough, before anybody realized it, he was

drinking with the pros after a fast-track training period during his heydays. Then, the high life started to take a toll on his education and overall welfare. He went from changing girlfriends to drinking straight vodka in tight set-ups, with the old guard. As he sank deeper into the bottle, Raj retreated, and was just a shadow of himself. He reached the dangerous point of no return. Once again, the community tried to save him without any success, as he drifted farther and farther away from reality. He pushed everybody away and sank deeper into drinking. The next step was to go home without a diploma, knowledge, or even a positive experience from the Union. Unfortunately, he was yet another bright mind compromised by vodka.

Now to Kasey, a born athlete from central Mali, whom, every soccer coach would want in his or her dream team. When he joined us in Kishinev, we admired his personality and really appreciated his talent as a defender in our soccer team. He was reserved and trustworthy from the start, which earned him a great deal of respect from the community. Later on, he was even elected general secretary of the Malian community. He stayed in shape by hitting the gym, pumping iron to build more muscles. The community was proud of his talent, decency and leadership. We were good buddies, and I never heard the slightest negative thing about him early on.

But two years later, to my surprise, one of the ancients told me that the general secretary himself touches "red," meaning red wine. At first, I was not worried and thought that it could just be a case of casual drinks on special occasions - a hasty denial on my part. But rumors kept coming about him buying his own and enjoying it in his room with friends and at parties. I was also told that when he got drunk he would stand on one leg, and lift the other one in the air like Jackie Chan or Bruce Lee. He would punch or kick windows for no apparent reason. He even cut a vein during one of these episodes, and had his hand in a bandage for quite a long time.

Staying up late and competing to get drunk with a bunch of friends naturally did not help academically. He lived in the same dorm as some of the worst drinkers in town, like two brothers from Sierra Leone, who were more unstable sober than drunk. Kasey never took an academic break but kept fighting, disturbing the peace in the dorms, hurting himself, and ultimately losing our respect.

His story shows how corrupting Kishinev's drinking environment was. He got sucked in, even if he never drank before and went astray in record time.

These cases demonstrating the disastrous effect of alcohol, are just from the small Malian community in Kishinev. A separate book would not be big enough to address the cases of all drinkers in Kishinev, much less in the whole union or within other communities. That number is unimaginable, and the toll on each represented country, unknowable.

There were many others who drank without endangering their own lives, or those of the community members, but who did not succeed academically because of it. Many would travel from town to town to be with their drinking buddies and binge night after night for days. From missed classes to failed exams or projects, these students were more dedicated to their drinks and drinking partners than to the purpose of their presence in the Union.

Some others drank just for machismo, or to go with the flow with the Soviets who needed alcohol to get in the mood. These students finished their education on time and without serious trouble with the authorities. One can only imagine how much more they would have accomplished academically if they were not in the grips of alcohol.

Due to the pervasiveness of alcohol many students went back home without a diploma. Unfortunately, these students were led by some elders who wanted to widen their circle just to feel better. I say shame on them for destroying young lives in the search for company while going downhill.

IV
Четыре

D. EASTERN JIM CROW

When the list of potential candidates for the former Soviet Union came out in the summer of 1986, many of us knew little to nothing about race relations in the Soviet Union. It just did not appear on our radar screen, especially during the thrilling atmosphere created by a potential trip to study abroad. The secrecy surrounding the USSR, the worthlessness of Malian authorities, and the deafening silence of current and former students, left us nothing to work with. All I knew was that Ottman was beaten drunk in the street and left for dead in Moscow, and my own mom told me someone rubbed her skin to see if the color would come off, during a visit funded by the Soviet Union in the 1960s. Besides those cases, the general perception of the "Internationalist Soviets" was better than that of shameless colonial-Europe and Jim Crow/Indian-genocide-America, when it came to race. Before my trip, I was more worried and intrigued about the unknown, the KGB and the restrictions in my host country, than any potential blatant racism or beatings in the streets of Moscow. If that were the case, Mom would not have let me go, no way no how.

During the cold war, the West constantly accused the

former Soviet Union of just about any sin under the sun, but racism was not one of them. The lack of freedom and Gulags full of political prisoners were the main flaws. The Soviet Union on the other hand, loudly professed peace, independence from colonial powers, and friendship among nations, while accusing the "soulless" West of imperialism and racism. I say kudos to the propaganda machine on both sides, for successfully solidifying these stereotypes about each other, at least in the developing world. In my mind's eye, I can still see the pictures of US Marines invading Grenada, police attacking African-Americans with dogs and fire hoses, or "white only" signs in US southern cities, decorating the hallways of our language school and dorms. However, the longer we stayed in the Union, the more we suffered from the difference between the Communist Party lines and what blue collar Soviets really thought of blacks or minorities in general.

A few hours after my arrival in Moscow, we were herded to the nearest cafeteria for lunch. On our way, we met two young men who looked at us, said something to each other and openly laughed at us. For those who would never experience what I am describing here, there is no more enraging and sickening feeling than being black on foreign soil, not speaking the language, and being overtly laughed at by passing whites. Only God knows how bad that first encounter hurt. Deeply angry as I was at these two punks, and as this seemed to be an isolated incident, I let go.

In the cafeteria a few minutes later, as if to neutralize this brutal episode, I met one of the Soviet teachers who used to cross our yard, to teach at an all-girl high school. She recognized me right away, smiled, and asked about my family and my trip to her country, before showing me the way to the buffet.

I felt good about that encounter, and was subconsciously looking forward to more goodwill in a country that never had colonies in Africa. The former Soviet Union, officially championed independence and self-determination on the African continent for decades. My heart and soul were just looking forward to a pleasant stay; I did not have the slightest reason to expect anything else.

162

We ate and rushed back to our hotel to learn about our next destination, which in my case was Kishinev.

The whole afternoon started off on the wrong foot. We arrived late at the railroad station as our train was departing. So we all ran and threw our luggage in the moving train, before jumping onboard without tickets or money. We then had to drag our luggage from the last car toward the front in the search of an empty compartment.

As we struggled through the hallways, our fellow Soviet passengers seemed very agitated and unable to calmly accept our presence. Every encounter turned into drama. Some passengers dashed into their compartments to avoid us as we came through. Others turned around to alert friends or family, who stuck their heads out of the door of their compartments, chuckled then retreated. Others said things in Russian as we approached, then exploded in laughter loud enough to send one's blood pressure through the roof.

In the restaurant, we could see the waitresses pointing at us and laughing before one decided to talk to us, trying to control her laugh by wearing a gigantic smile. We did not know what to do or say, but tried our best to manage our discomfort.

That long 36-hour trip felt like an eternity. The language barrier and the anxiety of the unknown ahead paralyzed our confused minds. Given the stares and mocking laughter we were subjected to, we felt like animals in a circus arena.

Ironically, we would soon discover that, while we felt like animals on display, most of the spectators on that train saw us just as that – sub humans, animals.

Once we settled in Kishinev, we asked the ancients about the Soviets' attitude toward minorities. I was told time and time again that the Soviets were condescending and deeply racist. As if to prove the point, the compound where our dorms and classes were was nicknamed "The Zoo," even though more Soviets than blacks lived there.

The picture I was getting day by day from the local population, and from my fellow countrymen and women, did not match the politically internationalist image presented by the Soviets. The teachers, neighbors and Soviet diplomats I had encountered in Bamako, had not displayed an ounce of bigotry.

163

There was no suspicion of harsh feelings toward others. But now, when I was in the 'belly of the beast," I was being rejected like the plague by people I thought were internationalists at best, or neutral at least. However, while there was no signs saying "white only", people refused to sit next to me in the cafeterias or restaurants. There was no "back of the bus" for us, but wherever I sat, nobody sat next to me, no matter how full the bus or how long and painful the ride was for any of the passengers. After only three months into the six-year long curriculum, we all had a pretty good idea about what we had gotten ourselves into: a profoundly bigoted society.

From day one, I tried to wrap my head around the obvious and yet puzzling state of race relations in the Soviet society.

The first year, our Russian language teachers were absolutely sweet to us, since they were our initial contact with the general population. They visited us in our rooms for one-on-one conversations, so while we got help with our homework and learned more about our hosts, they gathered our private information, which we gave away innocently. In class, they taught us proudly about their great history and the government's international involvement on behalf of developing countries. From the gifts the Soviet Union bestowed on Africa every year, to their assistance in the push for freedom and independence from the "colonial West", we heard it all.

But, when we stepped outside of these classes into the streets, we were laughed at and called names. Slowly but surely, our minds were no longer malleable. Our defense mechanisms started to work overtime to shield us against the new barbs coming our way. The ancients kept telling us their stories, and we kept experiencing new ones with every passing day.

All over the Union, black students had to deal on a daily basis, with the all-too-familiar classic expression of intolerance: a laugh in the face. More often than not, we would see an average Soviet citizen with a big grin, alerting his friends to look at us, before exploding in a laugh.

On the bus, people would not sit or stand next to you. While standing, a buffer zone would naturally be created around you by passengers who consciously refused to get close. When forced by circumstances, you could see the indignation or discomfort in their eyes. To counter or fight that behavior, I made the riding rule for myself to always sit next to someone. I felt like I always won, either by teaching my temporary neighbor that it was OK to sit by a black man, or by getting under his or her skin.

In town, catching a taxi was not a given, either. Many cabs would drive around you, and take the next client a few feet away. At the taxi station, cabbies would avoid the entire block altogether, if they saw black students in the queue. One day, when that happened to me and an ancient, we decided to do what the administration always told us to do: take down the plate number and pass it to the local militia. We never heard a word about the incident, despite reporting it.

There was obviously a deep uneasiness for different reasons on both sides of the racial line, which led to the peculiar lifestyle we did not anticipate. None of the returning or vacationing students warned us about the blatant racism that plagued the nation. They also neglected to warn us about the corrupt bureaucrats at the Department of Education and at our embassy in Moscow. We were also taken by surprise by the inhospitable atmosphere that greeted and pushed us deep indoors. We were tolerated in class and in the dorms; hated in the buses, restaurants, movies, bars, and nightclubs; robbed, beaten and killed in the streets. Therefore, as a community, we learned to protect ourselves by staying home as much as possible, and never to go out alone, especially after dark. Whether in Moscow or Dushanbe, there was this subtle and malicious feeling toward black students that still surprises. We were this complex creature, always on the defensive, that could do no good, nor be accepted as simple human beings by the Soviet society as a whole.

As time ticked by, I gradually learned what all the students and corrupt Malian diplomats knew all along about what it meant to be black in the USSR: "fucking niggers", "S.O.Bs Chasing Soviet girls" or "rich daddies' kids. Anyway you looked at the generalizations; there was trouble, resentment, even hatred, no matter how hard we tried to fit in.

a."Fucking Niggers"

To average Soviets, we were nothing more nothing less than "niggers". They made sure to call us as such, and also made damned sure to treat us as such. That deep-rooted racism surfaced at every turn of black students' lives, everywhere in the former Soviet Union, which may seem like an astounding fact to some. It was blatant and deliberate, but yet surprising, given the history of the Soviet Union. The Soviets were not known to the rest of the world for discrimination unlike Europeans and the US with their long history of colonialism and slavery. The former Soviet Union initially seemed guiltless in that department. This surprise effect added to the pains, and also to our vulnerability. At first, we kept guessing people's attitudes or motives by always giving them the benefit of the doubt. But to our own perils, as the insults and injuries kept coming back only crueler. We were called 'chimps", "niggers", "fucking niggers" and "fucking blacks" among other appalling epithets. Physical and verbal assaults kept us away from social life, and the Soviet government's paranoid rules kept us from renting apartments or working, therefore from really mingling with the natives. We could only be students, confined by circumstances to our dorms and away from movies, bars, clubs, stadiums or pools; in short, from life. So, we had to create our own universe in the dorms, a tricky undertaking that generated nothing but friction

166

with the authorities and our roommates. Here are some of the stories:

Moscow, Russian Federation, 1984
KT from Mali:

One early summer evening, outside our dorms at the University of Friendship - Patrice Lumumba, people were enjoying the cool breeze of the evening. Some were just sitting around; others were drinking or making BBQ. A young student from Zimbabwe was cooking some meat with a group of friends when patrolling militia men appeared with their dogs. One of the animals wondered off toward them, and they tried to chase it away without success. His handlers did not even attempt to pull it back, to the contrary, they got mad at the way the students were trying to chase the dog away from their meat. One of them subsequently pulled his gun and shot the Zimbabwean student point-blank. The poor student died right on the spot. All the foreign students got together and went to alert the authorities about this vicious racist crime. They analyzed the situation and said that the perpetrator would be punished with the full force of the law. A few months later, many witnesses saw the same militia man taking classes at another university. He just got moved from the environment of the crime to another part of the town without suffering any consequences. The life of a young African student was taken away for just trying to chase a dog about to eat his BBQ.

Moscow, Russian Federation 1986
MD:

As the president of the Malian community I dealt with an overwhelming number of cases of racism. One thing they had in common was the fruitless end of all the charges that got pressed. I personally witnessed a case in our dorm concerning a friend from Rwanda during the harsh winter of 1986. One night around five in the morning there was a lot of noise in the hallway, so we got up to see what the matter was. In fact, our friend from Rwanda, named Narciss got tossed out through his window, down from the fourth floor. He was lying unconscious in the snow, naked and covered with blood in minus 20 degrees Celsius weather. We called up the militia next door, but they took all their time to show up. Once on the scene, they started asking questions pointing in the direction of a suicide. They called the ambulance, asked a lot more questions and escorted the almost dead and frozen body of our friend. They did not arrest, or even briefly detain, anybody. When we got back up in the dorm, we met his roommate whom we questioned about the circumstances of the incident. He simply answered "Narciss was and is no more." That was the end of the near-death story of our friend, who we all know would have never attempted a suicide. No probe, no arrest.

With the pressure of the Rwandan embassy, they took good care of him at the hospital and he later even rejoined the basketball team of the academy.

Moscow, Russian Federation, 1989
KN from Mali:

My best friend, MC, with whom I shared a room and class in grade school in Mali, finished his PhD in 1989. He got his diploma and was getting ready to return home. I flew home earlier and was expecting him to come back any time for my wedding. The last time we talked, he told me to wait until June, when he gets home, to celebrate my wedding. Then I received a devastating letter informing me about his disappearance. Three months later, his body was found half-buried in a snow-covered park by the dorms in Moscow. When his body came home and during his funerals, his dad told me, "Open it son, this body belongs to you, do what you think is right," a pool of tears filled my eyes. His body was so badly damaged that we were advised not to open the coffin. That was another case without a single interrogation, much less an arrest.

Moscow, Russian Federation, 2001
MD:

In 2001 a refugee friend of mine from Zaire (Democratic Republic of Congo) was going to the HCR (United Nations High Commission for Refugees) to get his stipend with a bunch of friends. A group of Russians attacked them in the street right in front of Russian guards. They ran away to avoid the physical confrontation, but unfortunately he fell down. The Russians caught up to him and ruthlessly beat him. He died from his injuries, leaving behind a Russian wife and two kids. Nobody called the militia, nobody got arrested and as usual nothing happened.

Poltava, Republic of Ukraine, 1983
DT from Mali:

On September 14, 1983 we arrived in Poltava, a town of about 300,000 inhabitants, after three days in Moscow. The small railroad station was jam-packed as if a notable was stopping by. As we got out of the train and were finding our way to the bus, people were trying to touch us while making undecipherable gestures. The translators that came to get us started to panic themselves, and soon attempted to rush us through the devouring mob. We got swept away from the station and the "flesh eating looks", to the university buses. We later learned that the mob was at the station to satisfy some of their outstanding curiosities. They wanted to verify if our dark skin would rub off when touched, and if in fact we lost our tails after surgery in Moscow, as they all religiously believed to be true. Our group was only the third generation of foreign students in that town. Cannot imagine what the first two went through.

Moscow airport, Russian Federation, 1984
BD, a Student in Architecture in Kiev:

I was at the restaurant of Cheremetyevo Airport in the capital city, trying to get a bite while waiting for my flight. By coincidence, many big-belly high-ranking officers of the Soviet army also were at the restaurant savoring their meals. They were dressed in their eye-catching uniforms with a red stripe on the sides of their pants. You could just guess that there were up there somewhere in the hierarchy. They took up all the tables except the one I was sitting at by myself, right next to them. In the middle of the room stood a young man with his plate in his hands looking around for a place to sit. When our eyes met, I made a sign with my head that he could come and sit at my table. He looked deeply in my eyes and fervently said,

"Creatures like you should not mix with people." I did not say a word to avoid any escalation as he pompously continued hunting for a place to seat. I ignored him, ate my meal and went to get my winter coat hanging by the bigwigs. I grabbed my coat, turned around and said to the generals, "I thank you all for your sense of justice and your deafening support." Nobody said a word as I left.

Krasnodar, Russian Federation, 1987

HT, a colleague from Mali:

In 1987 during my language year, HIV/AIDS was just surfacing, at least in that main tea-producing region of the Russian Federation named Krasnodar. All foreign students were subject to an obligatory HIV/AIDS test. We went and shared blood-drawing needles right at the state clinic. After a few days, the Soviet authorities came with the results and said that many students tested positive and would have to pack up and go home. The targeted group was made up only of black students coming from Africa, mostly from Mali, Senegal, Congo and Togo. Mysteriously, the Arab, East-European, Latino and Asian foreign students were not even mentioned. The Soviets ordered an imminent departure of the "sick" group back to their countries. The communities of each affected country, started negotiations with the dean and faculty representing foreign students. During the brouhaha, a wealthy student from Congo went home in all kinds of shock. Her father sent her to France for a second opinion. Her test came back negative, and she made sure to send a copy of her second test to the Soviet authorities in Krasnodar. The news of the letter spread around at the speed of light. The targeted communities pointed at that letter to make their case. Facing a certain embarrassment, the Soviets authorities came out again and said that now, fifty percent of Malian students and a considerable number from Senegal, Togo, Congo and Mozambique, are infected and should go home. The Malian community held a secret meeting at 3 a.m. and decided to collect all Malian passports. In solidarity with the "infected", we threatened a mass departure home. We also asked other black communities to join the struggle, and put pressure on the Soviet authorities. The situation brew from bad to worse, as the representatives of many different embassies landed in Krasnodar, to closely manage what was heading toward a diplomatic showdown. Under tremendous pressure from all sides, the authorities, headed by the dean of the institute, decided to call a meeting with African students, the mayor of the city, and doctors from the state clinic. All African students came to confront the racist policy makers. The leader of the Congolese community said that he was not going to listen to a word from the local doctors. Tests and counter tests were on many lips, and some even demanded to send everybody to Western Europe, for a credible and reliable test. Flying in competent and trusted foreign doctors to Krasnodar, was also mentioned. The Soviet authorities then changed their story, and said that only three Malian students are infected, two women and one man. But the two had boyfriends from Senegal and Mali who were healthy, plus the boyfriend of the woman from Congo was also clean. Since all that sounded fishy, the Malian community said that the three Malians would go to France for further tests, but the Soviets refused to give them exit and reentry visas. Then, they added that those three would continue their studies, but could not go to Europe for vacations, which was their right. Later on, after the school year, one went to Mali and one to France, and both came back with negative results. Since their story was not standing anymore, the Soviet authorities backed down and let it go quietly. Why initiate such confrontation based on lies at all? Nobody had a clue.

Baku, Republic of Azerbaijan, 1987

DD:

In 1987 the government controlled-TV showed a Tarzan movie, which caught everybody's breath but foreign students. In the series, Tarzan had a little chimpanzee called Cheetah, which always hung around him. Since then, black students went from "niggers" to Cheetah in Baku. In the bus, the Soviets would whisper, "Cheetah, Cheetah, Cheetah," all along until one got off the bus. In Baku Cheetah became the nickname of every black foreign student, replacing the outright

171

"chimps" or "niggers" we were called before the screening of the movie.

Moscow, Russian Federation, 1987

AD:

Soon after landing in Moscow from Bamako, I had the misfortune to be sent to Tashkent, the capital city of the Republic of Uzbekistan, for my language year. A government minder accompanied us to the railroad station to help us find our train for the week-long trip. Our helper found my place in a compartment with three Soviets, one guy and a middle-aged couple. After realizing that I was going to travel with them, they balked. They refused to let me back in to take up my place, and moreover, put my luggage out in the hallway. My government helper tried hard to convince them to do the right thing, but to no avail. They were dead set against traveling with me, arguing that they did not want to travel with a "nigger" in the same compartment. The face-off brought out the rest of the passengers in the hallway, looking on like sports spectators. Frustrated and unable to persuade the bigots, my helper finally called the militia of the rail station. They stepped in and basically told the racists to knock it off and let me in; needless to say how tense and awkward the lengthy trip was.

Kiev, Republic of Ukraine, summer 1988

ALB and friends:

One afternoon of that summer of 1988, we invited a friend with his Soviet girlfriend to go eat at a pretty nice restaurant near a park, not far from our dorms. The place was well known and always full. Once there, we sat down and made ourselves comfortable. After almost an hour, nobody came to wait on us, so my friend decided to go talk to the first waiter he could find. He approached one and explained that we have been sitting for a while, and asked if he or somebody else could help. He was told to still wait, that somebody will be with us shortly. We waited close to another hour without being served. He went back again to see what was going on, only to be told by a waiter that "he was not ready to serve some 'niggers' with a Soviet girl." We then decided to leave before things got ugly, as they often do in charged-up situations like this.

Kiev, Republic of Ukraine, 1988
BAD, a childhood friend of mine:

One day, I went to the restaurant with a bunch of friends for lunch. We lined up just like everybody else, and fifteen minutes later, they told us that the food we wanted to eat was not ready. As we were weighing our options, one of two ladies next to us, asked me, "Do chimps also eat what is served here?" I refused to believe what I was hearing, so I decided to get closer and asked her to repeat herself. Without hesitation, she did, "Do chimps like you also eat what is here?" As she was finishing her racist comment, I slapped her without calculation. Next, I went to protest to the dean of foreign students and filed a complaint. Eyewitnesses helped me win my case at the militia station. I was later told that she got 72 hours of jail time for her comments. I would like to believe that she actually did serve her days in jail, but something is telling me that she never did. Seemed like the authorities just wanted to be seen doing something.

Kiev, Republic of Ukraine, 1988
BAD:

In the summer of 1988, we were at the stadium playing for the African Soccer Cup, organized every year between African teams. A group of young Soviets stopped by and started asking questions. "How in the world can two teams of chimps play soccer?" said one. An Angolan student upon hearing that, jumped on them and started throwing punches. The militia soon intervened, separated the two sides and took everybody to their station. We filed complaints again with some witness accounts. The militia threw them in jail as we left and we never got any update about the case.

Kharkov, Republic of Ukraine, 1988

BT, a colleague and neighbor:

One day I was going to buy an airline ticket, when I encountered in the bus some teenagers and their parents. One standing by his dad took a hard look at me and said, "Say, if I cut your black skin, will your blood be red like mine?" I got angry about the stupid remark and tried to scare him. His father stepped in and tried to hit me. I protected myself as we coasted to the bus stop. When the doors opened, a Soviet traveler yelled, "A nigger is fighting with one of ours." Impulsively, all the foreigners at the bus station jumped in the bus and started to fight. A big brawl ensued, but when a foreign student pulled out a knife, people backed off right away, as the militia showed up. They hauled everybody to their station for questioning. I then filed a complaint against the father who tried to slap me. A week later, they contacted me to say that I won my case, because their constitution itself forbids a man to raise his hand on a woman. They also wanted to know if I wanted to see him convicted. I declined.

Odessa, Republic of Ukraine, 1989
ABN, a childhood friend:

One day coming from the university by bus, I stopped to buy groceries and started to walk to my dorm. About halfway home, I met four Soviets coming from the park who started to call me names. "Hey chimp, hey chimp" they yelled, but I did not even look back much less answer. I started to walk faster and my heart began racing as I felt the peril closing in. They paced faster too, still calling me names. As they caught up to me, one punched me in the face and avowed that they will kill me. I started to scream and run as fast as possible. I called for help as some foreign students were passing by. Their mere presence deterred my assailants and saved my life. I suffered swollen cheeks and an indelible psychological scar.

Kolkhoz Tcherkaski, Ukraine, 1989
HD, a colleague from Mali:

During practice at one of the numerous and gigantic collective farms named kolkhoz, I went with fellow students to the cafeteria for a break. The place was packed with Soviet workers, and we became the attraction of the day, as always. Once at a table, a little toddler accompanied by his mom decided to join us and satisfy his curiosity. His mom aggressively prompted him, "Do not approach these blacks, they still live in their jungles, not civilized." The kid replied that he just wanted to see if the black color on our skin would stick to his fingers. I got up and touched his glass of water, just to show him that the color does not stay. His mom then, with a swift movement, angrily threw the glass on the floor and broke it. I managed to control myself and did not reply to her unbelievable verbal assault.

Kishinev, Republic of Moldavia, 1989

Me,

In late June that year, I heard on the radio that, the Soviet soccer star Oleg Blokhin from Ukraine, was retiring after a final friendly farewell game. The Soviet national team was to play an international one, made out of super stars from around the world. Among them, Beckenbauer (as coach), Breitner, and Forster from Germany; Rocheteau from France; Antognoni and Maldini from Italy. For those as young as I am to remember these world super stars, it could not get better than that. So, I decided against every rule the Soviets had in place, to try to make it there. We, as foreigners could not travel beyond 15 miles without permission, and without finishing with all our exams. I knew the deck was set against me, since we were in the finals and Kiev was way outside of the 15 mile-radius. So, getting an internal visa was out of question, especially in such a short time. Kiev was only 250 miles or about 5 hours away, from Kishinev. I decided to take the first train for Kiev, watch the game and return right after, in order to be at school the following morning. Once at the rail road station, I had to bribe a Soviet citizen to buy me a ticket, since I could not get one myself without a government issued visa. Once over that hump, I jumped on the train for Kiev. Few hours into the trip and at the first stop in a small village, ticket controllers came in. Sitting in the middle of a bunch of Soviets, I stood out like a sore thumb. Needless to say that I was to be among the randomly checked in that train car. My heart started to race but

175

I kept my poker face on. The controller came and asked for my ticket. When I handed it to him, he said right away that this was a ticket for the natives, not for foreigners and that I knew better than to try to fool him. He ordered me to follow him to the buildings and to the militia post. The chief of the station told me that without a permission, he would have to send me back to Kishinev, after signing an affidavit. I grudgingly wrote, as he dictated, that I knowingly broke the travel rules. I argued and insisted that Kiev is not far anymore, and that I would return right after the game, but to no avail. He then made me buy a return ticket and also made sure I got on the train going back. As the train started to leave the station, I jumped out and landed on the far end of the platform, dislocating my ankle. I limped away and hid behind a little shed, where I nurtured my swollen foot. Few minutes later, one of the militia men from the station, found me hiding and hurting in that corner. He stated "Are you soccer crazy? Look, my boss told me to come check everywhere, to make sure you were on that train and returning to Kishinev. I will not tell him anything, but if you get caught again, you will be in bigger trouble". I acquiesced, cracked a smile and promised to avoid capture at all costs. As he returned to his post, I approached and bribed another guy to get me a new ticket for Kiev. Hurting and hungry, I waited in my hideout for the next train. About an hour later, I limped into it and ducked until we completely left the station. Once in Kiev, I went to the dorms to tend to my ankle, then to the stadium to get my ticket. Watching Blokhin and the super stars with glee, I forgot about my foot and my affidavit, which the dean of foreign students would be reading before my return. As a soccer fanatic, I had the best time of my stay that far, and was ready to assume the consequences. Going to class the next morning as planned, the Dean saw and summoned me from a mile away to go see her. Once in her office and without even discussing the matter, she demanded to not do this again. I told her that time was short, finals were upon us, but that I badly wanted to go see the game. She then said what I always dreamed of, since I got to Kishinev. "Next time, let me know and I would give you a permission to travel", she said. I could not believe my ears and already started to prepare my next trip in my mind. She kept her promised, and I never wandered again without permission. I would eventually use her authorizations to go see George Weah and Monaco in Odessa, Maradona and Naples in Moscow, Tigana, Boli, Abedi Pele and Marseilles, in Moscow. To name just a few soccer super stars. Fast forward seventeen years, with Blokhin now at the head of the Ukrainian national team. According to the British magazine Mirror from June 8 2012, Blokhin voiced his opposition to Africans playing in the Ukrainian league. He went on to tell the New York Times, right before the 2006 World cup the following: "The more Ukrainians that play in the national league, the more examples for the young generation.

"Let them learn from Shevchenko or Blokhin and not from some zumba-bumba whom they took off a tree, gave him two bananas and now he plays in the Ukrainian League."

The Ukrainian authorities took no action against Blokhin, despite assurances given to UEFA (The European Football body) that they are campaigning against racism. What a disgusting being I jumped through hoops to go see.

Kharkov, Republic of Ukraine, 1990
ID, an acquaintance

At one of my exams (measurement techniques) in IT, I came early and got in the class among the first six students to pick my questions. The teacher stopped me and asked why I was among the first to enter. I told him that I was ready and wanted to pass the exam. He replied, "As a nigger, how dare you enter first, can you know more than our Soviet students?" I stood up and grabbed him by the collar swearing to destroy him, he tried to push me off, and we found ourselves behind his desk and against the wall. The students and other teachers came in and separated us. We went to see the dean of the institute and the dean of foreign students. They all said that the teacher is known for his racist positions, but that I should not have grabbed him. I said that even if they repeat what he said I would grab them too. They calmed the atmosphere and decided that I should go pass the exam again, but in front of a state commission given the beef between us. I passed in front of a three member commission, and the teacher himself for fairness sake. I passed that exam with the minimum grade and he told me that I was not off the hook yet, that he will be waiting for me at my graduation. A few years later, he was the first one to come to my graduation exam. As I started to explain my hanging tables all across the room, he interrupted me before my ten minutes were up with a question, against all ethics. I answered that one and continued with my tables. After my presentation, the president of the commission asked if anybody had a question for me, and he replied yes. I walked past the rest of the teachers and stood right in front of him. He said that my theme had a lot of math formulas, especially algorithms, and that I should have made a special table about the main formulas my theme was based on. I replied that the maximum of tables allowed is seven and I have eight. "If I had added another one, there would be no space for it, unless we put it in the hallway" I added. Everybody started to laugh at him, and I could see his face turning red. The head of the commission asked again for questions. He raised his hand again, but the head of the commission cut him short by asking me his own question. That way he got drowned out in the crowd and let me be. After the deliberation, all the teachers came to congratulate me, and when we faced off, he called me "colleague". I replied, "Yes dear colleague."

Kharkov, Republic of Ukraine, 1990

ID adds:

One early morning the militia descended and surrounded our dorm. They took all the documents and IDs at the front desk to assess who was staying where, and who played host to whom, overnight. They rounded up all the guests who spent the night, and all the hosts who allowed that to happen. That night my girlfriend stayed with me and found herself in the group of trespassing guests, and me among the trespassing hosts. We were all at the front desk waiting to know our fate, when my girlfriend said that she had to go to work. Since they had her ID, they agreed to let her go. She fought her way out through a group of militia men to the main door. As she left, the chief of the militia said, "Look guys, she yells at us but she does not even know if her host has AIDS?" I immediately shouted back, "If I had AIDS, I could have contracted it only from your mother." We then started to exchange insults and curses with people intervening to separate us. All the foreign students stepped in and the tension reached a fever pitch, prompting the militia to order more troops to the rescue. By now they outnumbered us and took everybody to their station. They separated us and threw the men in one room and ladies in another, but kept me in my own cell as a special case. Later on, two militia men took me in a big room for an interview. I told them that I would talk only in the presence of their chief who came to the dorm. They said that he already gave his side of the story, and that it was my turn to give mine. I refused to say anything without him present. Finally they called him in the room, I then told my side of the story. The head of the station then asked him if my version was correct, and he nodded yes. I was then told to go home and come back at 12:30 p.m. Once home, I called my girlfriend, and we shared the latest news on each side. She told me that she already called her father (an officer in the army), and that he promised to take care of the situation. When I went back to the militia station, a new team interviewed me, and I gave exactly the same answers as before. Then they started to ask about my relationship with my girlfriend, and I told them to mind their own business, this being my private life. They then told me to go home again, and come back at 5 p.m. Once out of there I called again my girlfriend who told me that they wanted her too at the station. We both then went at five, and met with the first team that interrogated me. Meantime, they checked both of our backgrounds, and said that I had a problem at the university with a teacher, whom I had beaten. That was the only thing in my files. They then said in a very friendly manner that I do not have the right to have guests overnight as the rules say. Their chief even proposed to come to the dorms and see how I live, before ordering me to wait outside while they talk with my girlfriend. After a while, she came out and home we went. A few months later he came to the dorm in civilian clothes, and I did not even recognize him until he introduced himself. "I am here to visit as I promised last time we met," he said. I was surprised by the visit and invited

179

him in my room. My girlfriend was there that day, too, and we all had coffee together.

Voronej, Russian Federation, 1990
DS, a Malian colleague:

One beautiful day, a young Malian student who just arrived in our town, paid me a visit. After a very pleasant and quiet time together, he decided to go home. I offered to accompany him out of the dorm and toward the bus station. Upon returning, a bunch of Soviet classmates, whom I just saw at the front desk while exiting, denied me reentrance and asked for my student ID. "Come on, guys, are you kidding me?" I said. "No, we do not know you, and you do not live here," they replied. "Come on men, you are our class leader aren't you? We all play soccer together, too" I said, pointing at one of them. "No, we want to see your student ID," they replied while encircling me. Before I knew it, they grabbed my hands from both sides, and my class leader himself, started to kick and punch me. After receiving a very painful one in my genitals, I screamed from the top of my lungs. Then I pulled forward away from the ones holding my hands, to punch my classmate in a crazy wrath. My knock opened a gushing gap above his eyebrow, and he fell on the ground, where I kept punching him. The rest of the group vanished, leaving the two of us and me still punching him. I then saw and heard Lucy from Togo screaming for help "Come on, come on all, the Soviets are beating DS!" The lobby of the dorm filled up instantly with African students, who yanked me to my room. Some advised to go file charges; others thought that could backfire like in many previous cases. "If you decide to press charges, the students may be fired and punished, then they will hunt you down in this town," somebody said. While we were weighing our options, a small delegation from the Soviets' side knocked at my door. They asked for forgiveness, and to keep this unfortunate incident between us here and not under any circumstances to press charges or involve the authorities. I acquiesced.

Rostov on the Don, Russian Federation, 1991

GJPK, a high school friend:

One day, I went with a group of friends to a bar named "Geneva." We got in and gathered around a high chair, then passed our orders. Quietly, we were enjoying our drinks when I spotted a group of suspicious looking Soviets. I told my friends that we seemed to be in some guys' crosshairs. "No way, you think you know and sense everything", they replied. I grudgingly said that we will see, and that I wish I was wrong. Just as I predicted, one of them approached us and insolently engaged me. He aggressively asked, "What are you doing here? This is a bar, and there is no banana here (for you chimps)." I told their leader that we are also Soviets but black, before a heated and unorthodox cursing argument started. They came to the conclusion that we will not lay down for them, so the very volatile argument turn into comradeship. I bought some beer for them, and we started talking, to the very displeasure of another more radical group. That latter group started to attack by throwing beer bottles at us from every direction. The four of us could not believe what was happening, and did not know how to protect ourselves in this sea of Soviets. My friends astonishingly dashed outside to safety. Meanwhile, I was being the target of beer bottles that kept coming. Fortunately, other Soviets literally shielded me like a concrete wall with their own bodies, moments later. They managed to safely get me out, and calm the situation inside. Once out, I saw a mob of African students rushing from the dorms towards the bar, obviously alerted and recruited by my three friends. Among them, I recognized the cultural secretary of African students of Rostov, a very close friend of mine. I panicked and feared the prospect of a potentially deadly confrontation between foreign students and Soviet groups, between blacks and whites. I called the militia right away, and upon arrival they led away the delinquents. The chief inspector of the militia then plainly told me to quietly find other places to socialize, not here. He added that this bar was not even safe for normal Soviets, much less for foreigners.

Another day, my girlfriend and I were both traveling, she, to her native town Novorossiysk (The main Russian port on the Black Sea) and I to Moscow. Our separate trains were departing five minutes apart from the same railroad station. So we got out of the dorm to catch a cab and ride together. After a while, a private owner stopped. My Russian girlfriend got in with her luggage and moved over to make enough room for me to get in the car. Faster than I could think, the driver drove away with my girlfriend and his opened door, leaving me behind. Since he clearly did not want me in his car, I caught a normal cab and followed them all the way to the rail station. There, without uttering a word, I politely paid him once my girlfriend got out. He calmly took the money and drove away.

Odessa, Republic of Ukraine, 1991
AD, a Malian student:

I knew two PhD students at the Hydraulic Institute of Odessa. Shortly after graduation, they were getting ready to fly home. Unfortunately, a group of Soviets attacked them in town with sticks. One of them got a broken jaw, and had to postpone his departure to stay at the hospital. The Malian community filed complaints with the militia of the neighborhood, only to be told to avoid empty streets at night in order to stay alive.

Tashkent, Republic of Uzbekistan, 1992
AD adds:

One day, I went grocery shopping with my friend at the farmers' market called the Bazaar of Tashkent. We were peacefully scouting the market grounds when I abruptly found myself locked in the arms of a muscled and stinking Uzbek trying to kiss me. My excessively racing heart almost came out of my chest. I freaked out and started to scream at the top of my lungs in the middle of the huge market. He panicked and let me go but kept following us. I then decided to ask him what that was all about. He pointed toward his friend who was at some distance from us, laughing his heart out, and said, "My friend there promised me a bottle of vodka if I kiss a nigger." I was speechless as they left.

182

Voronej, Russian Federation, 1992

DS, a colleague and fellow soccer player:

One night, I went out with two friends to a party in another dorm, several miles away from ours. Around 3:30 a.m, we decided to head home, when we encountered a group of about ten Soviets who started to march toward us. Once in our face they said, "Listen, friends, today an African fucked us and we do not know who he is and where he is, but we are on a mission to take revenge." We tried to bring them to reason by saying that not all Africans are the same or bad just like any other race or ethnicity. They reluctantly refuted that and said that they are going to make us pay. I knew that we were in trouble and started to back away from them, but they kept coming. We knew that our winning chances were very slim and that only an escape plan could save our lives. Suddenly, a random car passing by stopped about thirty feet away, certainly acknowledging our state of emergency. I understood that he was trying to help us, but I could not get away as the guys kept attacking. He drove ahead, turned around and parked just few feet from the scuffle. I immediately ran towards him, got in his car and rolled up the windows. In the meantime, a third African student appeared at the cab station and understood right away that we were in trouble, so without more ado, he too joined me in the car. Our last friend, though tall and notably built, was giving his last strength to escape the Soviet mob. Unfortunately for him, they had the upper hand, and were seriously beating him. He managed to get closer to the car with the hooligans still punching him. The driver started to move the car to give him a chance to hop onboard, or at least to hang on. By now he had his back against the car, facing the mob that will not let him turn around and get in the moving car. Then, they started to poke him with a knife hidden in a bouquet of flowers, anywhere they could. Now bleeding, tired and almost desperate, he hung on to the car and kept pushing back his attackers. The driver kept the pace and miraculously, he somehow got in, bleeding from his multiple wounds. Our savior sped away and stopped at a safe distance to tend to him. He was seriously bleeding from his legs and arms. The driver then kindly took us to our dorms, not to the hospital, where we took care of the wounds. No enquiry, no arrest as usual.

Moscow, Russian Federation, 1993

HD:

After graduation, I was training at the Veterinary Academia of Moscow under the supervision of a much-respected advisor. One day, a lady brought her cat to the clinic with a fractured rear leg. My advisor told me to go take a look at the poor thing. When I came from the back room to inspect the cat, the owner vehemently refused my intervention. "A nigger does not know shit about a sick cat, and will not treat my cat," she yelled. My advisor said that if I could not look at the cat, that nobody else would. She categorically refused and went home with her suffering cat. Two days later, she came back, hoping to convince my advisor to have somebody else take care of the cat, only to be told the same thing over again. Now, with her back against the wall, she decided to let me do the job, but reserved the right to sue for damages. I took care of the cat and put the leg in a cast. Days later, the cat got well without any complications. Since then, she would bring me treats any time she came for routine checkups.

Kishinev, Republic of Moldavia, 1985

MD, a Malian colleague:

I went to the park with another Malian student just to clear our minds for a while. A young Soviet was coming from the opposite direction, looking at us with hate and anger. When we got close to each other, he spat on us saying, "Since when do 'niggers' go to the park?" I turned around and ran after him 200 yards before catching him. I knocked him down and punched him in his face, and left him with a swollen forehead. The whole park came to see what was happening, and circled us without saying a word. Since he was alone I taught him a little lesson about respect he would never forget.

MD adds:

One summer day of 1987 I got on a bus to go do some errands. The bus was full and I proceeded to take the

184

last seat left. As soon as I placed my bottom down, my direct neighbor got up and everybody else moved away from me, isolating me on one side of the bus. I did not say nor do anything, just stayed in my seat by the big side window of the bus, with the sun right on me. After a while somebody got off and I took his seat, this time on the other side of the bus in order to be in the shade. An adult man sitting on that side started to smile and asked me, "Why did you change seats?" I said because of the sun that was shining directly on me. He said, "How can a nigger from Africa complain about the sun?" I replied that it was none of his business for one, and that we do not walk on embers in Africa. I got mad and started to insult him and call him all kinds of names. Realizing that I was reaching my boiling point, he got ready to get off at the next stop. When the doors opened, I got up and kicked him in the ass while he was exiting. He fell down on his face, and the bus took off. After that, I got more isolated in my seat and people really did not want to get close to me, rightly so this time.

Moscow, Russian Federation, 1990

ND:

As a junior, I went to a village for my practice and worked at the center of the Academy - Timiriazev. With me were a Nigerian and a fellow Malian girl. In that remote village there was only one bathroom where the entire village took a shower twice a week, Wednesdays and Saturdays. We foreigners were more than uncomfortable with that policy, and pushed to have at least one normal shower per day, without success. We then decided to take our showers in a room where people washed their clothes. Then Wednesdays and Saturdays, we tried to be among the first ones at the door. The first time when we got there, everybody got out of the bathroom, and we, without thinking twice, took our shower and left. At the only government restaurant in town also, things got rough. When we got there, everybody already inside and in line turned around and left the place, the ones after us never made it inside to be served. We took our plates, served ourselves and gave the government tickets to the cashier. We then sat

185

down to eat, alone in the restaurant. After we left, people came in and ate. So, we became the talk of the town.

Now came the time to actually work on the theme of our three-month practice. We had to work with other fellow students from our academy in Moscow, and also with some students from the village. We had to do a lot of physical work, among them digging holes in the ground to observe the profile of the soil and take samples. We needed help from the village labor force to get the job done in a timely manner. Once on the site we would dig with the many picks available, and move on to do other stuff. Back at the dorm, the geology teacher was complaining about missing instruments, specifically picks. He would send people to go find them, but they always returned empty-handed. In the morning when we would go by the holes we already dug, we would see the picks right by the holes untouched. It appears that nobody would touch the picks we used; therefore they were missing all the time, since nobody would take them back to the dorms once we touched them.

Karkov, Republic of Ukraine 1990

OC:

One night I was at the rail station with a fellow Malian and a friend from Benin, when a Soviet guy approached us with his dog. He then told his dog to take a very good look at us, so it would know what chimps look like. I did not know what to say or do, so I decided to go talk to the militia man standing not far from us, keeping peace at the station. I told him about the guy harassing us with his racist comments. The militia man bluntly told me, "You know, things have changed (since the fall of the Berlin wall in November 1989), either you knock him hard and he will let you be, or be ready to fight to the bitter end. The third option is to just ignore him. I myself can get in trouble trying to defend you guys these days". I was amazed but not shocked by his comments, which I reported to my friends. When the guy came back with his dog again and started to call us names, I approached him and asked what he wanted. As he was about to respond to my question, I punched him in the face so hard that he ran away with his dog. The militia man who was following the events from afar, came to congratulate and remind us that his advice was the right one. Later on, at the metro station where we exited, the guy with the dog came and threatened to find us in our dorms and get even. We never saw him again.

Varonej, Russian Federation, 1991
MS, a Malian colleague:
One night I was coming from visiting my girlfriend in the dorm #6, towards the bus station. A gentleman innocently approached me, leading me to believe that he was after a lighter or something. Unfortunately, he unpredictably kicked me in the stomach in front of several people. By the time I recovered from my pain, I saw an elderly woman ripping him apart for his behavior and giving him some civics lessons. The man was ashamed of himself and decided to come and apologize to me. I forgave him, thanked the woman and gratefully went home in one piece. It could have been worse.

Moscow, Russian Federation, 2001
MS:
One afternoon I was coming from the experimental farm of the University Patrice Lumumba of Moscow, after checking some lab animals. In the metro I sat with some fellow students and one of my teachers, minding our own business. At one of the stops, a group of young noisy boys entered our car and hung around us. All of a sudden, one of them grabbed the overhead bar, lifted himself up and kicked me in the chest right in front of everybody. I got up and confronted him head on. The rest of the group joined the battle, and after a few punches were thrown, an old lady, and only her, intervened and let them have it. At the next station they got out and nobody else seemed to care.

Kishinev, Republic of Moldavia,
SS, a fellow Malian:
In 1983 VB from Moscow and SSI, decided to go to the nightclub of the hotel "Intourist." At the front desk they were told that they could not enter the hotel, much less go to the nightclub. They argued with the concierge who then called the

militia. Upon arrival they got into a fight with them, and VB, built like a catcher, kicked their butt. They retreated and called for more help. A bus full of militia men came, and took VB away in a separate room. There, they stepped on his arm and broke it. Then they told him to sign an affidavit saying that he broke it while resisting arrest, if he wanted to get help. He reluctantly signed it, then they called the ambulance for him. They took him to the hospital, put on a cast and took him home, end of the story. We just did not have any right or protection and were at the mercy of the system.

In the summer a friend of mine went for a walk with his girlfriend to a park nearby. All of a sudden, he came running back into the dorm in his underwear, shaken and dazed. After calming down and getting himself together, he told us that they had been attacked, and the Soviets armed with a knife wanted to cut his penis for going out with a Soviet girl. Again nobody got questioned or arrested and as always nothing happened.

In 1982 my Zambian friend went to a nightclub. There, he joined some girls, started dancing with them and was evidently enjoying himself. After a while a group of Soviets approached him and said, "Hey nigger, what are you doing here?" After a scuffle they grabbed him, put him on a table in front of the whole club, and swore to cut his throat. Fortunately, a service man came in and yelled, "What the hell are you doing guys?" They got scared and ran away. His life was saved by a courageous militia man, but subsequently nobody got arrested or even questioned.

Another day the same guy went to drink with some friends and again, a group of Soviets attacked him. This time they took all his clothes off and left him naked in the street unable to catch even a cab. When he called the emergency number, and told them that he was naked in the street, they hung up on him. Luckily, a passing by ambulance took him to the dorm. Again, there was no arrest, no investigation, nothing.

Moscow, Russian Federation, 1992
SK, a Malian colleague:

Around 1 p.m. this wintry day, I went to buy bread at the grocery store near Tashkent Street in Moscow. Coming back with my hands full of grocery, a group of teenagers confronted and circled me, in a blink of an eye. I heard "fucking nigger" over and over again, before one of them hit me in the head. I broke away from them, and ran for my life. They all started to sprint behind me. Fortunately, I reached the main street that was a little crowded. They then abandoned their chase and went away. To this day I refuse to think about what could have been.

Moscow, Russian Federation, 1992
SK adds:

One June day, I was in a store minding my own business, until a Soviet man caught my attention. He walked slowly towards me as if he had a question. I gave him my full attention in that narrow alley, crowded with buyers. He then said, "Hey, comrade, what did you do to burn yourself this bad?" referring to my dark skin. The elderly in the crowd displayed a certain amount of shock and shame, while the not-so-old were enjoying this verbal assault by laughing out loud, and hoping for more bigoted jokes. I had to say something just to keep my head up and avoid any potential fight. I replied by simply saying that I took my last shower six months ago, before quickly leaving the scene.

Kiev, Republic of Ukraine, 1987
YT:

One night, we, as a big group, were coming from a party a little ways from our dorms. We all gathered at the bus station and waited for the next one to take us back to campus, named after the famous Soviet chemist, Lomonosov. This very large complex of dorms sheltering several thousands of foreign and Soviet students, was also nicknamed "Negrograd." Out of nowhere, a group a Soviet youths mushroomed and began to move toward us. My heart rate doubled and I could see the same fear and anxiety on my colleagues' faces, because we all knew from experience that nothing good can come out of such encounter. They started to harass us and shouted racist comments: "What are you doing here, Monkeys, Trees weren't enough for you tonight and you had to come down?" At the same time, they were pushing and shoving us around with their faces in ours. The ladies in the group got really scared, and were making themselves less visible by ducking behind the men. Next thing we knew, the first punches were being thrown. As some fought back, others parted from the group to hunt for taxis. The assailants left the ladies alone and kept punching the men. Soon, the guys came with three cabs and swept all of us away to safety.

YT continues:

Another day between dorms 4 and 11 of the same Lomonosov compound, I got my matchbox out to light up, when a group of Soviets attacked me. I still do not know how, but I found myself in the air before landing on my back. By the time I got myself together, they disappeared. I went and complained to the commandant of both dorms, to the militia and to the dean. But nothing happened as always, so I and two of my friends from Guinea-Bissau decided to do justice ourselves. Every time we could, we would attack any Soviet wandering around our dorms by himself.

b. SOBs chasing Soviet girls

Take a cab anywhere in the former Soviet Union, the conversation would always veer to the good old stereotypes of genital sizes and bedroom performances. A few minutes into the ride, the first question, just to get the conversation going, would be about your country of origin. The next one is guaranteed to be about your sex life. Just about any cab driver or private citizen using his car as a cab, would say "How about our Soviet bitches, have you tried one yet? I heard they prefer you guys, those bitches." If you happen to admit that you have a girlfriend, they next want to know what kind of things or goodies you are showering her with. The inkling being that the girls who dated us were all prostitutes, or were after things from overseas, or were trying to leave the country. To them, there has to be something else other than love or attraction, for a "poor fucking nigger" to date a pure-blooded Soviet girl. The stigma made dating a hellacious confrontation with the Soviet authorities and the population at large.

The Soviet males, aside from their disdain for us, did not befriend us in order to avoid being seen as wanting Western items from us, or worse, selling Soviet secrets to us. To the society in general, "niggers" have nothing in common with the Soviet youth, therefore there must be some material advantage for a pure-blooded Soviet guy to befriend us. That collective mindset and self-serving stereotype regarding blacks, soiled

191

every decision making process.

Here are some cases shared by other colleagues who agreed to open up to me, unlike many others who decided to suppress their pains.

Kiev, Republic of Ukraine, 1987

DT:

In the summer of 1987 we were having our practical training on a small farm outside of Kiev. Since living conditions in those rural villages were far from adequate, almost all foreign students would travel back to the dorms, every day after classes and return the next morning. In short, nobody wanted to sleep, eat or shower in the villages on government-run mega farms. Just like many ancients before us, I along with three fellow Malians, two Nigerians, and two colleagues from Madagascar, returned to sleep in Kiev every single night, unlike our Soviet classmates.

One morning, we entered the cafeteria to find all the Soviet students and our professor of epidemiology, whispering something under their breath. We sensed that something was up, but had no clue as to what the stir was about. Finally, the professor decided to break the news to us, foreigners who just arrived from Kiev. He said, "Look guys, we found a needle that is obviously not Soviet-made, who knows if it is infected with the HIV/AIDS virus? We will have to call the KGB for an investigation." The mere mention of "foreign made" and "HIV/AIDS" in the same sentence, was like calling us by our first names in the context of the Soviet Union. Since we were clearly the target, I jumped on the opportunity and also demanded to have the KGB handle the situation in order to clear our names. I made clear to the professor that if the needle was infected by HIV/AIDS, then it could have only come from the Soviet students. I reminded him that all foreign students are tested by the authorities at least twice a year, every year, and that the positive cases are sent back home. At the same time, none of the Soviet students has ever been tested, so it was clear where to look for the virus. I shouted all over the cafeteria, making clear that we were there in order to study, not to entertain their racist sentiments.

The professor started to dread our determination to push the story further, and wanted to drop the whole thing. I categorically refused, and wanted to pursue his own wonderful idea about bringing the KGB. Feeling that we would not let go, the professor sent the class leader on a mission to try to convince us to drop the case. It is during that mediation that we found out why the professor concocted the false story. He "hated the fact that you went back to Kiev, in his mind, to sleep with Soviet girls, instead of staying at the farm," said the mediator. The professor could not stand the idea of blacks dating Soviet girls. Unfortunately, he had also previously promised to a grade school that he would have his foreign students give a talk about their respective countries. But after the incident, we collectively refused to go talk, up to the last minute that afternoon. We then relieved the pressure that clearly was gnawing at him by agreeing to go. He was really worried about the reaction of the dean, an impartial man who never took sides, and expelled many Soviet students involved in harassing foreign students. Rumors had it that the dean worked in England for the KGB, hence his open-mindedness.

Kishinev, republic of Moldavia 1986
SHO:

After the summer break in Kishinev right before the school year, the Interior Ministry sent an invitation letter to all the Soviet girls hanging with foreigners. He did so after tracking them down from the log book at the front desk of every dorm. Among the letter addressees was my own girlfriend. The intimidating letter said: "HIV-AIDS is around and the black foreigners are the only carriers. So, in order to stop the spread of the disease in your own country, you should stop seeing them. This is about warning you, and from now on, anybody who goes to see these 'niggers' will hear from us". So, the letter momentarily scared some, especially when delivered to their work places. But many also have seen scare tactics come and go. It did not get the desired effect as most recipients of the letter went about their daily lives.

SHO continues:

In 1986, I had a girlfriend named NT, who taught my zoology lab classes at the university. Because of the very hostile environment to interracial dating, we used to meet at my friends' in other dorms, in order to hide our relationship from the authorities. Despite our efforts, the Soviet militia found out about us, and alerted the dean of the university about her "unhealthy" relationship. The dean's office called her up and tried to fire her from her position. She fought very vigorously and after a long and hard battle they kept her, but moved her from conducting our lab classes. After that we kept our relationship very secret and completely changed our meeting strategies. We decided that she would come to the dorm with other girls' IDs. Or, we would bribe some of the front desk guys not to register her name in the log book. That seemed to work since she was never bothered by the militia, but made her girlfriends very nervous.

Kharkov, Republic of Ukraine, 1988
BT, a colleague of mine:

During our second year in Kharkov, a disturbing trend was being observed around our dorms. Black female students were being increasingly harassed by the Soviets. It became so prevalent that we could not even go to the phone booth or the grocery store by ourselves, without being attacked and beaten. We would always have somebody escort us. The situation got worse as black males were added to the target group. The reason for the racially prejudiced violence was that, Soviet guys wanted to date black foreigners, just like black foreigners were dating white Soviet girls, even if that was veiled in the dorms as much as possible. Fed up by the aggression and the silence of the Soviet militia, black foreign students decided to march without permission from the dean's office straight to the city council building in downtown Kharkov. The State Agriculture University of Kharkov being far from the city center, we decided to march all the way to strike a chord. Overwhelmed by our determination, the Soviet authorities ordered the buses not to take us, since it was an unannounced march. We then marched several miles from Rogan, our city, to

194

the center of Kharkov in order to voice our anger directly to the member of the city council. They said that this was the first time in more than 45 years that students marched without permission. So they ordered us to return, ask for permission from our faculty, and wait till the faculty forwards the request to the city council which would give its final decision. Then and only then, could we march or not, depending on their answer. Our leaders said no and more vigorously asked to see the secretary of the city council. They refused and demanded us to go home and send back the leaders of our different communities. We decided to send in our leadership on the spot. The latter explained to the council that we were being targeted because we dated Soviet girls, but the Soviet guys could not date our black sisters. At first the council said that we should let the Soviets date our girls too, over which we obviously had no control. But since we would not budge they pledged to protect us with militia shifts around the dorms. They kept their word and the steady presence of the militia over time deterred more than one drifter.

Varonej, Russian Federation, 1990

MS:

One night, Maxim from Benin, his Soviet girlfriend Lena, Tito from Sao Tome and Principe and I were coming from a party organized by the African community of Kaznova in Varonej. As we got to the cab station, a small group of Soviets accosted us and addressed Lena: "Aren't you ashamed of hanging with these 'fucking niggers'?" Maxim, unhappy about these comments, replied. He suddenly found himself in the middle of a bitter fight. I instantaneously looked for a cab to get us away from this mob, while Tito entered the battle to help Maxim and Lena. As a cab stopped, a militia car on duty pulled over miraculously to our great satisfaction. But as in a nightmare, the militia, after calming the spirits, decided to arrest Lena and took her with them to their station. Maxim vehemently opposed that and started arguing with the militia. Finally after a tough and rough discussion, they decided to let us go without even questioning our attackers. That was another biased intervention from the "peacekeeper" militia.

195

Moscow, Russian Federation, 2001

MD:

I have a story about a friend from Sudan named Joseph, who just graduated with a PhD at the Vet Academy of Moscow in 2001. Shortly after his graduation he went for a walk with his Soviet girlfriend in the park Kuzminki next to the academy. They were having a good time and taking pictures when two Russians attacked them. They beat him and left him for dead in the pond of the park. When they vanished, he got up with the help of his girlfriend and went back to the dorms. He had two broken ribs and a displaced jaw, which caused him to stay in bed for a month. He went to the militia with his girlfriend to press charges against his aggressors. The police came to his room many times to ask all kinds of questions. By chance, he had the pictures of his assailants in his broken camera. The images were so clear, that the militia could easily catch them if it wanted too. But they did nothing and au contraire, begged him to withdraw his charges. He said, "No, I want to see them arrested, so I could confront them and ask why they did that to me." His Soviet girlfriend insisted that they should go do their job and bring these bigots to justice. They are still waiting.

c. Rich daddies' kids

Some Soviets had this wild idea that foreign students were all from well-to-do families. The logic being that, since we were from poor countries, only rich kids could make it out and to the Soviet Union. The stereotype was sometimes reinforced by some foreign students themselves, who implied as much to taxi drivers or other inquisitors. To feel better about themselves and look good to the average enquirer, some students made up stories about their family standing. Daddy holds a cabinet-level position or Daddy is a rich businessman, were some of the common stories told to strangers. Some Taxi drivers even thought that everybody's father was a secretary in the government of the Republic of Congo.

Another reason why this erroneous notion survived was the fact that many foreigners were better prepared to enter their universities and outperformed the indigenous students. Consequently, they assumed that we graduated from expensive prep schools paid for by our rich parents.

Also at a time when Soviet citizens could only dream about traveling abroad, foreign students took numerous trips to Western Europe, bringing back items they only saw on TV. That further cemented the "rich kid" stereotype and drew a lot of bile in some segments of the society. The Soviets as a whole, resented us for what they imagined we all had, and compared that to their own pitiable standard of living. Many of them attacked foreign students out of jealousy and sometimes fatally, comforted by the blatant racist criminal justice system. Here are some of the stories:

Gorky, Republic of Byelorussia, 1989
AT, a high school colleague:

One day I went to get my clothes from the laundromat, only to be told that somebody broke in and stole my belongings. Feeling that I could not get any further with the lady behind the counter, I went to the militia and filed a complaint. Afterwards, they sent two militia men to the laundromat to assess the damages and enquire about the matter. A few days later, beyond my wildest dreams, I received a phone call to go back and recover my belongings at the laundromat, without a report of their investigation on what exactly happened to my clothes. A week later, coming from a soccer practice, I found two inspectors waiting for me. They said that they were looking for somebody whose name sounded close but not quite like mine. So I told them that I was not the one they were looking for. They then began asking all kinds of bizarre questions, like how much my pair of Levi's jeans cost me back home? Or if I were from a very rich family? I told them that all depends on what they understood by "rich," which had nothing to do with my being in Gorky. Then, they asked about my entertainment center, my furniture and other belongings in my room. Finally one of them added "how do you (foreign students) get all this expensive stuff given that your monthly stipend is only 80 rubles per month?" I got sick of their stupid questions, and told them that I was going to call my embassy in Moscow. They both grabbed me, begging for forgiveness, and would not let me get out of the room to make my call. So I yelled from the top of my lungs, "Aren't we supposed to live well and have nice and expensive stuff?" They left my room and disappeared.

Moscow, Russian federation, September 1992

GD, a Malian student:

In the fall of 1992, we were supposed to change dorms, but since I had graduated that summer, I could not have a room in the new dorm. So I stayed in the old dorm waiting for the return of my girlfriend from the former Czechoslovakia. One night, a Russian acquaintance of mine came to visit and we decided to watch TV. After a while he excused himself, saying that he will be back in few minutes. Twenty minutes later I heard a knock; I opened the door only to be face to face with two armed guys. One had a pistol and the other, a metal rod. They pushed me in my room and locked the door from inside. They asked for money and/or gold. I told them that I do not keep any valuable of that order on me. So, they decided to tie me down and take whatever they pleased in the room. They packed all my main belongings: TV, VCR, clothes, shoes, stereo etc., and vanished. Fifteen minutes after their departure, I managed to free myself to report the assault to the Russian authorities. I am still waiting to hear from them.

Moscow, Russian Federation, 1982

KN:

I had a friend from Cameroon named JMT, he did a lot of business between Europe and the Soviet Union as mentioned above, and made quite a fortune in Moscow. One day he was having a fellow countryman over in his room when a Soviet classmate, Ruslan, showed up accompanied by his buddy. They knocked at the door and courteously got admitted. The two sat on the bed close to the door as opposed to JMT and his friend who were quite a ways inside, near the window. They were all enjoying the notorious Russian tea when JMT decided to put a tape in the tape player located by the window. In a split second, Ruslan got up and knocked JMT down, pulled out his knife and with the help of his friend, started to stab JMT'S guest in his face. They grabbed the stereo and threw it through the window from the ninth floor and got out, leaving the bleeding man on the floor. JMT got up and ran after them trying to stop them and get help. But at the front desk everybody was tight-lipped. Nobody saw the two hooligans running away. JMT recovered his broken stereo and assisted his bleeding guest. As usual, that was the end of the story. No investigation, no arrest, nothing.

Moscow, Russian Federation, 1992

MD, a Malian student:

One night around 12 p.m., two Chechens came in our dorm, knocked at the door of three Malian students and held them up with knives. They told them that from now on, they will have to pay 5000 rubles each for their security. The three students implored them and made clear that they do not have that kind of money. One of them said that he was not from this room, and that he could pay them some money if they let him go to his own room. They implausibly let him go and held the others captives. He came running to my room and explained the state of affairs. We decided to call the militia, so we run downstairs to ask our concierge at the front desk to make the call. She freaked out and said that she will never mess around with the Chechens, fearing retaliation. She said "I am out of here; you guys call the militia, meet them here and do what you have to do. When the dust settles I will come out and take my post." She left and we called the militia next door (there was one post just about everywhere, especially where foreigners lived). They came and we went upstairs together. They broke down the door and arrested the assailants, but never found their weapons. They handcuffed and led them away. One militia man took us aside and said, "Guys, it is your choice to press charges or not. If you do, we will convict and throw them in prison; if you do not, we will ask them few questions and let them go". He pondered a bit and said, "Here is my private advice to you, remember you are only some ill-protected 'niggers' here. If you press charges and have us throw them in prison, their friends will come back to get even, and your next call to the militia will be about dead bodies. So just drop the case". We considered his advice very seriously and did not press any charges for the sake of our own pathetic security.

Moscow, Russian Federation, 1990

ND, a colleague and fellow Malian:

I had three good friends at the Moscow Institute of Dentistry. Unfortunately they were the only blacks among thousands of natives. In 1990 one of their professors made them repeat their exams time and time again. Every time he would say, "Guys you did well but you need to work a bit on your Russian language, ok, so go study and come back again." After so many tries, they finally decided to confront him and find out honestly what the matter was. Irritated, uncomfortable but defiant, he replied, "You foreigners travel abroad all the time, bring back stuff for sale and never give anything to anyone; you should pay me some money in foreign currency before I sign your exams". Baffled and out of options, one of the trio came to see me. I gave him $50 for the professor and wished him good luck. The next day he came back to tell me that he got an "A" this time and that the matter was closed.

Moscow, Russian Federation, 1990

Again, ND:

I went on a business trip to Turkey to buy some merchandise for sell in Moscow. At the border of Romania and Moldavia, the custom officers checked my luggage and saw some denim jackets and pants. They pointed at some of my articles to be given to them, if I wanted to avoid paying duties on them. I told them to figure out the cost and that I was ready to pay. They stepped away for a while and came back with a colossal amount that I could not pay. So, they decided to confiscate my stuff until I paid the duty on them. I decided to play hard ball by pulling the "call to my embassy" card. You can keep everything here until my embassy contacts you to solve the matter, I said. They freaked out and told me that "niggers" never give anything away to anybody. They backed off but turned to two young men and charged them of extorting some of my goods. The two went to drink some vodka and confronted me two villages after the borders. They threatened to beat me if I didn't give them something. I politely told them that I had nothing with me, much less to offer to them. They said that they know what I have got and that I should stop pretending and give them some clothes or they will beat me up. Seeing that they were getting pretty serious, I started to open my bags and pretended to be looking for something for them. I played that game until the next station where the ticket collectors came in with a militia man. I complained to that one and he advised them to let me be. They told him that they do not want to do anything to me, that they were merely following orders from the customs officers. He lectured them to leave the foreigners alone because we were their guests. The two petty delinquents vanished.

Kishinev, Republic of Moldavia, 1992
NE, a friend from Sri Lanka:

In my final year at the university, I was having all kinds of difficulties with my advisor. The Soviet Union had fallen, Bessarabia was talking independence from Moldavia, and the universities were trying hard to get rid of "burdening" foreigners. My advisor was avoiding signing my book of exams without which I could not graduate. After turning around the pot for quite some time, she flatly came out and said: "if you want to graduate on time, you should give me some of the beautiful jewelries you always wear to class." She unambiguously pointed at one silver set of necklace and earrings, my mom gave me as I was leaving Sri Lanka for Moscow. I really agonized over that proposition but did not have an array of choices. My back was against the wall with no way out. I grudgingly gave in, mindful of the potential retributions on my path to graduation after six long years, had I refused.

In school, deans, teachers and students were forced to respect us because of our preparedness, intellect and overall performance compared to the natives. Unfortunately, that respect stopped right at the door of the class, and did not even extend to the corridors or hallways. Our classmates would drastically change their attitude and demeanor as we met outside the classroom. The same student or roommate you feed or help with home works would not even say hello to you in the streets. They frantically avoided being seen with us even within the walls of the university; when we met in the hallway they looked away and avoided eye contact. But when it was

202

impossible to ignore us, they winked or sometimes barely nodded, without giving away any sign of association.

Befriending black foreigners even remotely could result in a sentence of public shame. Even our roommates behaved like that, leading us to wonder why in the world these guys we shared a room with, helped out, or even fed sometimes, would actually look down on us. The phenomenon was so prevalent that it became a normal part of the social landscape.

The case was worse with our female classmates, because they could not even come close to talking to us in class, much less in the halls, not even by mistake. I spent five years with about six girls in my class and we never talked, said hello, or randomly sat close to each other. I never knew their names and they never knew mine, killing the whole idea of cultural exchange. The schools were not segregated, but unfortunately they were not conducive to blending, either.

Somehow, in spite of the stereotypes, the endless examples of racism and bigotry, and the societal boundaries, we learned to live among the Soviets. After all, twice a year, winter and summer, we would be forced to seek each other out for illegal trading.

In December 1992, I visited several embassies in Moscow in order to collect some data about their respective students. I started with my own embassy and managed to get a one-on-one meeting with our grudging consul, Mr. C. I told him that I needed access to some of the records of beaten, missing, maimed or killed students for this book. He told me that I could not see those records, period. My persistence would only have made the matter worse, so I left without obtaining any information. What was he afraid of?

I met the same resistance at all the foreign embassies I visited or called to plan a visit, except Ghana. There, Mr. Babington told me that, overall, a third of his 900 students were physically attacked one way or another. He stressed that the embassy was still waiting for the results of the autopsies of seven students that the Soviet authorities refuse to provide. Five were killed in town (from drowning, during surgery, or at home) and two were found hanging at the airport while in transit. Fifty students went to the West on vacation and never returned. In 1989, there was a false case of HIV/AIDS which was debunked by three clinics.

The numbers would be staggering if every embassy were to release their statistics as Mr. Babington from Ghana courageously attempted to do as I interviewed him. They would be more astounding if more students were to open up and recount their experiences too. Which could call more attention to the subject and save lives.

Knowing the Soviets, not one of them would face up to these facts, especially if you talk to them here in the West, where they try very hard to shed their Soviet skin. To them by choice, and to the average world citizen by ignorance, Soviet bigotry is a non-issue. Blacks are held to such a nonhuman status, and with such condescension that racism or intolerance does not exist to them. Black students existed in the former Soviet Union when the Soviets wanted them to exist. We were beaten and killed at will, ignored when convenient, and acknowledged only when necessary. The bottom line is, we were disposable, and as I write these lines in this 21st century, many more blacks are being battered in the streets, stadiums and dorms without mercy. No police to protect, not enough good Samaritans to speak up.

After six years with the Soviets, I dare say today that President Obama has a pejorative nickname, not only in the streets, but within the Kremlin itself. Where racist Americans (even some lawmakers) have bigoted attitudes toward the President, the Soviets would have hundred nicknames. It is a fact that President Obama is adored overseas; wherever he goes thousands line the streets, even in Eastern Europe (i.e. Prague). By contrast, his trip to Russia was a non-event in the streets of Moscow. The Russians simply could not bring themselves to respect a black man, even if he is the most important leader in the world (and a damned good one, by the way).

Given the fact that the Soviets did not have a colonial past in Africa, and that Alexander Pushkin, their greatest poet and the founder of modern Russian literature was half Ethiopian, you would expect the Soviets to be at least fair. I am still looking for the origins or the reasoning behind their bigotry.

If you think that race relations are a lot better today after a generation, think again. A simple Google search of "racism in Russia" may surprise you.

Mr. Gorbachev and Mr. Putin, would you address this plague and in the public arena? Ignoring it will not make it go away and please do not say that you did not know about it. Which side are you on?

V
Пять

E. GORBACHEV and I

In the summer of 1986, as we were getting ready to leave for the Soviet Union, Gorbachev was making his mark after only sixteen months in power. In Bamako, he was seen as a fascinating being, young and charismatic, as opposed to all his half-dead, foot-dragging predecessors. In my circle of invincible high school graduates, he was referred to as Gorba, or even "the one with the map of the world on his forehead," in reference to his port wine birthmark. He had the world's attention like no other Soviet leader before him. Even apolitical citizens like my sisters were intrigued, and talked about him from time to time. My second sister, a flight attendant at the time, used to say that Gorba was getting a lot of international press time and would stand up to the US, a position that still pays dividends worldwide.

We did not know much about him, and I do not think we cared much about his past and upbringing. Unlike in the West, his private life was not for sale on front pages around the world. All that mattered was his youth, charisma, and his bold ideas of transparency and complete reorganization of the Soviet system. For those who knew a little bit about the Soviet

Union in 1987, these ideals were exactly what the USSR had stood against for the past seventy years. So, a fresh and smiling communist leader, uttering words that would otherwise sound hollow unless spoken in an atmosphere of freedom, accountability, and justice, represented a world-shattering policy shift. Everybody was intrigued and eager to see how he would implement these changes in such a corrupt, brainwashed and, by some criteria's, backward society.

I, for one, could not wait to get to the Union were all these actions would take place, even if we were warned by the Soviet Embassy in Bamako to stay clear of politics. The minute I arrived, I asked to see the Kremlin, the symbol we had all heard and read so much about, and where the political focus of the world would be for the next decade.

When I arrived in Kishinev, the capital city of the Republic of Moldavia (one of the fifteen republics that formed the Soviet Union), I found that all the ancients were very much mesmerized by Gorbachev. That blind love was also expressed in the political science classes among some Soviet colleagues; others were ambivalent. That ambivalence came from a combination of the relatively scarce information available about his past and his accelerated ascent to power. Later, a BBC documentary film called "The Second Russian Revolution" would try to shed some light on his background, path to power and mindset, for those who wondered about this new "chosen one."

Here are some excerpts: [14]

Mikhail Serguievich Gorbachev was born on March 2, 1931 in Privolnoye, a small agrarian village of the Russian Federation. A high-ranking official once told a group of foreigners in Moscow that he knew Gorbachev as a student. What was he like, a journalist asked? The official paused, smiled, and said, "I do not remember." His official biography talked only about the different positions he held within the Communist Party and skipped over some basic information. For example, it was unclear if he had siblings. It was said that he had a brother who

[14]Award-Winning documentary the "Second Russian Revolution", 1989-1991.Produced by Brian Lapping (Brian Lapping Associates Ltd) and the BBC-British Broadcasting Corporation.

worked in agriculture, but nobody seemed to know his name or age. Rumors about a sister were never confirmed.

He was inspired by the revolutionary doctrines of Lenin himself who, according to our teacher, once said, "From small private farms were born Capitalism and Bourgeoisie every day, every hour, endemically and at a grand scale

Growing up in an agrarian village, he tasted early the hard work in the huge government farms and the long hours accompanying his father on combines. Already at the age of 14 he was driving combines after school and during summer breaks. Summers were very hot (90° F) and winters so harsh that Gorbachev covered himself with straw during harvest.

He became a member candidate of the Communist Party and General Secretary of the law school Komsomol (Union of Young Communists). Already, he showed an acute Intellectual curiosity. "I cannot even recall my favorite subject," he told an Italian journalist. "Finally I wanted to major in physics. I liked math, but also history and literature. I can still recall poems learned in school." But he flunked the entry exam for the physics faculty, so he decided to go to law school. The choice was a bit awkward because, during Stalin's rule, law was meaningless and often ridiculed by many Soviets.

Gorbachev took some classes on the history of political ideas and studied the works of Aquinas Hobbes, Locke, and Machiavelli. Then, the personality cult of Stalin as the "all-time greatest genius of all people'" reached its climax, and Gorbachev was not immune to it. "He was also a Stalinist just like everybody else," said Mlynar, a classmate from Czechoslovakia who later became a party official of his country.

But Gorbachev displayed a strict realism regarding Soviet life that had never been seen before. Once, he and Mlynar were watching a Soviet propaganda movie named "Cossacks of the Kuban," showing happy peasants around tables full of food. "It is not like this at all!" shouted Gorbachev, recalling the hunger in his own village.

He demonstrated such a particular interest for Lenin that he even studied what was not in the program for the school year. He was fascinated by Lenin's doctrine, "one step forward and two steps back" (the ability to maneuver and to retreat, if necessary, in the pursuit of a goal). This theory inspired him, and was an integral part of his career.

Regarding students who were portrayed as criminals for disagreeing with Stalin's ideas, Gorbachev told Mlynar that Lenin himself did not arrest Martov (the leader of the Mencheviks, the opposition party), but allowed him to go into exile.

Gorbachev had his own ideas, different from the status quo. He had his doubts regarding some political tactics, but when it came time to praise Stalin lines, he did so with obvious conviction.

At twenty-one, he became a full member of the party and was assigned to Moscow.

Lev Yudovich, who graduated two years after Gorbachev, said that someone pointed Gorbachev out to him as somebody to be afraid of. "For good reasons," declared Neznansky, another classmate. If Gorbachev found out that the parents of any students were not in line politically, he asked for their expulsion from the Komsomol, and even from the university. Michel Tatu, a French Soviet specialist, was convinced that he might have even joined the vicious anti-Semite campaign that started well before Stalin's death in 1953.

In 1955, Gorbachev's graduation year, Kruschev repudiated Stalinism. His reports on Stalin's crimes came out, and the entire country was in shock. Kruschev's secret speech to the 20th congress of the party in 1956 opened the door to some limited freedoms.

Gorbachev went back to Stavropol, where he was nominated as Secretary, then First Secretary of the Komsomol after only a year. He had no choice but to return back home after an unsuccessful run for a position within the Komsomol of Moscow. He became a specialist in agriculture, the main activity of the region, through correspondence courses. In 1967, he added a degree in agriculture to his law degree from Moscow.

He was particularly interested in the press. Contrary to the other leaders, he believed that, for journalists, it was not enough to write politically correct articles, but they had to be interesting also. "Do people read your articles?" he used to ask. He enjoyed the remoteness of Stavropol from Moscow by taking local opinions and pushing through his own ideas. He thought that Moscow interfered too much in local affairs. Once, after being denied government help to finance the building of a circus, he raised the funds from local institutions and organizations and built it anyway.

His rapid exit out of provincial obscurity remains a mystery, since few had heard of him outside Stavropol. Conversely, he attracted and won over many dignitaries, Fyodor Kulakov first of all. Kulakov considered him promising; he succeeded him as First Secretary of Stavropol. Kulakov left for Moscow to become the Secretary of Agriculture of the Soviet Union. Apparently, he made sure his protégé became known among the leaders in Moscow.

The Opatovsky method (a new and faster harvesting technique) became a success in 1977, which boosted his reputation, although it was probably an idea from his predecessor Kulakov.

Christian Schmidt Hauer, a German journalist, observed that Gorbachev also gained from the geographic position of his region. "If Gorbachev was boss, let's say of Murmansk in the far north, he would not have ever become General Secretary," he said. In Stavropol, he was able to welcome vacationing or treatment-bound Moscow bosses on their way to the Mineralnye vody and Kislovodsk spas. As Soviet historian Roy Medvedev said, "They (the bosses from Moscow) found their host very impressive in many ways because a smart and congenial regional secretary was then considered marginal. Instead if Gorbachev yelled, swore and was a drunk, a player with a datcha outside of town where officials were entertained by beautiful waitresses, he would not have been noticed."

An acquaintance, a poet, contacted Gorbachev as a young official of the Komsomol regarding the purchase of a Volga sedan. Gorbachev used his influence to bypass the waiting list and accelerated the delivery of the car. The poet sold the car on the black market and showed up for another favor to get a second one. "Gorbachev, who generally keeps his cool, started to yell and chased the poet out of his office, ordering him to never show his face again," Maximov, a writer who worked for the Stavropol newspaper, recounted.

Two important visitors were also impressed by the reputation of the young party chief. Mikhail Suslov, head of the Soviet Ideology, and Youry Andropov, head of the KGB, were both disgusted by the corruption of the Brejnev era.
When Kulakov died in 1978, he left vacant the post of Secretary of Agriculture.

On the 19th of September 1978, Brejnev's train made a brief stop at the small railroad station of Mineralnye vody. During one of the most remarkable moments of the Soviet history, four men who would serve as General Secretaries of the party met on the same platform: Brejnev, Andropov, Chernenko and Gorbachev. Less than a month later, Gorbachev was pulled from Stavropol to become the 47th member of the national hierarchy, positioning him 20th among all the Soviet leaders.

As Secretary of Agriculture after the death of his mentor, he maintained a mediocre level of 155 million tons of cereals produced in 1981. Bad weather was blamed for the poor performance, as well as Brejnev, who announced a sweeping reorganization of the Department of Agriculture that ended up creating more problems than it solved. It is still remarkable that Gorbachev managed to avoid bearing the blame for the agricultural fiasco, and at the same time climb the party ladder.

After only one year in Moscow, Gorbachev became a member candidate of the politburo. The following year, at age 49, he became a permanent member of the politburo. He was eight years younger than the youngest member of the politburo and twenty-one years younger than the average member of the party.

At this point, Brejnev's health was deteriorating and his eighteen-year-old regime was stagnating. He would die on November 8, 1982

At Brejnev's funeral, the old guard thought it had a legitimate successor in Chernenko. Gorbachev was not yet a member of the supreme elite, but apparently had not long to wait. Andropov took over and immediately attacked corruption, the economy, and civil servants, and Gorbachev became his right-hand man. According to Rijkov (Gorbachev's chairman of the council of ministers), Andropov chose Gorbachev among many other older and more experienced leaders, and he trusted him.

Another man who emerged from the group, Igor Ligachev, helped Gorbachev fight corruption and purge the party from the "dinosaurs." His mission was to crisscross the entire Union in order to uncover and target potential candidates. "Andropov sent me to Ukraine for my first trip. I stayed for a week, visited two counties and headed back. Upon returning, my wife informed me that a parcel has been waiting for me since yesterday. I asked myself what parcel? Who could send me a parcel? Surprisingly it contained all kinds of goodies sent by Cherbitski Vladimir (General Secretary of the Ukrainian party) as souvenirs. I personally called him up and asked how he got to this point? Then I related the incident to Andropov, and we declared an open war to practices like it."

The old guard hated this campaign led by Andropov and Gorbachev, but they still had Chernenko, Brejnev's old crony, as second secretary of the party. Two camps were soon created.

As Andropov saw the first fruits of his tenure in less than a year, his regime was nose-diving. Bedridden because of health issues, he was preparing his speech for the next party plenum from his hospital bed. Each of his advisors had a day and time slot for visitations. Arcady Volski came on Saturdays from 10 a.m. to 3 p.m. He had been working with Andropov for two weeks on his upcoming surprise speech to the plenum of the central committee. One Saturday, as he was returning home around 4:00 p.m. he received an urgent call from Andropov asking him to immediately return to the hospital. Andropov gave him the secret speech with some additional handwriting at the end. In the speech, he expressed his inability to preside over the meetings of the Communist Party in the near future, and asked members of the Politburo to consider the question of his replacement by Gorbachev.

The message was clear and straightforward, and his speech was printed and handed out to all the members of the central committee. To Volski's surprise, the handwritten part regarding Andropov's replacement by Gorbachev was missing. When he asked why, the old guard told him that he talked too much and asked too many questions. "Mind your own business," he was told. "We swallowed our tongues," he recalls.

The trio, Chernenko (Second General Secretary), Oustimenko (Secretary of Defense) and Tixonov (President of the Council of Ministers), simply took out the relevant paragraph.

Unfortunately for Gorbachev and his allies, Andropov died sooner than expected, "muddying the waters" that were just starting to clear up for the "kids" of the 20th Congress. Tension was rising, the fate of the Union and the world, for that matter, was being decided behind the red walls of the Kremlin.

The conversation, as noted by Arkadi Volski, went like this: They were all standing in the orexovaia Komnata (Apple room) with doors wide open, and members of the Politburo were exiting followed by members of the council of ministers. All of a sudden, Oustimenko (the Secretary of Defense) and Tixonov (the President of the Council of Ministers) came out. Oustimenko laid his hand on Tixonov's shoulder and said, "No worries, Kolia. Kostia (short for Konstantin Chernenko) announced to all that during vacancies due to illness or vacations, it was clear that Gorbachev would head the plenum of the politburo." Gorbachev's nomination as Second Secretary would make him the informal successor to Chernenko.

The old guard was worried about what was happening behind their backs; in fact, so worried that Tixonov sharply replied, "Why Gorbachev? He already is regional secretary and takes care of Agriculture, why should he also be second secretary of the party?" Other politburo members expressed their support for Gorbachev and replied, why not? Tixonov, in a firm voice, said, "Then I am categorically against the proposal, because it would lead to too many plots and disorder for the country."

To everyone's surprise, Chernenko intervened decisively and replied, "You think like this and I think like that." To overcome the impasse, Secretary of State Gromyko chimed

213

in and said, "Comrades, both suggestions are worthy. Let Gorbachev head the sessions of the central committee, since he is used to doing it, and we will see."

Even as second in command, Gorbachev's limited power was not enough to pull the country's economy out of the chaos that was evident only to him. Nothing else seemed to be changing; Brejnev's cronies were still pulling the strings. On TV, they were still touting the successes of the economy: 500 Zil cars, 190,000 meters of fabric, 180 tons of legumes, etc. But only a few reformers knew the real economic situation and kept Chernenko updated. Rijkov saw that there was no interest, no support from Chernenko. "I felt like an intruder," he says.

It was obvious to the average Soviet that Chernenko's days were numbered. There would be a ferocious fight for his succession, but an open campaign from either side was suicidal. With Rijkov's help, Gorbachev set out to weaken his adversaries within the politburo.

One of their first targets was Viktor Grishin (a Moscow boss), a scion of the old guard that Brejnev had nominated seventeen years earlier as first secretary of the urban committee of Moscow. Shady dealings and other underground machinations in the city were rumored, and the old guard wanted to take care of this embarrassing story. When asked about the situation, Grishin admitted that some corruption and theft cases happened, and unfortunately continued to happen. The press, muzzled and controlled as in any Communist country, tried to address the issue. The popular paper Izvestia, in print since 1917, tried to shed some light, but the article was censured. Ivan Laptiev, its editor, decided to seek advice from the second general secretary of the communist party: M. C. Gorbachev.

One day, in a private meeting with Gorbachev Laptiev decided to reopen the question of whether to publish the article or not. Gorbachev jumped at the opportunity and said, "Publish, but under your responsibility." It was the kind of gift politicians dream of: an opponent's dirty laundry. And his role in the publication of the material would not be known.

Izvestia published the article without delay. Reactions

214

poured in to the paper. Call after call came in from everywhere - from secretaries of the central committee to Grishin himself - all asking the same question: Who gave you the authorization to publish this article? But Laptev kept his word and said that he had published it on his own authority as editor-in-chief.

Gorbachev the strategist started a series of trips within the Union, the satellite countries of Eastern Europe, and in the West. The international community was getting used to seeing him, especially since he was seducing more than one leader. As Z.K.Brzezinski said, "They were all zombies, Khrushchev pounding the podium with his shoes, and other leaders looking like the living dead. And there was Gorbachev dressed by the Brooks Brothers." [15]

Domestically, Gorbachev's adversaries (with Grishin in front of the pack) were cozying up to Chernenko, hoping to follow in his footsteps to power. Chernenko's days were numbered because of the terrible pulmonary illness he suffered. His respiratory tract was so damaged that you could barely hear him when he spoke or read his speeches. For the third time in two years, it was becoming impossible to hide the worsening health of a Soviet leader.

Chernenko informed his comrades that he was checking into the hospital, and asked them to reduce his duties in the politburo and the central committee. He wished everybody good luck and said he was going to fight not for life, but death. The old guard did not like the sound of that. Their future did not look bright as Chernenko entered the hospital.

Once again, Grishin and his clan tried to shape the course of events regarding the succession. Who will become General Secretary this time? It seemed that the dying Chernenko was leaning toward Grishin according to the images broadcasted over and over again on the central channel. Grishin could be seen offering flowers to the dying leader at the hospital. Gorbachev's team could not believe what they were seeing, and tried to guess who was behind it all. Two days later, Arbatov Georgui, who suspected the

15 Z.K.Brzezinski, United States National Security Advisor to president Jimmy Carter from 1977 to 1981

central committee, asked Gorbachev if he had seen the terrifying images on TV. "Which images are you talking about? I have no idea," he replied. In fact, it was organized under special orders from Grishin, who was trying to propel himself to the coveted position.

On March 10, 1985, at 7:20 p.m. Chernenko died. Gorbachev, who had squandered the previous opportunity, found himself in a better position this time. As second general secretary, it was up to him to set the date for the crucial meeting to nominate Chernenko's successor.

At 9:30 p.m., only two hours after Chernenko's death, Gorbachev summoned the members of the politburo to the orexovaia komnata of the Kremlin. On such short notice, only eight of the ten members could make it on time. Gorbachev then made a daring and audacious move by proposing that Grishin, his most fervent adversary for the post, head the funeral. Grishin refused, and the task naturally fell to Gorbachev as second secretary. Grishin was being courteous, but in reality they were both playing a dangerous game. The president of the funeral commission always becomes secretary general.

The two empty chairs at this meeting would forever influence the course of events. They belonged to Kouniaev and Cherbitski, two old power-hungry anti-reformists. Cherbitski (first party secretary of the Communist Party of Ukraine) was in the USA, specifically in San Francisco, when Chernenko died. He and his delegation were immediately summoned to the Soviet Consulate, and were told that Dobrynin had called to announce the news. Unfortunately for Cherbitski, Moscow and San Francisco are eleven hours apart, making it impossible for him to attend the decisive meeting of the politburo.

Without those two conservatives, Gorbachev mustered the majority of the votes in the politburo to lead the funeral commission. But it was not a done deal yet; that same night, team Gorbachev, led by Ligachev, beat all records by summoning all 300 secretaries of the central committee for the following day, therefore taking charge. At 4 a.m., Gorbachev, Ligachev, and Chebrikov went out into the street, and one of them asked, "What will tomorrow bring?" Gorbachev would later tell some students that this was the night he told his insiders that, given the current state of affairs, his candidacy was inevitable. The country could not go on this way.

The sun was still rising on the capital as the delegates arrived, but victory was not clear yet. Even if Cherbitski would not make it for the meeting of the politburo, he could still make it to the plenum of the central committee and influence the course of events. First, his flight was delayed, then postponed more than once. A pilot problem seemed to be the cause, but some in Moscow believed that all that was organized to make sure Cherbitski and his delegation got home only after the plenum. The politburo met without Cherbitski and maintained the Gorbachev candidacy proposed by the Central Committee. Aside from some criticism here and there, the majority of the delegates upheld Gorbachev's candidacy.

Finally, Gorbachev was elected Secretary General of the Communist Party of the Soviet Union. The news made it to New York, where Cherbitski and his delegation were finally boarding their plane for Moscow. They toasted the occasion. Once elected, Gorbachev promised members of the central committee and the politburo to follow the path of his predecessors. Will he?

This fascinating story of ascension looked like the prelude to a politically tumultuous reign. Gorbachev, by promoting seismic changes in the society, boldly engaged his fellow Soviets and the rest of the world. In the same breath he declared war on just about anything previously considered "Soviet." Soon there would be no dearth of enemies even in this tightly-controlled empire.

By the time we reached Kishinev, it had already been a year and a half since Gorbachev took power. With only a month as General Secretary, he launched his bold program of reconstruction, or perestroika. Already, a lot of old things were under review and new ideas proposed or passed into law. Economically, politically, and socially, Gorbachev attacked the status quo as I, along with tens of thousands of other foreign students and diplomats across the Union, settled to witness history.

Already by late fall of 1986, Gorbachev was preparing

his October meeting with President Reagan in Iceland that ultimately did not break new ground. The two sides blamed each other for the failure, with Reagan's SDI (Strategic Defense Initiative) being the stumbling block. They pledged to meet again with bolder initiatives the following year.

Earlier that year though, Gorbachev led the 27th Congress of the Communist Party (his first as Secretary General), dealt with the explosion at the Chernobyl power plant, and pushed through a number of new economic initiatives. In November, he took a successful trip to India; in December, he freed Nobel Peace Prize winner Andrei Sakharov from his six-year exile in Gorky. He had no time to waste, it seems.

We could not help but notice some positive changes on the ground even that far from the center of power - Moscow.

In 1987, perestroika (reconstruction) became the word of the decade on just about every lip, domestic or foreign, generating a tremendous amount of buzz. Everything that Gorbachev intended the Soviet Union to be, was packed into that simple word. As a slogan, perestroika was a hit; it was so popular that it also entered our everyday jargon. Fellow Malians would use the term to describe anything new, uncommon, or defiant. Even in a tease, perestroika would be blamed for causing someone to disrespect his elders (a huge deal in Malian society), or to not show up at an appointment, or even for just rearranging one's room. Abroad, there was a lot of "wait and see" in many political capitals, but there was a sea of enthusiasm and hope in the streets.

Domestically, the Soviet society itself was about to enter the longest transition period since the revolution in 1917. The political, social and economic cataclysms triggered by the birthing process of perestroika, were being felt around the country. On the ground in Kishinev, away from the cameras, we witnessed some tectonic shifts right before our eyes as Gorbachev pushed his reforms through.

At the time, Socialism had been unequivocally following its long course towards communism, and it seemed that no soul or outside power could derail it. Just a year earlier, Gorbachev had pledged to continue in the footsteps of his predecessors, but obviously, he did not intend to do so and made a lot of enemies with his radical changes. He was even accused of abandoning the communist system and being a C.I.A plant. (The US Central Intelligence Agency)

The economy was struggling along the good old Soviet way, as it had been for the last 70 years. Products seemed to be plentiful and extremely cheap in all government stores (the only ones around, by the way). A thirty-minute line to get basic produce was common and considered normal. After the daily delivery to the local store, if you did not get what you needed, you would come a little earlier the next day and be just fine.

Government five-year planning was the sole economic theory, not supply and demand, hence some major miscalculations. It felt like the government always erred on the short side when it came to perishable products, which led to periodic shortages. "We have everything," our teachers always reminded us, and never missed an opportunity to do so. That was certainly true if you left out the headache it took to buy anything and the mediocre quality of "made in U.S.S.R." at the time.

Behind the scenes, the Union was headed toward a cliff due to its gargantuan military budget and what was finally recognized as the unsustainable, artificial Soviet economic system. By 1987, the defense burden, estimated at 15% of the gross domestic product, was about two to three times that of the U.K and the U.S.[16] This, while they were telling us in class that their weapons were being built by volunteers instead of expensive defense contractors, like in the U.S.

The clock was ticking for Gorbachev as he tried to steer resources away from weaponry and back into this unsound economy before it collapsed. On the road around the country, he bluntly warned time and time again about dire consequences if new and sweeping measures were not taken. The Soviet economy was lagging behind the West's year after

---

16 Encyclopedia Britannica. 1988 Book of the year, events of 1987.P-476.Special Report: USSR. Perestroika and Glasnost- A Progress Report by Martin McCauley-Senior Lecturer in Soviet and East European Studies, University of London

year and was comparable to that of some developing countries. His proposed overhaul of the economy was coupled with legislation designed, in the long run, to make the USSR competitive.

Simply making a nice pair of shoes, underwear, or even socks was too much to ask for this economy living in the past. A pair of Adidas sneakers, a Puma sweatshirt, or a simple jacket from Wal-Mart turned heads in the street and unfortunately also invited burglars. In the dorm, our toothpaste, underwear, soap bars, watches. etc., were to be treasured or never to be found again once misplaced or left behind in the bathroom.

We were puzzled by the discrepancy between the light and heavy industries that found themselves at opposite ends of the priority list. Here was a proud nation that was first in space, and had destroyed Hitler's war machine, but could not make bubble gums or even grocery bags.

To steer this backward economy away from its approaching doomsday, Gorbachev began by tackling bureaucracy, waste, fraud, corruption, lethargy, and alcoholism. He said that the production and retail costs were completely disproportionate, and that something needed to be done about them too. The government could not keep on subsidizing just about everything by printing money or controlling the price. During one of his numerous speeches, he even talked about kids playing soccer with loaves of bread because they were so cheap.

On a daily basis, workers robbed their government without hesitation or retribution, because everybody did it. Those working at a TV plant would take home the latest brand before it even hit the shelves. And those working on government farms took home meat and milk with no questions asked. The same phenomenon plagued the bike, watch, bread, shoes and clothing factories. Working in those plants also gave a certain power to workers, who never hesitated to use and abuse them. They would sell items they had access to at work to the highest bidder, with interest. That is also how foreign diplomats and students got all the items they needed to use in the country, or for sale abroad. We would order generators, air

220

conditioners, speakers, or even huge, beautiful carpets from the south from acquaintances who worked in the plants, or who knew someone who did. Through their connections in town or in their villages, Soviet go-getters would fill our orders by any means to make some rubles. Sometimes even in the stores, the clerk would refuse to sell a needed item until you paid him or her first.

To tackle this broken system, the law regarding private ownership was enacted on May 1, 1987. People could own and run businesses for the first time in their lives. On the ground in Kishinev, we witnessed it take hold, first with private cabs just like today's Uber taxis. People were allowed to register their private cars and carry passengers around town for a nice fee they could keep after taxes. But it was meant to be a part-time job on top of the full-time, public job these owners had, and they were not allowed to hire any employee. All of a sudden, government cabs were experiencing competition, and we found ourselves less discriminated against while trying to get home. People could also have their own bakeries, grocery stores, repair shops, etc.

The capitalist notion of agricultural cooperatives, that Lenin himself had outlawed, was reappearing and could potentially lead to privately-owned farms. "Private property" was subtly entering the Soviet jargon without anybody being sent away for life, as "capitalist" or "rich bourgeois." These baby steps prompted people to think for themselves instead of relying on the Communist Party. Potentially, these new forms of private enterprise would displace the government's old dinosaurs and gradually satisfy the huge domestic demand in goods and services. These privately-owned businesses that were seen as the key factors for revitalizing the economy were also permitted to import and export.

To encourage workers, the notion of self-financing was peddled by the party in order to give factories greater financial freedom and be liable for their own management. The idea was that this would eventually free the bosses to fire recalcitrant workers and motivate others with bonuses.

Timidly, but surely, people started to open shops and work for themselves. Initially, prices were almost double those of the government, even if the quality was comparable. When affordability became an issue, many citizens found themselves in the same place again; if they could not buy something in the past because of the rationing; now they still could not buy it because of the price. The businessmen were doing better and could afford the new products on the market. The quality of life was not getting better for average earners like teachers, factory workers, bus drivers, and specially retirees living on a fixed income. Perestroika did not have much to show for itself, and the government kept talking about all the good measures they were putting in place, to borrow a little time.

For foreign students and diplomats, life was still good economically because we could still bribe clerks in order to buy products in short supply. There was nothing that we could not put our hands on if we wanted to. Because of the trafficking, our buying power could not be matched. That unfair economic privilege bred some resentment that many Soviets sometimes displayed right in our faces. On the other hand, the damage inflicted upon the work force and the populace by alcoholism was reaching its breaking point.

In May 1985, only two months into the new regime, harsh anti-alcohol laws were passed as an attempt to get a handle of this "cancer." Gorbachev even ordered Soviet embassies around the world to hold alcohol-free parties and dinners. No one could ignore the damage it was doing to the economy in lost hours, and also to families. Many Soviets would go to work drunk, if they made it there at all; others would skip work all together. Either way, the loss was incalculable. Rumors had it that during one of his factory visits, Gorbachev asked workers about a common saying regarding alcohol and work. He asked if it was true that one could not work after two drinks, and the crowd replied "not true, it is possible to have that many and still work". How about three glasses? Asked Gorbachev, "We are all here and working just fine", replied the crowd.

Ironically, Moldavia, because of its wine production, found itself in the forefront of Gorbachev's battle against this scourge. One of the comprehensive measures was to uproot thousands of acres of grape vines to reduce the supply.

Moldavia was to lose about 10,000 acres, a great setback for its wine industry. Across the nation, the price of all drinks doubled, and clerks were supposed to ration the per capita sale of alcohol even further. Fewer and fewer bottles were being distributed to countless government liquor stores that adorned every neighborhood.

The Soviet society as a whole, at that point, did not seem to appreciate why Gorbachev was taking such draconian measures against "innocent drinkers." In the street, some random drunk would "flip the bird" to the measures and to Gorbachev, swearing that he would never be able to control their drinking. Some of my colleagues were also getting nervous that these measures would seriously curtail their supply, sending them into unfamiliar territories far away from our dorms in search of alcohol. We could all feel the pinch coming because drinking was a way of life in the Soviet Union, and talk about rationing it, sent people scrambling. In the dorms, foreign as well as native students were grumbling while preparing for the coming drought. The paranoia led to the proliferation of homemade and dangerous alcohol drinks called Samagon (self-brewed).

Politically, Gorbachev started by enforcing many laws and rights already on the books that were considered taboo to even discuss, much less implement. Freedom of speech and press started to mean something to the average Soviet, who could now criticize the government without being sent to Siberia and never to be seen again. The government press timidly began to show some teeth by chipping away at censorship and actually naming names, even from the politburo, in their criticisms.

For starters, the father of the nation, Stalin himself, became the target of a scrutiny unseen in Soviet history as files were being declassified. Article upon article in newspapers around the country examined the many shortcomings of the leader of the people. Historians were licking their chops over the treasure troves being declassified regarding Stalin in particular, and the nation as a whole: Massacres of Polish POWs in Katyn in 1940; uprooting and deportation of entire villages of political opponents to labor camps; purge of the

Communist Party leaders etc. Previously censured negative news and statistical data about the Soviet Union saw the light of day, as well as numerous books and films critical of the system. TV programs and movies also started to have their dose of glasnost by showing more international news and programming, even if those criticized the Soviet Union and its way of life.

That change was a bittersweet adjustment, depending on who you were in the Union at the time. The West was now being shown in a much better light, particularly in terms of the introduction of rewards for individual accomplishments, into the Soviet psyche. If the population was previously encouraged to watch striking workers in Paris, for example, (although they were really checking out the cars, shops, buildings in the background, and strikers' clothing), this time, citizens came away with an inkling of what was achievable with some Western attitudes and policies.

Africa, Latin America, and parts of Asia, however, were being cast in the worst possible light. Famine, diseases, wars, and poverty were the only themes covered when it came to news related to those regions. No surprise there, considering the fact that the Soviets were only perpetuating what some mainstream media in the West is still doing today: painting a dire picture of anything that does not fit their narrative; a subtle agenda fueled by racism and condescension.

I am not saying that unbiased reports do not exist, but the ratio of negative-to-positive news about developing, non-white countries is characteristically one-sided. When we host the Olympic Games or a major tournament here in the US, we never see a news report about the crime rate, the ghettos, overcrowded jails, or Catholic priests raping young boys in the context of the event being hosted. It all would be about the event in question, period. When Canada hosted the winter Olympics, there was no special report on drug addiction, kids killing their parents, or the condition of the native peoples of the land. When Germany hosts major sporting events, no channel airs a special edition on Nazism, Neo-Nazism, or racism directed against South Asians in the context of the game. When it is France, there is no TV report on the ghettos around

Paris, police brutality against immigrants, or the deeply rooted and subtle racism that still plagues the French society at its core.

However, when South Africa hosted the World Cup in 2010, there was no shortage of news reports on crime, dangerous suburbs, HIV rates, or the worsening drug problem, all in the context of the game. Why? ABC sent reporters all over the country to dig up the dirt and splash it all over its morning news. Robin Roberts could not miss the opportunity to once again link Africa to animals by doing a special edition on her visits to parks or zoos. Another reporter invested all his time and energy on young black teens in jails talking about redemption, etc.

As I write this, Brazil is in line for hosting the FIFA World Cup and the Olympics Games in 2014 and 2016. By now, we have all heard about the crime rate in the slums called favelas. Since Qatar won its bid for 2022, allegations have flared up about bribes, human right abuses, and poor working conditions for the migrant workers who are building the infrastructure. Some trade union activists are even pushing FIFA to remove the tournament from Qatar if working conditions do not improve. Again I am not suggesting that these things do not happen or are not true.

When was the last time though, a month-long sport tournament was used to pressure a Western country to improve its labor laws? I strongly doubt that they are perfect though. In this regard the Soviet media was just following in the footsteps of its counterparts in the West.

Since political truths were coming out, thanks to glasnost, all the major focal points and events of the history of the Soviet Union were now under a huge cloud of doubt. For example, we learned that not all the decisions reached by the Communist Party were passed by unanimous votes, but sometimes by a simple majority after heated debate with dissenting politicians. We also learned that many of the dates given for the peaceful adhesion of several republics into the Soviet Union were in fact the dates when they were simply annexed by the Russians or the Soviet army.

Because of glasnost under Gorbachev, the truth about the creation of the U.S.S.R. became an integral part of the demise of the Union itself. In the past, only the elderly knew the truth about what had really happened. Now, more and more people discovered that their respective countries had been taken by force by the Red Army, which led to more and more demands for independence. The genie was out of the bottle, and Gorbachev, at that point was struggling to get it back.

In class, every assumption in our history books was challenged so significantly, that new books that did not peddle the party line were printed. Our Soviet classmates began challenging teachers more aggressively, and foreign students ramped up their already confrontational attitudes. Democracy was taking painful baby steps in a totalitarian society right in front of our eyes. There were some powerful enemies, a lot of confused citizens, and a majority of supporters. The old guard and its like-minded followers, though in the minority at this point, were dragging their feet to slow down the burgeoning reforms. Many were afraid of the unknowns of democracy pushed by Gorbachev, and preferred to remain in their comfortable positions while controlling the lives of the average Soviet. They pushed back hard, but without success, on new election proposals that included secret ballots or multiple candidates for different posts.

Glasnost (transparency or openness) was the next unwelcome initiative that frightened many secretive Communist Party leaders, who just wanted to stay in the shadow and continue with their abuse of power. Every one of them was a kingmaker in his area, a position they were not ready to give up. They had never known what it was like to stand in line for hours just for milk, butter or shoes. They always had their goodies delivered right to their houses or offices, and received kickbacks for helping people acquire cars and apartments without standing in line for years. Meanwhile, next door in East Germany newlywed couples got the keys to their apartment as they exchanged vows.

In Moscow, old party bosses were doing their best to undermine perestroika and glasnost, prompting Gorbachev to change personnel and bring in some new blood he could trust.

When the young German Mathias Rust landed in Red Square in May 1987, he consequently helped Gorbachev affirm himself as commander-in-chief. Alexander Koldunov, in charge of the Air Defense of the Union, was let go, and Defense Secretary Marshal Sokolov's resignation was also accepted.

The reaction of many Soviets to Raissa Gorbachev's appearances alongside her husband on submarines, gave us a slight inkling of what the military thought of the couple. In this macho society, I heard a great many unflattering comments about Raissa being the first woman to "wander" onto a military ship. They would fume every time she appeared well dressed in fur next to her husband, whether on a warship or a plane going abroad. But, historically, Lenin himself said that you cannot be in politics without your spouse by your side.

Gorbachev's proposal of the total denuclearization of Europe rubbed top military brass the wrong way. They were not fans of perestroika to begin with, and saw it as a retreat or concession to the U.S. However, after a successful trip to Czechoslovakia in April, and a snubbing in Romania by the dictator Ceausescu in May, Gorbachev ended his trips by signing the Intermediate-Range Nuclear Forces Treaty, or INF, with the U.S.

Socially, many Soviets and classmates did not know what to do about this new era that I call the longest transition period in Soviet history. Not only were the old habits hard to break, but the new order was unknown and very foreign to the average Soviet. There was no preparation or "manual" for it, hence the uneasiness. They went from not owning anything, to being able to own whatever they wanted; from leaving everything to the party and the government, to becoming masters of their own destiny; from not daring to criticize the government, to being able to openly criticize anybody and anything; from spying on their neighbors and relatives, to becoming anonymous free citizens minding only their own business; from being stuck physically and mentally in the Soviet Union, to being able to travel around the world and learn; from government-imposed atheism, to religious freedom; from one government-run party and union, to freedom to associate; from suffering from the law, to being saved by the law; from demonizing the West, to envying and looking up to it. It was like telling them to forget and bury the previous 70 years of the life of the country since its founding by Lenin in 1917. All these changes felt abrupt, too much to handle, and alien to the formerly-subjugated indigenous population.

Ironically, with the exception of the laws pertaining to private property, all of the aforementioned changes in the law brought to bear by perestroika and glasnost, were already imbedded in the laws of the land and guaranteed by the constitution of the Soviet Union. Gorbachev just had the political courage to bring them to light and enforce them.

Let's address some of the laws that might shock the average world citizen, who had heard about the Union of Soviet and Socialist Republics: the USSR.

- Statute 49 stipulates: Every citizen has the right to propose to government entities and organizations, better solutions and to critique their shortcomings. The concerned authorities must look at the proposals, answer them in a timely fashion and take necessary measures. Persecution for critics is unlawful and those doing so will be called upon. [17]

Before perestroika, people were thrown in jail or gulags in Siberia for criticizing the state, or singled out as an "enemy of the people."

- Statute 50 takes it further: In the interest of the people and in order to strengthen and develop the socialist system, the citizens of the Soviet Union are guaranteed: freedom of speech, print, association, protest, rallies and demonstrations. These political freedoms should be facilitated through workers and their organizations, with access to public buildings and spaces, streets and widespread information, press, TV and radio. [18]

---

[17] *Constitution (Main Law) of the USSR (adopted at the Seventh Extraordinary Session of the Supreme Soviet's ninth convocation on October 7, 1977). Moscow Law books 1986. P-18*

Here I am reminded that each and every student wrote down all the questions, one by one, to our multiple tests dictated by the teacher or the leader of the class. Why? Because there were no copy machines, much less computers, to print out the questions and distribute them to all students. Why? Because printers and copiers were still forbidden in order to slow down or eliminate the spread of anti-government leaflets, underground papers, journals, etc. Lessons were learned the way Lenin himself communicated with his followers before the revolution, while in exile in Europe (Germany, Finland, England) or in jail. He printed a lot of articles in his newspaper called Iskra, or Star, as he organized his associates for the revolution in 1917.They even wrote in invisible ink on papers hidden in women's undergarments, to be later soaked and read by his co-conspirators. Seventy years later, the Soviet government was still doing everything in its power to suppress any means of mass communication that domestic or foreign oppositions might utilize to widely spread their message. A suppression in complete violation of Statute 50 of the revised constitution voted only on October 7, 1977.

- Statute 51: In accordance with the goals of Communism, citizens of the Soviet Union have the right to unite in social organizations, encouraging the growth of political participation and self-reliance, according to their different interests. Social organizations are guaranteed all necessary conditions in order to successfully pursue their goals.[19]

In the old Soviet Union, that would be true as long as the organizations exclusively accepted and promoted government lines. Here too, one could be deported to Siberia for organizing and creating opposition parties or movements.

---

[18] *Constitution (Main Law) of the USSR (adopted at the Seventh Extraordinary Session of the Supreme Soviet's ninth convocation on October 7, 1977). Moscow Law books 1986. P-18*

[19] *Constitution (Main Law) of the USSR (adopted at the Seventh Extraordinary Session of the Supreme Soviet's ninth convocation on October 7, 1977). Moscow Law books 1986. P-18*

Statute 52 addressed the thorny question of religion that everybody avoided.

- Statute 52 stipulates: Citizens of the Soviet Union are guaranteed the freedom of conscience, meaning the right to practice any religion or none, be member of religious cults or propagate Atheism. Inciting enmity and hate because of religion is prohibited. Church in USSR is separate from state and schools from church. [20]

Statute 52 could not be clearer about freedom of worship and the separation of church and state. You would think you were reading the US or Malian Constitution.

Besides this constitutional guarantee of freedom of religion, we were taught that one could proselytize only inside mosques, churches and synagogues, but could promote atheism everywhere else but in mosques, churches and synagogues.

The dictates of the party, individual perceptions, societal allegations, and urban myths all trumped the fundamental laws of the land. Everybody cowered under the iron fist of the state, and no one even dreamt of challenging the authorities about these straightforward rights. The persecution of religious leaders or individual worshippers drove religion out of sight and mind. Ironically, the only violations of institutionalized atheism were the relentless use of the very popular expressions, "Bojé Moï - Oh my God" and "Ne Daï Bog - Heavens forbid". All Soviets used them without making the connection.

- Statute 54 dealt with privacy in these terms: Citizens of the Soviet Union are guaranteed the integrity of their beings. No one can be subjected to an arrest, except on the basis of a court order or the approval of a public prosecutor. [21]

---

[20] Constitution (Main Law) of the USSR (adopted at the Seventh Extraordinary Session of the Supreme Soviet's ninth convocation on October 7, 1977). Moscow Law books 1986. P-19
[21] Constitution (Main Law) of the USSR (adopted at the Seventh Extraordinary Session of the Supreme Soviet's ninth convocation on October 7, 1977). Moscow Law books 1986. P-19

- Statute 55: Citizens of the Soviet Union are guaranteed the integrity of their property. Nobody has the right to enter a home without a warrant and against the will of the occupants.[22]

In reality, many people got arrested and sent to gulags or forced labor in many frozen camps of the North East. Intellectuals, critics of the regime and many innocent people disappeared without charge. The militia and all other authorities from party members to the commandant of a dorm, could order any door opened upon simple request. Occupants trembled in their boots just at the sight of any authority figure at their door-step. Nobody dared challenge the regime even at the lowest level for fear of being deported.

- Statute 56: Citizens' private lives, personal notes, telephone conversations and telegrams are protected by the law.[23]

Compared to reality, this statute was laughable at best. The entire socialist system in the Eastern bloc stood on unlawful eavesdropping on citizens by citizens and their governments. A trip to the post office showed that exactly the opposite of this statute was the de facto law of the land.

- Statute 57: Respect of individuals, protection of rights and freedoms of citizens are the duty of all federal authorities, social organizations and officials. Soviet citizens are protected by the court from assaults on their honor and dignity, life and wellbeing, on personal freedom and property. [24]

---

[22] *Constitution (Main Law) of the USSR (adopted at the Seventh Extraordinary Session of the Supreme Soviet's ninth convocation on October 7, 1977). Moscow Law books 1986. P-19*
[23] *Constitution (Main Law) of the USSR (adopted at the Seventh Extraordinary Session of the Supreme Soviet's ninth convocation on October 7, 1977). Moscow Law books 1986. P-19*
[24] *Constitution (Main Law) of the USSR (adopted at the Seventh Extraordinary Session of the Supreme Soviet's ninth convocation on October 7, 1977). Moscow Law books 1986. P-19*

This statute was like a dream perched out there, a pie in the sky, but Gorbachev at least gave it a chance to be dusted off and revisited by lawyers.

Surprisingly enough, even the environment was mentioned in the very first statutes of the constitution.

- Statute 12, in its third paragraph states: Kolkhoz (big communal farms) and all other producers have a duty to effectively use the land, treat her with care and raise her fertility.[25]
- Statute 18: In the interest of present and future generations in the USSR, all necessary measures should be taken to: Protect in a scientific and rational way, the land and its mineral and water resources, fauna and flora, to preserve clean air and water, ensure the production of natural resources and improve the environment.[26]

Greenpeace, Departments of Natural Resources and Environmental Protection Agencies around the world would have been proud of the tenets of this statute, if it only made sense to its "enforcers" in the first place. Unfortunately, the monoculture in the south and the abuse of fertilizers and herbicides in the West of the country, led to unprecedented levels of pollution.

As students, we saw some of the best soils in the world in Moldavia, Ukraine, etc., turned into some of the least-productive ones due to the careless use of chemicals and poor stewardship. In many republics in the south, the monoculture of cotton under irrigation "killed" thousands of acres that once sustained millions of people. Once again, the narrative did not match reality. Not even close.

---

[25] *Constitution (Main Law) of the USSR (adopted at the Seventh Extraordinary Session of the Supreme Soviet's ninth convocation on October 7, 1977). Moscow Law books 1986. P-8*
[26] *Constitution (Main Law) of the USSR (adopted at the Seventh Extraordinary Session of the Supreme Soviet's ninth convocation on October 7, 1977). Moscow Law books 1986. P-10*

These rights and freedoms could not be clearer, but the successive regimes trampled them to sustain their grip on power and subjugate an ever-more terrified population. From the start, Gorbachev decided to enforce the laws as an inherent part of democracy and a civil society, crucial in his view, to perestroika and glasnost. The trouble laid in that stubborn lag between the passage of laws in the Douma, and subsequent implementation where the average citizen could see and feel the changes. Not to mention the mental resistance from those who would not and could not accept change.

Our first year, which was the second one for perestroika and glasnost, was hectically dizzying for everybody in the Union. Foreign students and diplomats alike were pulled in every direction as we tried to follow the moving targets of consequential reforms without tangible progress.

First and foremost, foreign students wanted to see the end of the restrictions in the dorms, and on travels within the country. Since our entire existence in the Union revolved around dorm life and traveling, a major change in those areas would have been remarkable. We wanted to be able to simply receive and socialize with our guests without registration at the front desk. We also wanted to be able to travel freely around the country beyond 15 miles, without having to apply for an internal visa, a process that took the fun out of any trip.

Since we knew what the final product should look like, any delay in the delivery felt like inertia. We were impatient to see meaningful changes in our day-to-day lives, but at the same time supportive of the new leader we all adored, and who we thought knew what he was doing. By contrast, the indigenous population was split among those who doubted yet pessimistically followed the General Secretary as their only hope, and those who would not have any part of those "sell-your-soul-to-the-West" changes that they thought weakened the Union.

By 1988, results were mixed, and in some areas the situation seemed even worse. This was the weaning year, one of the most difficult of this long transition period. The country was at a point of no return in terms of its old ways, having let go of them in most areas, but not quite yet in full perestroika and glasnost modes. I dubbed it the "anything goes" year, as the country seemed to be navigating blindfolded, without a blueprint on how to get there. The Soviet 'slaves' were being 'freed' overnight, and they did not know what to do with themselves and their new freedoms. All along, the only master they had known was the Communist Party, and the only thing they knew was how best to serve it. Now, it was up to all citizens to be their own master and plan their own destiny, building along the way a "more perfect Union". Gorbachev, perestroika, glasnost and all the newly passed laws blazed the trail, set new boundaries, and establish a lot of buffer zones. The community of foreign students and diplomats were still on board with the General Secretary, but the dynamic was slowly changing, potentially not in our favor.

Economically, change was definitely in the air after seventy years of government planning. Some sectors showed higher productivity, and others, unfortunately the ones that could make a concrete difference in people's lives, shrunk. According to Martin McCauley, during the first nine months of the year, industrial production was up 4.3%, but no republic or industrial branch fulfilled its plan. In the important machine-building sector, 47% of enterprises did not meet their contractual obligations, and in the chemical industry, 42%. Labor productivity rose 5.4%, compared with 2.5% in 1987. The grain harvest was smaller than in 1987, necessitating more grain imports at a time when the Soviet revenues from oil, gas, and war material exports were falling. The minister of finance stated in October that the 1986 Chernobyl nuclear accident had at that point cost the country over 8 billion rubles. Food subsidies came to 91.5 billion rubles and would climb to 103 billion rubles in 1989. About 20% of budget expenditure covered various subsidies, with food accounting for approximately 90%. [27]

At this point, people did not need to know these

---

[27] *Encyclopedia Britannica book of the year 1989, World Affairs: Eastern Europe and the USSR. P-495, by Martin McCauley, Senior Lecturer in Soviet and East European Studies, University of London.*

statistics to feel the pinch. The standard of living was declining fast, and some dramatic actions were needed.

Travel and import permits gave rise to a new army of entrepreneurs, foreign and domestic, tasked to help the party satisfy the giant appetite of the country. If the government could get away with rationing the supply in the past, now, with those controls gone, it became overwhelmed. Produce and domestic goods were in very short supply. As a direct consequence, prices went through the roof, trapping the average Soviet and all retirees in sudden poverty. Now everybody was selling and buying without producing.

With that, the number of speculators grew exponentially, choking the supply lines. Those working in government grocery and appliance stores became very greedy and doubly powerful. They would artificially create a crisis by not displaying or selling tons of meat, butter, sardines, onions, oil, refrigerators, etc. People would then panic and offer their entire savings for a few pounds of meat or a few cans of powdered milk. At the farmers' market, the Bazaar, you could find fresh produce right from the farms, but the cost was out of reach for the middle class. Such corruption gathered steam as people were getting more desperate by the hour. It became virtually impossible to buy basic produce without bribing the clerk or somebody you knew in a given store.

It seemed and felt as though, on a personal level, the economy was not going in the right direction, despite the numerous measures Gorbachev was taking to avoid a crash. "A simple repair of an apartment would take weeks before the plumber shows up, and then he would use 40% of the material the government provided for the repairs, and robbed the remaining 60%," Gorbachev once stated during a televised visit in Leningrad.[28]

For foreign students and diplomats, the situation was very different from the locals. Our trips abroad brought in more money, because of what we were still smuggling into the country. We imported things we would use and wear ourselves, from nice wide-screen TVs, video players, women's clothes

---

[28] Gorbachev, Televised speech in Leningrad, 1987.

and cosmetics, jackets and shirts to designer shoes. The new Soviet businessmen, who were making money left and right in this evolving environment, also started to place specific orders with us. Business was booming. Some Soviets were finally able to buy what they really wanted while others did not have enough to eat. Our behavior did not change due to the harsh economy: fake birthdays and improvised parties were still in order.

In 1988, with the new prohibition law previously pushed by Gorbachev, vodka and other alcoholic drinks became rare commodities. Just like with groceries, the solidarity among drinkers saved many weekend drinking escapades. They would spread through town, scouting for vodka or beer. Once somebody located a drop, the message would go out to drinking buddies. Like ants, the reinforcements would come in for more bottles. In the winter, the picture looked bleak and brutal as guys waited in the frigid cold with huge bags full of booze, for buses that sometimes never came. Cab drivers, in turn, would have a field day when they came across four or five frozen foreigners, clearly underdressed for winter and dragging a heavy bag.

Days like that were doubling in number, and lines were getting longer as the new law dubbed sukoi zakon (or dry law: no alcohol consumption) took root. As alcohol became rare, or at least rationed, the need for drinking gatherings also became crucial, as drinkers who could not find alcohol would seek out and join those who unearthed some. If you could locate any alcohol, the price was astronomical. That pushed our colleagues out of their dorms to travel long distances and join others, if they hoped to drink to their former capacity, as they did a few months earlier in the comfort of their rooms. These circumstances dangerously exposed them to vicious mob attacks late at night, or when returning drunk, or both. Almost every community suffered losses or maiming of fellow countrymen in street beatings.

Before my stay in the US, I could not understand why people would put themselves through hell, just to locate a bottle of alcohol. I mistakenly thought that it was just a matter of will power to quit drinking oneself to death, or to avoid the beatings and the humiliations. The words addiction, help lines or rehab were not used when it came to alcoholism or sobriety in my native Mali. The Soviet population grew more irritated as prohibition took its toll. Considering the fact that many Soviets could live on vodka, bread, and salty fish alone, the elimination of vodka from their diet constituted a serious decline in their standard of living. The anger could be seen on buyers' faces at the liquor stores, and the frustration in the long lines was at a boiling point. An anecdote even had it that a drunk was loudly complaining while in a very long line for vodka. Tired and angry, he left the line swearing to go kill Gorbachev at the Kremlin. A few moments later, he returned, seemingly disappointed, to reclaim his spot in the queue. When asked why he was back so quickly, he replied, "The line is even longer over there."

A few years earlier when vodka was plentiful, some fans used to brew their own in the backyard. Now, with the tightening of the rules, homemade and underground vodka production kicked into high gear. The illegal and unsafe vodka producers were now trying to fill the vacuum left by the new regulations, and had sickened many. The extensive underground production of samagon (self-brewed) started to pull sugar away from the market, where there was not enough of it to start with. With no new source of sugar, the price of samagon, vodka, and sugar itself shot up, pushing people to other alternatives. In the dorms we used honey for our sugar needs, but vodka lovers and underground producers looked even further afield to feed their addiction. Their next target was medical spirits from the pharmacies, a product very close to vodka in alcohol content. All of a sudden, the demand for that grew exponentially, and pharmacies saw their inventories shrink. Clerks found themselves in a position of power and started smuggling it out of pharmacies and selling it to desperate alcoholics. The government, still playing catch-up with all the unattended consequences of the sukoi zakon, put a band-aid on the problem by requiring a doctor's prescription to buy spirits at pharmacies.

Next, biology substances at universities and colleges fell prey to vandalism, for the varieties and quantities of spirits they

237

held for students' experiments. Here again, many people got sick for drinking toxic laboratory products. This time, lab technicians were the culprits for stealing or sending their accomplices to break in and steal experimental spirits. We heard of two gentlemen who brought home some lab products they gave to their cat first, as a precautionary measure. Unfortunately for them, the cat, with its nine lives, did not show any adverse effects and survived the ordeal. They, however, ended up in the hospital.

Alarmed by the epidemic, the educational institutions started to move their spirits and toxic experimental products from their shelves to safer places. Squeezed from different directions, desperate drinkers and their underground alcohol producers turned to rodenticides and insecticides; in short, to anything that kills. Somehow, they found a way to make and sell drinks from these poisons to make up for the scarcity induced by the new law.

People were spinning in a vicious cycle of alcoholism, a bad economy, and the anxiety of the transition period. The worse peoples' problems got, the more they drank, so, in the failing economy with exorbitant sticker prices, alcohol became people's best friend if they could find it in any shape or form.

Obsession with alcohol was at its height. In its third year, Gorbachev's new law was taking hold, but at the same time was exacerbating the problem it was supposed to cure: the loss of productivity due to alcoholism, not to mention the health consequences.

As another unintended consequence, the law also enraged the majority of Soviet citizens who did not have a drinking problem, but enjoyed their vodka very much during their leisure times. This no-win situation made everybody's life miserable, dimming another starry aspect of perestroika.

On the political front, things were moving so fast that it was impossible to focus on even the major policy changes. Gorbachev was everywhere, especially on TV, his favorite new medium of communication. In a way, he was trying to engage a shapeless, confused, and disengaged citizenry. Selling perestroika and glasnost to a hungry public was not getting any easier, as basic goods were disappearing from shelves or remained financially out of reach.

Politically 1988 began with a big personnel loss, then Gorbachev himself nominated Yeltsin to be head of the Communist Party in Moscow. Yeltsin's unorthodox crusader attitude, his shrill criticisms of the pace of perestroika and of the Gorbachevs' themselves, made him some powerful enemies in the politburo.

A month later, a major political upheaval got underway in the Nagorno-Karabakh Autonomous region. It took all of us a while to understand the core issues of that turmoil so far away from Moscow. Before I even understood the underlying problem, most of us knew that this was a very serious situation, being the first of the kind. We were puzzled by the fact that such defiance was bursting wide open in this tightly-controlled country. On the one hand, Moscow should have seen this nationalist riot coming, in order to quell it. On the other hand, this was what perestroika was supposed to be all about: freedom of expression.

The Armenian majority living in Nagorno-Karabakh demanded that the area be attached to the Armenian republic, away from Azerbaijan. Moscow sent troops to the region with reports of many casualties and the imposition of a night curfew. This seemed to be the first crack in the cement that had kept so many tribes, ethnicities, and nationalities together since 1917. As declassified documents later showed, many tribes and ethnicities had gotten transferred, deported, or put under others' control all around the country. We also learned that borders were redrawn and many other ethnicities or nationalities were taken into the Soviet Union against their will. Moscow saw the Nagorno-Karabakh rebellion as a test case, aware that other regions were also keenly watching. Moscow did not give in but reinforced its presence there, while negotiations were underway to at prevent a potential rift. Moscow removed the leaders of the two belligerent republics, a move that sent more people in the streets of Yerevan-Armenia. Gorbachev would later reject the redrawing of the borders to avoid a domino effect in this huge country with many tribes.

In the summer of 1988, turmoil started also in the three Baltic republics in the North-West: Estonia, Lithuania, and

Latvia. People took to the streets to denounce the key element of their integration to the Soviet Union: the Soviet-German pact, or Molotov-Ribbentrop pact of 1940. It mirrored the Berlin conference of 1885, designed to divide Africa into spheres of influence between European powers. This one freed the two signatories to invade and share Eastern European countries with neither one challenging the other. They divided Poland, and the Soviets annexed some Finish territories and the three Baltic States.

Speaker after speaker denounced the pact and repudiated the official version in history books of their "peaceful" admittance to the Soviet Union. Angry party members laid charges of invasion and occupation and started to demand autonomy from Moscow. Others talked about making their native languages the official ones instead of Russian. Old national anthems, flags and emblems were dusted off and propelled to the forefront.

The problem was complicated by the sheer number of Russians in those republics, who found themselves "abroad" in their own country. All of a sudden, the Soviet army, largely made up of Russians, was unwelcome in many regions, especially the border republics that hosted military bases.

The independence and sovereignty fervor started to fill the air across our host republic, too. In Moldavia itself, talk resurfaced about the Soviet annexations of Bukovina and Bessarabia into the Union. By now, Bukovina was part of Ukraine and Bessarabia was still in Moldavia. The first thing on every lip was the recognition of the native language, Moldavian. People started to speak it in the streets, on buses, and in stores without looking over their shoulders, which was the case just a few months earlier. Calling someone Moldavian, considered an insult before, suddenly became a badge of honor; no more shame to be a Moldavian, and no more "big scolding Russian brother" to be afraid of. Our colleagues in class and in the dorms started to speak Moldavian, and some of us French speakers found it easy enough to throw some words around, to the delight of store clerks and cab drivers.

The numerous ethnic Russians, Ukrainians and Gagauz were now feeling in their own republic exactly what the ethnic

Moldavians had felt since 1940, not at home.

Not only a clear-cut conflict between the republic and the central government, the Moldavian situation was also complicated by its great ethnic diversity, now turning into a curse. Non-ethnic Moldavians started to gravitate toward each other, demanding some autonomy or outright independence from Moldavia in Transdniestra. Meanwhile some of the Moldavian-speaking population were talking about reunification with Romania. All of a sudden, our Russian and Ukrainian teachers were being looked at suspiciously, and sometimes challenged by students who answered their questions in Moldavian.

A complicated political and historical feud was brewing in this tiny agrarian republic, sandwiched between Romania and Ukraine. Foreign students sat on the sidelines and observed the in-fighting that could not have a happy ending, given the apparent irreconcilable nature of their differences.

In April, in the midst of all these evolving tribulations, Gorbachev courageously announced a plan to pull out Soviet troops from Afghanistan, which they had invaded a decade earlier. With more than 10,000 dead and more than 30,000 wounded, the human cost was getting too high, not to mention the billions of rubles going down the drain for a fruitless occupation. Our Soviet colleagues, who were either there or on their way, thought the decision was long overdue. They talked about the atrocities that were being committed there and what the war was doing to the boys. Many of the vets had become drug addicts; others could not study anymore because of their trauma. To make matters worse, there was no arrangement to help them reintegrate normal social life upon returning. There was one Afghan vet in our class named Anatoly; he was very quiet but always smiled when you made eye contact. His friend told us that the war had messed up his head and now he "runs" on opium. I can still see him with his golden teeth, calmly coming and going without saying a word.

To me, the nine-month withdrawal plan of the 115,000 soldiers was a key decision that separated Gorbachev from other ego-driven world leaders. Essentially, he swallowed his pride, cast aside his military super-power ego, and decided to cut his losses and bring the boys home. Most chest-thumping presidents have difficulty admitting mistakes (a proof of sanity, leadership, and character) in order to save lives. The warmongers would rather keep sending somebody else's children to die, than stop a lunacy they started in the first place, just to feel potent or win elections.

I have always wondered, who is supposed to pay for the killings of not only the innocent people the fighting powers call "collateral damage," but also the patriots who try to protect their families and countries after an illegal aggression? Since many of these wars were based on lies and egos, where is justice when you really need it?

In late May, Gorbachev received Ronald Reagan in Moscow to ratify the Intermediate-Range Nuclear Forces Treaty (INF). This visit really boosted Gorbachev's standing as a world leader seeking to engage his archenemy for peace, and softened the image of the U.S.S.R. around the world. Who does not remember the pictures of the two smiling presidents on Red Square carrying a little Soviet girl? The subsequent visit of Chancellor Kohl from Germany in late October only underscored that trend of goodwill, crucial to Gorbachev and the West's readiness to do business with him. Later, Gorbachev would also disclose at the UN that he planned to withdraw half a million troops and thousands of tanks from Eastern Europe, yet another bold move aimed at reducing tensions in the world and diverting these savings to his ailing economy.

In this quest to reassure the world about his country and shake off the "evil empire" stigma, Gorbachev also overlooked some fundamentals at home. In the summer, while traveling to France through the two Germanies, I learned from some unhappy Soviet troops packing up in Berlin, that there was no housing for them to go back to in the Soviet Union. All these troops and their poor families were heading home to some inadequate barracks from their nice bases in Germany. Given the uncertainty of the time, only God knew how long the waiting period was going to be until they could get their own homes.

As if he were not opening his society fast enough, Gorbachev also decided in early summer to allow the commemoration of the millennium of the Russian Orthodox Church with fanfare, significant guests and ceremonies. He even met with the Patriarch and other members of the Orthodox Church, an unimaginable event just a couple of years earlier. Given the sensitivity of this issue, we thought that religion would be the last thing affected by perestroika, but once again Gorbachev proved many of us wrong. Churches, that had never closed their doors but maintained a very low profile, were officially open for business again. The shift was amazing to witness as churches and their ringing bells became part of the landscape. Conversations about beliefs and prayers were not hush-hush anymore, and the sight of people going to church and carrying religious documents and artifacts seemed surreal.

The religious movement around the country, emboldened by this newly-found freedom, joined the demands for autonomy and self-determination everywhere it could. Outside influence, the most feared opponent of the pre-Gorbachev era, started to get a foothold in the Union through religious charitable organizations that flew under the radar of the paranoid central government. Peace and democracy movements from abroad helped create domestic groups, and positioned themselves very early on to be major players later in the new life of the Soviet Union.

In late June, the Communist Party held a huge conference that was televised worldwide for the first time in decades. It was chaotic at times, and very lengthy to watch it all and draw conclusions. There were a lot of personnel changes, a deck-cleaning of sorts, in order to make it easier for Gorbachev to better maneuver his policies. One shocking replacement got everybody's attention, that of Gromyko, the eternal Foreign Secretary of the USSR, and later Soviet President. He was the face of the Soviet Union on the international scene for forty years.

There were other proposals for the reform of the Communist Party and how it does business, but Gorbachev still clung to it as the primary entity for setting all the major policies of the country, albeit through local committees. There was talk of a multiparty system, but the General Secretary would not even entertain the idea that could have cemented his chief political signature: perestroika. That stand would eventually have dire consequences for him and his position at home in the eyes of his former ally, and now main critic, Boris Yeltsin.

To make matters worse, a terrible earthquake of 6.9 on the Richter scale devastated northern Armenia in December as Gorbachev traveled to the US, Cuba, and the UK, triggering a massive relief effort from the international community. He cut his trip short and headed home to yet another battle front not of his making. The nearly 25,000 death figure was numbing and indicative of the scale of the tragedy. The mighty Soviet Union was caught off-guard, clearly unprepared to deal with such a calamity so far away from Moscow. With dropped jaws, we watched on TV as foreign countries brought blankets, sniffing dogs, and other first-responder emergency supplies, to a so-called world superpower. The tragedy showed the world how vulnerable and impotent the Soviet Union's first line of civil defense was.

Fortunately, Gorbachev's glasnost was having the same effect, exposing the vulnerabilities of an empire that once breathed fear into the rest of the world. By letting in the foreign press and emergency relief groups, and by showing the disaster on live TV, he stayed true to his word. The disaster at hand also proved his point about the necessity for a profound political, economic and social reorganization. If this tragedy had happened under any of his predecessors, the first step would have been to aggressively censure the news and tightly control the flow of information from the region. As a consequence, the relief effort would have been jeopardized, leading to greater loss of life, since the country was clearly unfit to face this urgent state of emergency.

The international mobilization was swift and robust, but the Soviets were overwhelmed by how to properly channel the huge donations of money and goods, pouring into the country. The TV clips were shameful to any Soviet with a conscience and a sense of pride. They also should have had a motivational effect on the citizenry, pushing them all to work harder and lift the country from this "armed-banana-republic" status. The hectic situation was a con-man's paradise, and rapidly bred corruption while exposing an unimaginable incompetence, all the way from Moscow down to local authorities on the ground. When the dust settled months later, a string of complaints followed, with nobody in a position of power taking responsibility for botching the reconstruction and the aid redistribution efforts. People were left in makeshift tents for months, and most of the roads and buildings never saw a contractor. A quarter century later, Armenian towns and cities still show scars of the earthquake.

Moscow had one eye on the management of the disaster and the other on the fierce ethnic unrest in the region and around the country, but in the end mishandled both. To buy time and put out multiple smoldering fires, including the one between Armenia and Azerbaijan, Gorbachev agreed to guarantee some freedoms, but not independence or redrawn borders.

By 1989, as we entered our third year in the Soviet Union and were old enough to be called by the ubiquitous nickname "ancients," Gorbachev's tribulations were multiplying in scope and severity. Unfortunately, his problems were directly linked to ours as never before. If in previous years we sat unaffected on the sidelines, now we were as affected as they were by the realities of life in the USSR, despite our relative wealth. Every way you turned, there was an entrenching crisis that nobody seemed able to counter. We were now all knee-deep in the quicksand, foreigners and natives alike.

The economic reforms in the private sector that were supposed to reverse habits and fuel production, were losing steam amid the transition chaos. Overnight, everybody became an entrepreneur, venturing into the complicated world of the marketplace, a genuinely revolutionary concept to every Soviet citizen without exception. The new laws regarding the private sector were very vague, nearly indecipherable and not backed by stringent, enforceable rules and regulations. Take the example of private cabs. The drivers were supposed to register and pay taxes on their revenues, but there was no mechanism in place to monitor the generated incomes. Both kinds of cabbies, the government and private drivers, constantly haggled with clients about the fare for a particular ride, ignoring the meter. Once they had negotiated their "fair price" (twice or triple what the meter would read), they would give their standard happy "Poekali" (let's go), knowing that they'd just cheated the state out of at least 60% of the total fare.

Some citizens did not even bother to register their cars as a licensed cab, but rode around town transporting passengers all day long. Thus, made close to their monthly salary per day never to pay taxes on it. They were always jittery when they picked up black foreigners because of the high probability of being pulled over. Why? Because chances were, a private car with a black passenger was unmarked, unlicensed, and above all, not paying taxes. Since no Soviet citizen well-off enough to have a car would have a black friend, seeing them together always raised suspicions. Is he illegally transporting him, or are they going to illegally sell something to each other on the black market? To fend off any potential face-off with the police, these private taxi drivers had an inventory of cooked-up stories for their passengers. There was no lack of alibis for them to make money and not declare it.

Here are some of the lame stories both driver and passenger would agree on:

- Oh, I am just showing you where to find a specific store you have been looking for, since this morning.

- With no bus in sight, you were hitchhiking to your dorm and I am giving you a ride since I was going the same way.

- We attended the same university.

-We live in the same area and I am just giving you a ride to town.

The tax and banking systems were too weak and outdated to allow the government to streamline and tax the new revenues. Cold cash was king in the street, therefore out of sight of the government. There was no entity or enforcement mechanism in place to go after the delinquents, period.

The number of privately-owned stores also went through the roof. Called Commertcheski Magazines, these outlets full of imported cheap rubbish from neighboring countries like Romania, Poland, Turkey, etc., opened their doors everywhere. The hope was that they would supplant government stores and provide urgently-needed products and produce to a disillusioned population.

Instead of sparking fresh competition among new small businesses countrywide, as intended, the trade laws would have unexpected ramifications. Now that they were permitted to travel, many new Soviet businessmen focused on importing basic things that the people craved and could not get (clothes, shoes, underwear), but not edibles. At the border, the corruption of customs agents was still rampant, which deprived the government of any significant income from tariffs on imports, or even exports, for that matter.

Once inside the country, a good percentage of the items were sold directly to impatient consumers without touching the shelves of any registered stores. If the merchandise did get into a store, prices were marked by hand and rose daily. Bookkeeping was done on the side, and a huge side business itself grew out of paying off law enforcement agents for not enforcing the law. Corrupt clerks assisted businessmen in buying hard-to-find government items, only to sell them in the new private stores for a fortune just because the store was not state-owned.

Few made anything per se, but everybody sold something with at least a 200% profit margin in those Komercheski stores and co-ops. There simply were not enough products to go around, and the newly-formed business enterprises were primarily middlemen instead of manufacturers or producers. Those who did produce were only a drop in the bucket of the GDP (Gross Domestic Product), even if their numbers did rise year after year. Agriculture, even in Ukraine, the bread basket of the Union, did not live up to expectations. The lack of management skills and stewardship doomed those family co-ops and repossessed government farms, before they ever got off the ground. According to Martin McCauley, Gorbachev's speech to the Central Committee plenum on agriculture included some daunting facts: 22 million hectares (55 million acres) of arable land and 3 million hectares (7 million acres) of irrigated land were written off; 20% of agricultural output was lost through mismanagement (30 to

40% for some products). [29]

As if the situation was not bad enough, angry miners took to the streets live on TV for the entire labor class to see. With empty shelves in the stores and wages wiped out by inflation, the miners decided to take on the central government. They had nothing to lose. Every night, we watched in awe as the nightly news broadcast the historic pictures of miners sitting down in protest. As the fever spread to other mines, Moscow gave in to most, if not all, of their demands so that they would return to work. That quieted them down for few months and allowed the miners an opportunity to organize better for the strikes that would eventually come.

Yet another battlefront for Gorbachev as he watched his economic reforms fail. Meanwhile the population lost faith in his capacity to even put food on their tables - A basic but impossible undertaking for Gorbachev to fulfill at the time. What had the mighty Soviet Union come to?

Our Soviet classmates started to lose interest in education. They argued that they could make more money in a few days by speculating on goods, foreign currencies, and all the other stuff in short supply, than they would in six months as government employees. The demand for dollars and other currencies skyrocketed, fueled by all the new travelers and businessmen. The black market for foreign currency claimed by foreign students and diplomats started to change hands.

To the detriment of Soviet manufacturing, the market was flooded with very cheap imported goods. These items were not of good quality, and unfortunately, not vital to the day-to-day survival of average citizens. All of a sudden, young and old found themselves in a position where, they did not have enough income to keep up with inflated market prices of desperately needed food and medicine. Produce from private or semi-private agricultural enterprises, could not only satisfy the demand, but also were out of reach for the majority among the working class. Starvation became a reality for many of the elderly who resorted to street begging. War veterans and other

---

[29] *Encyclopedia Britannica 1990 book of the year events of 1989. World Affairs: Eastern Europe and the USSR. P-495*

retirees bitterly complained about their dire conditions. Before the crisis, they had their pensions and a discount card that allowed them to get into any store and be served without delay. Now, the cards were obsolete and their meager pensions could only buy a few days' worth of groceries in either private or government stores. They could not believe that the country they gave so much to and for so long, could not even make sure they did not go to bed hungry. Many would recall the Second World War and how much they had sacrificed, only to starve a generation later.

In the dorms, word of a particular store selling chicken, butter or bread would spread like a bad rash. Everyone would grab a bag and dash down there in a flash to secure a particular item. Sometimes, the clerk would tip one foreigner off, telling him that his store would be getting a delivery of frozen meat, cooking oil or sugar. The lucky foreigner would then alert the others in the dorms and tell them to go see a given clerk exclusively. We would then trickle over there and buy the stuff for double the price, either through the back door or by giving a bag to the clerk. Of course, that rightfully infuriated the Soviets, but we all needed to eat.

That summer on my way overseas, I stayed with some friends in Moscow. An acquaintance of theirs came by with some US imported chicken, and pointed the grocery store out to us. We hurried to the designated store and stood in a long line for about an hour. The numerous wooden boxes of frozen chicken were disappearing right in front of our eyes, as we got closer to the clerks. By a miracle, we took the last pieces, as dozens of Soviets looked on. All of sudden, a bunch of them started shouting, "Go back home to your villages! You leave your villages starving to death, and come here to steal our food! Go home, 'niggers'" We did not know what to say or do; we just kept on going, leaving dozens of them still standing in line, hoping for a miracle delivery. We were lucky to leave all in one piece, and with the chickens, because in such circumstances violence was often the first recourse.

One by one, all essential produce became rarer and rarer. Groceries we all used to buy down the street every other day, were not to be found anymore. Cooking oil and butter disappeared at the same time, and bread and meat would trickle in when we least expected. Next, we lost beverages, soaps, sugar, and canned foods. People who had avoided being seen with a foreigner before, would now strike up a conversation with us about the pending disappearance of such and such item, and where to potentially find supplies. I still remember sitting on a bus bound for a small village for training, and listening to a colleague's rant about the Soviet Union not being able to feed its people. He could not also come to terms with the fact that he could not even buy a bar of soap to shower with.

Lines were getting longer at the stores with empty shelves, and people fantasized about sudden deliveries of something, anything they could stand in line to buy and save the day with. The government was failing its people in front of the entire world and, as in any crisis, one thing led to another, creating a downward spiral. As a desperate and temporary fix, the government issued coupons for indispensable items like oil, butter, or sugar. Again, the government clerks who handled those coupons started to speculate on them, copiously serving their own families first, then selling or exchanging the rest for more favors. Still, because of the corruption and speculation on either the coupons or the products themselves in government stores, there were not enough goods for all the coupons out there. The coupons did not guarantee anything but the right to buy a certain amount of something, if that thing was still available, after the speculation by the clerks.

Joint ventures emerged, especially in the food industry, from bakeries and pantries to dairy products. Again, at that point it was like a drop in the bucket, and the prices were too high for the average worker. Many foreign companies jumped with both feet into the new and lawless Soviet market. Some got badly burnt, many others ran out of patience and bribe money, but others dug their hills in.

The difficulty of the situation drove people to survival mode, and there was no shortage of ideas. Underground passages, sidewalks, and metro hallways became marketplaces. Private items that we normally see in garage sales in the US, medals and even pets (especially breeder dogs) brought in badly needed cash for food. Many even started exporting puppies to Asia without proper documentation. We heard that many got caught by custom agents, as the puppies made noise from suitcases. To avoid being betrayed by unruly puppies, the smugglers resorted to vodka to quiet them down. People were getting desperate by the minute, with no end in sight.

Film footage of the long lines and empty shelves on TV made the whole world aware of what we were going through. Worried about her boy's well-being, my mom sent me some rice all the way from Bamako, Mali, 3770 miles away. Others brought their supply upon returning from vacation. To make matters worse, foreign students were no more the king-makers they once were, when the natives could not travel. Now, with travel and imports allowed, the Soviets all but took over the activities that were once our illicit gold mines - imports, exports and currency exchange. With that loss of unwritten privileges, we lost our buying power as money got tighter and produce rarer. For the first time, we had to watch our spending and could not buy whatever goods we wanted. There was not enough items to go around anymore and the prices were prohibitive. Students began exploring their connections in other cities, this time not for items to export, but for basic necessities. Many would travel to other towns just to load up on cooking oil, sugar, rice, or soap, if alerted by a friend. Talk about tightening our belts. No more lavish parties or taxi cabs waiting outside for hours, no more fake birthdays and unnecessary feasts, to name just a few. Collectively, the society entered a prolonged survival period where everybody wanted to just have something to eat, no leisure, pleasure or luxury, just food and medicine to subsist.

The depression brought out the best of African solidarity, as fellow students shared the little they had to spare with no second thoughts. It also brought out the worst of our hosts as, in this economic downward spiral; we became even more the target of their anger, verbal and physical abuse. Just like in many countries in the West, foreigners were the root of all evils across a bankrupt Soviet Union that could not feed itself anymore. We suffered from hateful looks, bigoted comments and beatings. Evidently, nothing was working as the government kept trying new ideas and programs. Gorbachev was losing the domestic economic battle and the respect of the nation.

Socially, as a frightened, disillusioned, and genuinely confused citizenry scrambled to survive, the Soviet Mafia was being born. The newfound freedoms and the sense of lawlessness, exacerbated by unprecedented economic turmoil, became fertile ground for the very ill-intentioned. Slowly but surely, organized crime (a la Mafia) took hold in main cities and towns in the face of an under-resourced and corrupt militia force.

Their first targets were the new komercheski stores that imported cheap items from neighboring countries. Organized groups imposed a kind of monthly tax on them, in exchange for staying in a particular area to do business. With time, they became stronger and infiltrated the militia itself. They subsequently controlled the cabs that operated at every main railroad station and airport. Government and private ones could not even take a client until the Mafia-controlled ones left with a passenger. According to several drivers, some of their friends had their tires slashed and were threatened for not abiding by the unwritten street rules. Train tickets also were controlled by them with the help of corrupt and frightened clerks. The later set aside thousands of seats and would let the train leave empty rather than sell tickets at government price.

Airport rides were next and became dangerous, especially for foreigners. Innocent-looking cab drivers started to target foreigners for extortion, especially the ones flying in from abroad. It was assumed that those international flyers had a lot of foreign currencies and luggage full of Western paraphernalia. We heard stories of cab drivers veering off course and taking passengers in isolated areas to rob them. Sometimes, accomplices would take off behind the targeted cab and assist the driver in assaulting unfortunate passengers. A word of caution reached all of us to not load or unload suitcases into or out of the trunk of the taxi. But, to take them inside the cab with us, to avoid being knocked out with the door while bending to reach inside the trunk.

With the Soviets free to travel now, the lines at foreign embassies too became a focal point for organized crime. They took over foreign embassies by controlling the very long lines that travelers formed to apply for visas. Early mornings, before 6 a.m. people came and wrote down their names on a sheet of paper that was later handed to embassy officials as they opened doors for business at 9. The Mafiosi would write down dozens of names and later sell the spots to latecomers.

Survival by any means necessary seemed to be everybody's motto, especially the Mafia. There was no lack of ingenuity from a Mafia that was cementing its grasp on various supply and service areas of the economy. They even targeted the transport coins of the metro systems. With all the economic woes, the metro system was getting short on coins, as people were melting them for the bit of precious metals they were partly made of. To remedy that and raise the fees of an otherwise extremely cheap fare (5 kopecks, about 5 cents), the government introduced a particular token just for transport. The Mafiosi decided to make millions of similar tokens to be sold in the Moscow metro, alongside the government ones.

Nobody could describe what was happening to them individually, or to the country as a whole, and certainly nobody knew how to fix it. The deep pride that was left over from the victory in the great patriotic war against Hitler, and from building the first socialist country that stood tall against the US, was dissipating in front of our eyes. For the first time in their history, the Soviets were ashamed of themselves within their borders. We had witnessed in the past how uncomfortable and embarrassed they were abroad, but this time it hit home. The conversation within the Union turned unbelievably pragmatic, with no harsh words spared for the communist party. The proud Soviet citizen helplessly mourned his own economical demise in the face of a powerless government. It stung even more after learning about a better life in the West, especially in the US, the sworn enemy. All kinds of information gushed in from everywhere, allowing the average Soviet citizen to daily compare his mediocre life to that of the West. Despite all the brainwashing that went on for decades, even the most patriotic Soviet could not contain his or her disgust anymore.

Politically, Gorbachev was having paradoxical results in domestic and foreign policies in 1989. At home, he plowed ahead with the reforms that fewer and fewer people believed in due to the worsening of most aspects of life, since the onset of perestroika. Some of the early tangible results in everyday life were being overshadowed by the political gridlock he and his team found themselves in.

The year 1989 started with an announcement that the Soviet Union would unilaterally destroy its chemical weapons stockpiles and would also recall 12% of its military hardware from Eastern Europe. While these were steps toward peace-building as well as confidence-building for the Secretary and his policies, they were primarily ways to continue to free up more resources for a dying domestic economy. But the political turmoil all across the Soviet Union was far from over; to the contrary.

In mid-January, the presidium of the Supreme Soviet of the USSR decided to place the Nagorno-Karabakh region temporarily under Moscow's direct rule, in an effort to end ethnic violence there. During that time, it would continue to be an autonomous region incorporated in the Azerbaijan Soviet Republic. Despite the virtual imposition of martial law, the earthquake of December 1988, and numerous efforts to diffuse demands by ethnic Armenians that their region be incorporated into neighboring Armenia SSR, the turmoil had continued.

On the other side of the country, the Estonian legislature approved a new law making Estonian the official language of the Republic. The lop-sided vote underscored the growing resentment against perceived efforts by Moscow to impose the Russian language on minority groups within the Soviet Union. Supplementary legislation, if passed, would compel Soviet officials to respond in Estonian to any question asked in that language. The following week, Lithuania, another Baltic republic, passed similar but more rigorous laws.

As Moscow closely monitored these stubborn ethnic tensions, another earthquake struck in Tajikistan, killing 1000 people. This, only a month and a half after the one in Armenia, further over-stretched the modest means of the Union. Even with the help of the international community, the region would greatly suffer from inadequate coordination and allocation of funds, leaving many in dire conditions.

In February, foreign secretary Chevernadze visited China, melting the 39 year-old ice between the two countries, and by mid-February, Moscow confirmed the exit of the last Soviet soldier from Afghanistan. According to some Western experts, one Soviet soldier died every 5 hours during the nine-year occupation, whereas one Afghan died every 3 minutes. On that day in February, the carnage was over thanks to Gorbachev's courage in saying no to a war of choice.

The following month, 200,000 Latvians staged the largest anti-Russian demonstration in the republic's history. The crowd marched in support of the people's front, which sought to establish Latvian as the dominant language of the republic. Although some demonstrators called for independence from the Soviet Union, the group was committed to work with the communist party to achieve reform. Two days later, Estonia was the sight of a very different demonstration, this one by non-Estonian ethnic Russians who claimed to be victims of discrimination. They also decried Estonia's "creeping counterrevolution." In Lithuania, the third Baltic republic, local leaders withdrew the candidacy of two persons running for congress, fearful that the movement for greater Lithuanian autonomy would be suppressed by hard-liners if the two leading Communists were defeated. [30]

By the end of March, perestroika and the democratic process were put to the test as national elections took place. It was closely watched by many pundits outside the country as a gauge of political progress since 1985. But from within, it was seen as a window into the future direction of the communist party in particular, and the socialist system as a whole. The deeper the crisis, the less people were interested in the one-party system and its grip on just about every aspect of their lives. So, in March, in the freest national election since the 1917 revolution, Soviet citizens went to the polls to elect the Congress of People deputies.

Although there was never any possibility that the

---

[30] *Encyclopedia Britannica book of the year 1990. Chronology: March. P 37*

communist party would lose control of the government, the stunning defeat of certain high-ranking officials caught everyone by surprise. Among those who failed to win were the first and second most powerful communist officials in Moscow, the party leader in Leningrad, the top two officials in Kiev, both the president and premier of Lithuania, the head of the KGB in Estonia, the commander of Soviet troops in East Germany, and the commander of the Northern fleet.

The most talked-about candidate was Boris Yeltsin, the deposed party chief in Moscow and a critic of government policies, who won in a landslide.[31] Subsequently, a vigorous political debate took the country by storm, pulling even the most reluctant into the conversation. I watched the process with skepticism, given my bias against the communist party. I must admit, the process pleasantly surprised many of us who thought that the "invisible hand" would ultimately decide the outcome at the polls. Instead, a great deal of history was made through the votes of the citizenry.

In April, before the dust of the election settled, Gorbachev travelled abroad to lay out his vision for a peaceful world. After visiting Cuba and Ireland, he unilaterally declared in London that Moscow would stop enriching uranium, in hopes of further chipping away at his colossal military budget. Upon his return, he found the Caucasus in turmoil. On April 7, the Soviet government deployed troops and armored personnel carriers along the streets of Tbilisi to stifle strikes and demonstrations in the capital city of the Georgia SSR. The people, demonstrating peacefully, were demanding greater political and economic independence from the central government in Moscow. On April 9, at least 19 persons were killed and many hundreds injured when troops moved against a crowd that had refused to disperse. The next day, Foreign Minister Chevernadze, the only native Georgian of the politburo, flew to Tbilisi in an effort to restore calm. He later declared there was "no justification for the death of innocent

---

[31] *Encyclopedia Britannica book of the year 1990. Chronology: March.P38 Martin McCauley, Senior Lecturer in Soviet and East European Studies, University of London.*

people." [32]

In the midst of this upheaval, Gorbachev and his allies in the communist party, voted to remove 74 of the 301 members of the powerful central committee, all of whom had full voting rights. In addition, 36 other high officials were also voted out of office; some were voting members of the central committee, while others were members of the auditing commission. In general, younger men were appointed to take their places. The overall size of the Central Committee was simultaneously reduced to 251. All those dismissed were called "dead souls" and considered impediments to the Soviet leader's program of reform.

A month later, Gorbachev was elected president of the USSR by the newly- constituted Congress of People's Deputies, with tenure limited to two five-year terms. The result of the secret balloting was 2123-87. Before the vote, Gorbachev was publicly and sharply questioned about his policies and defended, among other things, his use of a plush official home in the Crimea (something all his predecessors did). During the debates, certain deputies contended that Gorbachev would rival Napoleon in power if he were both leader of the Communist Party and head of the government.

Boris Yeltsin, the former party leader in Moscow who had become a celebrity by challenging Gorbachev, had failed to win a seat among the 542 members of the Supreme Soviet. The congress responded to public indignation and voted on May 29 to allow Yeltsin to accept a seat offered to him by one of the victorious candidates.[33] Inevitably, the relationship between Yeltsin and Gorbachev went from friendship and admiration to open contempt for each other. Yeltsin publicly pressed Gorbachev on the slow steps of his reforms and accused him of clinging to a Communist Party soon doomed to collapse. His harassment of the General Secretary, unfortunately, looked

---

[32] *Encyclopedia Britannica book of the year 1990. Chronology: April. PP. 38-39*

[33] *Encyclopedia Britannica book of the year 1990. Chronology: May.P-41*

exceedingly disrespectful, and encouraged others to publicly stand up to him.

In mid-May, despite the high political tension at home, Gorbachev flew to an even more politically-charged atmosphere in China to normalize relations with his brothers-in-arms there. Protesting students camping on Tiananmen Square forced the Chinese authorities to change the protocols of the visit. The perestroika-supporting crowd had warm words of welcome for Gorbachev, and was determined to continue the protest. But by now we all know what the unrest led to, on June 4th, 1989 on Tiananmen Square.

Upon his return, another conflict broke out, this time in Uzbekistan where at least 57 people had been killed during clashes. The Uzbek government turned on native Uzbeks who in a wild frenzy had used wooden sticks and metal bars to kill 40 Meskhetians in Fergana on June 4. Hundreds of homes were also looted and set ablaze. The Meskhetians, a minuscule Turkish minority, had been relocated on Stalin's orders in 1944. Their previous home had been in Southern Georgia, along the Turkish border. Although thousands of Soviet troops patrolled the area, they were unable to contain the marauding bands of Uzbeks. On June 9, there were reports that Uzbeks carrying automatic weapons, hand guns, and knives had caused some100 casualties in Koland. On June 19, the Tass news agency reported that armed youths had gone on a rampage in Kazakhstan. Their anger seemed to be an expression of frustration over economic hardships and what they considered to be better conditions for migrant workers.[34]

As if there were not enough turmoil in the country, on July 10, three weeks later, a massive and contagious miners' strike started. Coal miners in the Siberian city of Mezhdurechensk, went on strike to reinforce their demand for better living conditions. On July 13th, Pravda, the communist party newspaper, reported that work at all five mines had come to a halt. Although the government agreed to certain concessions, the strike spread to other areas and eventually involved some 100,000 miners. On July 17, the Soviet press

---

[34] *Encyclopedia Britannica book of the year 1990. Chronology:June.P-42*

reported that eight mines in the Ukraine had also closed. [35]

During a televised address on July 23, Gorbachev told the miners he was inspired by their determination to take matters into their own hands to bring about changes that were necessary for the success of perestroika, his program for restructuring the nation's economy. Many strikers, heartened by Gorbachev's promise that their grievances would receive a positive response, began returning to work.[36]

Thanks to glasnost, all these strikes were televised and reported on without a sliver of censorship. On one hand, this incited others to take note and act, but on the other hand, it helped involve and educate a distrustful population.

By the end of July, the Supreme Soviet voted to allow economic autonomy for Lithuania and Estonia, a move seen by many of us as a slippery slope. It could open the door to political independence, not only in the Baltics, but for every one of the 15 republics that made up the USSR. To add salt to the wound, in August 22, the Soviet takeover of the region was voided: A commission of the Supreme Soviet officially declared that the 1940 occupation and annexation of Lithuania, Estonia and Latvia by the Soviet Union was invalid. The next day, hundreds of thousands of citizens in the three Baltic republics linked hands across their countries to dramatize their demand for independent statehood. The massive demonstrations were held on the 50th anniversary of the non-aggression pact signed by Stalin and Hitler. Which included secret protocols that had paved the way for the Soviet annexation of the Baltic States and Eastern Poland. [37]

By the end of August 1989, the Supreme Soviet voted to make Moldavian the official language of Moldavia. This was a very significant development in Kishinev, given the growing rift with the non-Moldavian speakers, who aspired to secede as a group. The central government was inadvertently making

---

[35] *Encyclopedia Britannica book of the year 1990. Chronology: July. P-43*

[36] *Encyclopedia Britannica book of the year 1990. Chronology: July. P-43*

[37] *Encyclopedia Britannica book of the year 1990. Chronologie: August. P-46*

their case for them, to unite on a friendly territory in the Transdniestra region and ask for independence from Moldavia. The language vote raised the tensions that were boiling just under the surface, and subsequently undermined any peaceful settlement of the issues of nationality, territory, and culture.

Moldavia, the "successful" multicultural Soviet republic, was at a crossroads in its rich history, which goes back to the 15th century, when it was governed by Prince Stephen the Great. Since then, Moldavia went through multiple status changes: princedom (supervised or autonomous), annexed or ruled territory; you name a status, and chances are that Moldavia experienced it. If the land called Moldavia had been tossed around in the past by external powers, this time the leaders of the internal forces stood at the brink of two historical choices: They could agree to form a "more perfect union" of all tribes in a would-be state independent from Moscow, or they could fight to the bitter end and tear the tiny republic apart.

As foreigners, we were reliving the post-colonial history of many African, Arab, and Asian countries, right in the heart of Europe. The difference was only in the language used to describe the facts on the ground. On one hand it was "savage killings," "tribal wars," even "terrorism," and on the other it was "fight for self-determination," "autonomy," "independence," or "freedom." Again, the mass media stayed true to its biases.

In Moldavia, the differences between the parties were unfortunately allowed to burst and metastasize, because of the rights and freedoms brought about by perestroika itself. Moldavian-speaking factions wanted to be independent and potentially join Romania, which pushed the non-Moldavian-speakers to claim the Transdniestra region. An area more developed and multi-ethnic, where Russians and Ukrainians were in the majority. The tribal purge was in its infancy, creating a situation of high anxiety palpable in the streets, schools, and stores. Any position held by a non-Moldavian-speaker became untenable, except in the Transdniestra region.

The economic and social prospects of such a partition looked dire for all parties. Transdniestra had a solid industrial and manufacturing base in addition to the main power plant, but had a limited agricultural output. The rest of the country was bigger in territory and housed the main institutions of power and education, headed mostly by minority Russians and Ukrainians.

Transdniestra naturally aligned itself with the Russian big brother for protection, whereas the Moldavian troops were galvanized by nationalists, eager to air out their anger with the minorities. The writing was on the wall but it was now up to the leaders to shape the future of Moldavia for the better. Could they?

In the meantime, the foreign students nervously observed the rise in tension at the university and in town, as anybody who spoke or looked different was becoming the enemy. If the white Russians and Ukrainians were considered occupiers, told on a daily basis to "go home," what about us? The rumors were that, with secession and independence talks from Moscow, we might have to go back home or to the Russian Federation, the heir to all the problems of the decaying Soviet Union. Moldavians falsely maintained that our countries paid our tuitions to Moscow and that they did not see a dime of that money; therefore, our logical refuge would be there. Our stay was not getting any easier, and it seemed like a perfect storm was brewing. As the economy tanked, the bigotry worsened in a Moldavia on the brink of disintegration.

By pushing for democracy and glasnost, Gorbachev had genuinely wanted to open the socialist bloc to the rest of the world, improve the standard of living, and still stay true to communism. Earlier, he had dropped many hints regarding other communist countries' self-determination, and showed no appetite for intervention in their domestic affairs. He even told the East Germans, that the decisions regarding their country would be taken in Berlin and not in Moscow. The withdrawal of troops and hardware from Afghanistan, Hungary, and Eastern Germany only confirmed that non-imperialistic ambition. It seemed to me that, deep down, he wanted to step back, scale back, and roll back the USSR's grip over Eastern Europe and parts of Latin America, in order to lessen the economic burden and focus on his own domestic problems.

The Kremlin found itself in a catch-22 between concessions and the unrest engulfing the republics. Moscow slowly gave in to all kinds of demands from labor, ethnic groups, and religious organizations in order to buy time and appease an enraged population poised to break out of the status quo.

Meanwhile, Eastern Europe itself, started to disintegrate under street pressure in many capital cities. Later that fall of 1989, a revolution swept through the streets, taking down communist regimes one after the other. Ironically, the domino effect the US had feared in Asia when it invaded Vietnam, was happening in Eastern Europe, only backwards. Instead of countries falling to the Soviet bloc one after the other as the US dreaded, they were now falling out of the communist bloc en masse. The rest of the remarkable events of the fall of 1989 in Eastern Europe is history.

Domestically, independence movements became emboldened by that fall of the Berlin wall, and its reverberations across the communist bloc. They had just observed the blueprint of how to get rid of the communist regimes that oppressed their own populations. In the Union overall, that regime was the communist party in Moscow. Locally, in respective republics or regions, that regime was made up of citizens living in the region as a minority, but wielding some power or authority. Russians and Ukrainians became the villains in the case of Moldavia, with us foreign students, in the middle of it all.

Overall, Gorbachev and his team were like firefighters, rushing to the four corners of town to attend the wildfires that kept reigniting after being put out just few days earlier. They did not seem capable of preempting, containing, or solving any of the major conflicts or the economic crises they faced.

By the end of the year, Gorbachev managed to make a trip to the Vatican and meet with President Bush in the waters of Malta which we all followed live at school.

As we entered 1990, the economic situation was clearly hopeless, with no relief in sight. The shortage of basic

262

foodstuffs worsened, which led to more speculation, more contraband, and, of course, more suffering for the average Soviet and retiree. It was Darwin's theory of survival of the fittest in action. After cutting back on foolish expenses, foreigners could ride out the stubborn economic crisis because we had alternatives. Our influence and wealth diminished by the day, but we could still travel home or to Europe at least twice a year to stock up, which was something most of the natives could not do. If in the past we sold most of our merchandise to desperate Soviets, now most of our items were for private consumption.

The country was in a deep depression, with no respite from the frustration. The underground passages, the metro alleyways, and the sidewalks were crowded with more people than ever, selling household items in order to survive. Beggars became more obvious and aggressive, despite the ban against solicitation in the streets and metros. We could see the social fabric changing in front of our eyes, as poverty gnawed at the most vulnerable.

By now, corruption was second nature, exacerbating an already dire situation. At school the secretaries and deans also became more vocal about gifts from abroad, if students' visa applications were to be approved on time. No commerce, transaction, or exchange of any kind went without a bribe or price-gauging.

It was then that the rift between the corrupt rich and everybody else widened and solidified. Those exploiting the chaos could afford the newly-imported goods and did not want to see an end to their new-found prosperity. The lawlessness was also a blessing for the rapidly-spreading mafia that controlled more and more territory.

The rest of us looked up to Gorbachev and his ever-changing team of economic advisors. They continued to push for more economic reforms, liberalization, and foreign investments. Unfortunately, despite the huge demand for goods, the power to buy or invest was just not there, due to underemployment, mediocre savings, and the lack of lines of credit. The archaic Soviet banks were never meant to play a stimulating role in the old communist economy, and were not about to start now. It was a catch-22 that even economists from around the world could not unlock, and had to tread carefully, given the unprecedented circumstances. The economy was in a precarious state, teetering between the now hated government control, and a free market that only yesterday, was considered the source of all evils. One part of the society wanted to return to the stable and predictable years, another wanted to completely liberalize the economy, and everybody else was in between. Meantime, the lines were getting longer and the shelves emptier, except at the bazaars, where few could dare to shop for groceries because of the astronomical prices. Talk of economic reforms, decentralization, cooperatives, perestroika and glasnost, sounded hollow to a disillusioned population that needed to eat. Hopes and dreams faded as fast as the trust we all had in the young and charismatic Secretary General, 4 short years earlier. All these years they were trying to transition from government five-year, top down and mandatory plans, to a free market based on the recalcitrant supply and demand law. It was a fact that nobody knew how to do it in the most market-illiterate country, with 300 million hungry and angry souls. No wonder Gorbachev changed economic advisors like he changed shirts.

The ounce of decency that remained got wiped out, as the Soviet society sank deeper into economic depression. With the growth of all the core problems of the society, morality went out of the window. Prisons grew overcrowded, security in the streets and our dorms was fading, and the corrupt militia ignored piles of complaints they were bribed to shove under the rug. People did not know what to do anymore, but to drown their problems in the bottle, also now hard to find. It felt like the Soviet society had hit rock bottom. By now, every class of the "classless" society was fatally wounded. Salaries could not support families anymore, so parents were to somehow make up the difference. Many joined the army of new businessmen who bought and sold every type of goods between villages and urban centers. Others became middlemen between government and Komercheski stores, or between cities of different republics. That was evident when, traveling by train, one could see loads of consumer goods being dragged by ordinary citizens from city to city. An entire society seemed to be suffocating with no chance of finding an air pocket. Every day, governed and governors alike, wondered what to do next.

Some of our Soviet classmates dropped out in order to survive in the worsening rat race. The best minds of the Russian and Ukrainian academia started to pack up and were replaced by any Moldavian with connections. Despite the decadence of the state of the Union, third-world governments kept sending young students to the lion's den, while we prayed for a safe and orderly exit. Thousands more students came and were welcomed by ancients all across the union with a smile and a good luck wish. Education, along with the society itself, was going to hell, at least temporarily, as the best minds fled and the resources dried up.

Politically, the powder was dry and there was plenty of fire to ignite it, from the Baltic republics to the southern ones in Asia. The fall of the Berlin wall a few months earlier only emboldened Soviet independence fighters, who did not want Moscow deciding their fate anymore. Gorbachev's struggle to keep the country together was doomed by the irreconcilable political, tribal and religious differences, he did not seem to foresee, understand, or accept. By now, people had enough of the Communist Party with its five-year plans, draconian rules, and choking grip on powers governing their lives.

To my surprise, that was also the time that Gorbachev decided to openly dig in and stubbornly fight for the redemption of the party, albeit modifying it around the edges. Every republic, region, or entity at this point, wanted some kind of independence from Moscow. They passed anti-Soviet legislations or loudly screamed in the streets for the Russian "Yankees" to go home. The writing was on the wall, but Gorbachev kept believing in his impossible dream. He hoped to keep the USSR intact as a Union of loosely-tied republics with himself as president, and with a degree of decentralization never seen before. Such an arrangement would look a lot like the U.S.A and its states, under one monetary and defense system. His biggest enemies were, ironically, his own key policies of freedom of assembly, speech and glasnost. Freedoms, the citizens used to protest and petition for more autonomy and independence from him. With free and fair elections, the old communist guard was being replaced with younger, unreservedly West-crazy lawmakers, who did not want to hear a word about Socialism.

Anticipating a string of defections, and feeling the winds of independence blowing across the Soviet Union, an irritated Gorbachev resorted to the use of force. In January, he sent troops to Baku to crush a popular revolt, aimed at ousting the communists from power in Azerbaijan and gain independence. A bloody and horrible scene unfolded in downtown Baku, resulting in hundreds dead or injured, as all of us who idolized Gorbachev watched speechless. This event showed us a suppressed side of a man who had both talked and walked peace, but who succumbed to the compulsion of keeping his communist house together at all costs. This was the old Soviet way of doing things, not the new way under Gorbachev, we thought. But, that dreaded scenario of a popular movement overthrowing a communist government and proclaiming independence, was not to start anywhere in the Union. The images from Eastern Europe after the fall of the Berlin wall were not to be replayed in the Soviet Union, if Gorbachev had it his way.

As the Baltic Three (Estonia, Latvia and Lithuania) pushed harder for, and declared their independence, the Russian Federation also started to demand more sovereignty under the guidance of Boris Yeltsin. As the biggest, mightiest, and most populated, Russian sovereignty would mean a de facto end of the country. Other powerhouses like Ukraine and Belarus followed suit by declaring their own sovereignty and independence respectively that summer of 1990, as a restless population demanded more freedom from big brother Moscow.

Gorbachev dug in and warned of the disintegration of all that had been built with sweat and blood for 72 years. He maintained that the country was on the right track, and that every effort should be made to preserve the gains of the last five years: Democracy, glasnost, and political and economic reforms. It was painful, at least for me, to watch him plead for restraint when no one, especially the defecting leaders bent on secession, listened. There was a feeling that everything was slipping away while meaningful changes were happening, even if they were not felt by the masses. Gorbachev could not understand why anyone at this juncture would entertain the radical idea of leaving the mighty Soviet Union. What a mess it would be to sort out questions of borders, currency, military bases, tribes, and nationalities scattered throughout the four corners of the country, he warned.

But it was evident why he was losing ground in this ideological battlefield. Simply put, he had not been able to deliver what the people wanted in terms of the economy, political reforms, and the ever-growing corruption eating away at the future of the country. With the fall of the Berlin wall and the exodus of many other nations from the communist bloc, any oratory on the worth of socialism was destined to fall on the deaf ears of a citizenry looking West.

In Moldavia, we were in the eye of the storm as local politicians geared up for autonomy, cessation, or a war for independence, as was happening everywhere else in the Union. Internal contradictions and divergent interests were about to make Moldavia even tinier, as different sides pulled the republic in many different directions. The ultra-nationalists, who cared only about Moldavian speakers, wanted to break away from the Soviet Union. Some wanted to join Romania, and others wanted a stand-alone independent Moldavia. The disenfranchised non-Moldavian speakers then bonded together and contemplated the idea of an autonomous region West of the Dniester River. They, along with us foreigners, were fearful for their safety, jobs, and status within a future Moldavian state, given the racist and xenophobic rhetoric coming from the nationalists. The latter were grabbing all the rights and privileges that they were denied by Moscow for so long. With Moldavian as the official language, all non-speakers became second-class citizens in a republic where they had lived, served, and raised their kids. Professors, deans, even top researchers preemptively left in order to avoid their inevitable firing and replacement by Moldavian speakers. The future of their kids was definitely not going to be in the part of Moldavia, bent on joining Romania or pushing out those who did not speak the language.

By now, all sides were on the collision track, and only a miracle could spare them from a big bang that would tear the republic apart for generations. With each passing day, we witnessed the further closing of the peace window, and felt more and more sandwiched hopelessly between the fighting parties.

Malian diplomats, among many others, just sat on their bottoms in Moscow. They did not even contact the students throughout the Union to reassure them that they stood with them, or to discuss any contingency plan in case of an emergency. All they cared about were the containers and other contraband items they continued to send abroad. Their inaction in the face of an imminent danger was immoral. They cared not a whit about the thousands of faceless students scattered around a Soviet Union about to implode. This utter disregard for duty, the total submission to former colonial powers and that fatalistic attitude of waiting for destiny to find you sitting at home, are still among the root causes of the economic woes of Mali and other African countries. Malian diplomats in Moscow and other capitals were and are still richer than the embassy itself, due primarily to thievery and corruption. Calling, faxing, visiting, or meeting face-to-face to discuss the welfare of their fellow countrymen did not even cross their egocentric minds. There we were, left to our own devices in a republic on the brink of civil war and a Union at a crossroad not seen since World War II. Before we knew it, the situation escalated all around us, ratcheting the tension to a climax.

After a referendum, the minority non-Moldavians' territory on the left bank of the river Dniester, finally declared its independence. At that point, the majority Moldavians passed a resolution to change the name of the republic from Moldavia to Moldova, and also declared their autonomy from Moscow, eyeing unification with Romania. Immediately, and to nobody's surprise, bullets started flying between the factions in a town called Dubasari, populated by minority Russians and Ukrainians. The civil war was on.

As a direct effect, fewer agricultural products made their way into our bazaars, and rumors of rationing spread again. By now, foreign students and other minorities were keeping a very low profile, and the majority Moldovans avoided the troubled regions in Transdniestra. This political stalemate aggravated the already dire economic crisis, sending the whole populace of Moldova scrambling for food and shelter. The different factions all believed that they could survive without each other after 50 years of cohabitation and intermarriage.

By the end of 1990, the economy was not any better, and the political crisis had deepened as more and more republics declared some form of independence or autonomy from Moscow. The central government resisted calls from every corner for ditching the communist party, and even threatened to reign in some republics by force. As Gorbachev lamented, the unity of the once mighty Union of Soviet Socialist Republics seemed closer to its end than ever.

By 1991, six years after Gorbachev's appointment and five years since I landed in Moscow's, the Soviet Union was not any better. The economy could not have been worse, given the lack of basic food items and the high prices of what was available. Despite the numerous laws and regulations passed to jump-start the economy and turn it into a market-based system, we were all still suffering. Our buying power was crippled because of imports by Soviet or joint ventures and the widening of the black market base. Now, the lion's share of legal sales belonged to the countless Komercheski stores and those illegal markets and transactions run by the Mafia. Foreign students and diplomats became less relevant in overall sales, but maintained some black market share of the foreign currency exchange. The Vietnamese community, better organized and discreet than any other, ended up being the go-to fellows. In the dorms, they had several layers of security at any given time to prevent falling prey to the numerous criminals lurking the currency black market. Any potential client was checked at the door and then led behind a curtain where at least two people were in charge of exchanging the money. After agreeing on the rate and amount, somebody would then leave the room to get the necessary amount from an undisclosed room while the clients waited. They changed their location from one day to next, so that all potential clients were led to them by somebody they knew, thus avoiding any surprises.

Our financial status continued its nosedive as the country opened up, and we could not come up with other clever alternatives. At that point everything we used to sell illegally was legally available at a very high cost for those who could afford it. The only way to make money, was to import some items through the new Soviet businessmen at a huge cost and risk, or to export some durable goods to Africa. Most of us were hanging there, hoping to graduate before the country imploded, which would cancel our education.

To make matters worse, Gorbachev, still on a mission to salvage the economy, decided to devaluate the ruble in order to boost exports. At the same time, new banknotes were printed to replace the rampant counterfeit notes in circulation, and people were given very short notice to exchange a limited amount. That move made many criminals very poor overnight by halving their illegal millions, but also hurt students, diplomats, and average Soviets, who innocently kept many of the targeted banknotes under their mattresses.

The economy designed in 1917 was not relevant any more. It was not a market economy, but a hybrid that only crooks and criminals could navigate. Nothing seemed to be improving as calls for abandoning the socialist system got louder. Gorbachev's economic team pushed for more privatization and deregulation in order to transition into a market economy. The direct consequence of that aggressive process was the birth of the Soviet nouveaux riches. The old, wealthy and well-connected party leaders sold bankrupt Soviet factories to themselves, their families, and their close friends, for literally nothing. The speed and subtlety of these corrupt transactions did not register with the average citizen until new young millionaires started to pop up out of nowhere. Classy foreign cars, once reserved for diplomats, began filling the streets of Moscow, along with five-star hotels.

For a time, women's clothing and real estate were the hottest businesses in town, and it showed. Shiny and expensive foreign department stores filled the mall right on Red Square, a few feet from Lenin's mausoleum and the Kremlin. If the renovation of decaying buildings was an eyesore in the past, now it was an unmistakable proof of a changing society building anew. At this point, these minor changes suggested that the future looked bright, if the people only stuck to the glimmer of positive trends.

Small businesses, joint ventures in banking, bakery, catering, and even sex trafficking were underway, to the delight of Mafia extortionists. Business was "anything goes" in order to draw an income, since real government jobs could not support a family anymore, and were disappearing at a lightning speed. A tiny emerging minority in the cities took advantage of a scrambling majority running out of their last refuge: hope.

A third-world trend was rapidly developing in this Union that had been a superpower five short years ago. A small group of corrupt bastards was getting richer than the country itself, careless and almost gleeful of the utter misery of others around them. They stole from the government, drove big cars, built big houses, and had sex left and right. At the same time the infrastructure was crumbling in all the now unsafe cities. Vices like drugs, alcohol, prostitution, and crime multiplied, overwhelming a depleted health-care system in transition. The West would also pump millions of Dollars into the system to bail out the former "evil empire"

The toll of the crisis on the society as a whole, was heartbreaking to see and experience. By now, families had sold everything they could and used up the meager savings they may have had, in order to put food on the table. The guaranteed government job was no match for the high prices, and most did not have the resources to retrain themselves in order to enter the hyper-volatile private sector. As the poverty pool grew, physical attacks became viable options for many former decent citizens. Many proud war veterans resorted to begging in the streets or selling their medals and packs of cigarettes, while others brewed and sold vodka or became middlemen for a more established brewer. The most common survival activity was to buy or steal from the government stores through connections and resell in the streets, through Kommercheski stores or to close neighbors. The youth, in turn, were torn between sticking to their classes or getting out there and fending for themselves in the murky system to support their bankrupt parents.

More and more students abandoned classrooms to join the growing army of businessmen who travelled locally or abroad to make ends meet. To Moldovans, Romania and Turkey were the prime destinations for the import of clothing and shoes for students, native and foreign. Other go-getters around the country focused on used cars from Poland, the then- Czechoslovakia, or Germany. Some even exported rubles in cash in their back pockets to East Germany, where they would exchange them to buy used cars. Many others joined forces to set up bus companies taking the new travelers all across Europe. The bosses of these new bus lines eventually joined forces with organized crime to export vulnerable girls for prostitution across Europe. Also, new agencies promising to find quick jobs or husbands overseas, mushroomed, only to turn into criminal enterprises. It was during these dire times that a new and open bigotry was born, aimed at all Soviet southerners with dark hair or complexions, mirroring exactly what we saw and still see in the West. The concept is simple: When the economy tanks, security deteriorates, and foreigners or non-whites get the blame. This convenient broad brush gets dusted off and carelessly used against minorities, most often for political gains. Sounds familiar? It should, because it is still happening at you read this.

Unfortunately, this same selective bigotry became rampant in Russia, and particularly in Moscow, as survival became more and more difficult. Any dark-hair gentleman from the south became the target of an aggressive anti-southerner campaign. Because some Southerners committed crimes in

Moscow and got convicted for them, they were now all presumed guilty of every transgression. The umbrella term Chechen was readily thrown around because many of them, along with other southerners, came up north in the quest for a better life. In the streets, the average Moscovite avoided close contact with them, and the militia checked their IDs at every opportunity. Then, it got worse as the Chechen's apartments were raided first, anytime there was a crime in the vicinity. Finally, getting an apartment in Moscow became almost impossible for anybody who looked different from the white Russian. This aggressive discrimination only added to the brewing tension between Moscow and Chechnya, as it contemplated its independence from Russia.

It was like the old south in the US all over again. If one black commits a crime, then all blacks are criminals. If one Arab or Muslim kills, then all Arabs or Muslims must be killers. If one Latino gets busted with drugs, then all Spanish-speakers are tagged as drug dealers. If some priests molest children in church, then all priests must be child molesters... Oh wait; it does not work this time, does it? If one Christian sets off bombs in the Oklahoma Federal Building, or abortion clinics, or Olympic stadiums, then all Christian males must be terrorists and murderers, right? Oh no, it does not apply in cases like this, does it? If some white church leaders get caught exposing themselves or soliciting gay sex, well, then, all white church leaders must be perverts. Oh, wait a minute; painting every church leader with the same brush does not do justice, does it?

Given the history of slavery, where would the US be if the black community had bitten into what I would call the ignorant logic of guilt by association? Given the history of colonialism and slavery, where would Europe be if African countries had adopted this ignorant logic? Given the history of World War II, where would Germany be if the Jewish community had fallen for this ignorant logic? Given the history of the Crusades, what would Europe look like if the Arab world had fallen for this ignorant logic? Given the history of apartheid, what would South Africa look like if Mandela had abided by this ignorant logic? Let us all think again and get educated, before judging an entire community because of a few.

With all the unbelievable upheavals of 1990, there was an expectation that the New Year would see political crescendos during this long transition period the Union had never seen. By now, many republics and regions had battled for or unilaterally declared their independence or autonomy from big brother Moscow. Unfortunately, the more people pushed for independence and the abolition of the communist party, the more Gorbachev clung to it, as the cement keeping it all together. He strongly believed that socialism was a just system that needed some tweaking, but was overall a good idea at its core.

Desperate in the face of an avalanche of pending and declared mayhems around the country, Gorbachev again threatened the use of force to reclaim renegade republics. In January, such threats became reality in the capitals of the Baltic republics, when Soviet special troops and tanks captured key buildings and demanded the repudiation of their vote for independence. After a few days of confrontation, and many deaths and injuries, the Soviet troops withdrew while Gorbachev denied any prior knowledge of the invasion and the shootings.

That was my idol at his lowest point grasping at straws. It was ridiculous for him to suggest with a straight face that he, the General Secretary of the Soviet Union, did not know that his Secretary of Defense was planning a military operation in the Baltics. That, after having just refused to rule out military intervention when he addressed the leaders fueling the independence fire in the North-West.

After the Saturday massacre in Baku a year earlier, people were bracing for a far worse showdown with the first republics that had started the independence movement in 1987. The facts were clear: all the republics wanted to be independent, to democratically elect their governments, and chart their own futures. A course Gorbachev did not approve of. Ironically, it was exactly what he wanted for the Soviet Union, as long as it remained one country, and not fifteen separate republics.   Regardless of all the setbacks and humiliations he suffered while trying to preserve the unity of the country, he stubbornly refused to accept the facts on the ground.

At this point, no number of blockades, special troops, or armored tanks could deter a freedom-hungry populace unwilling to take one more order from communist Moscow. After a six-year war against the anti-reformists, this continuing battle between the central government and the republics, was consuming Gorbachev's waning influence.

In the dorms we maintained that the Soviets did not know what they were throwing away, by not following Gorbachev. The common perception was that he was going to lead the country to a kind of Promised Land where the Soviet Union would be a respected democratic, military, and economic superpower. A force for good that would always put its people first, while remaining wedded to the core principals of socialism.

But that road got tougher, reaching an insurmountable height in 1991 with record demands for independence. Unfortunately, Gorbachev had not much to show on behalf of a system that appeared to ruin people's lives instead of improving them, a fact that undermined his endeavor all along. There also was a big faction of nostalgic communists who would like nothing better than to get back to where the country was in 1985, when Gorbachev took power. This latter group never bought into perestroika or glasnost from the get-go, claiming that the Soviet Union was steering away from communism, the inner core of its might. And they had a point, considering the abundance of goods in government stores and the relative peace among all the tribes when we arrived in 1986. Nobody starved, begged in the streets or sold belongings to make ends meet, which is what many wanted to return to. Even if people lacked basic freedoms, with many of them sent to concentration camps, or killed for no good reasons. The new-found democracy and perestroika did not sway those who could not afford heat in their apartments during the atrocious winters.

Our beloved leader now found himself trapped between the political camps without a base to sustain his position, the classic case of an Emperor without clothes. He kept trying in vain to reason with his fellow Soviets to be patient, to continue to build a stronger democracy and a better life for the next generation within the Union. As a last-ditch effort, he suggested that all the leaders sign on to an economic and political agreement to avoid the disintegration of the Union. Meanwhile, Yeltsin discussed border issues, money, the future of the communist party and defense with Russia's neighbors. They agreed to seriously take up the question in the Supreme Soviet upon Gorbachev's return from vacation in Crimea.

Unexpectedly, the other shoe dropped that summer of 1991, when the old guard from the army attempted a coup while the first family was vacationing in Crimea. All of a sudden, a group from Gorbachev's entourage, led by Vice-President Ianaev, called a press conference and declared that Gorbachev was "unable to communicate and fulfill his duties as president. He stated that he would assume all of Gorbachev's responsibilities. While reading this famous communiqué, his hands were trembling, and the whole band appeared nervous. Anybody who saw the video clip knew that something was really amiss and expected more to come. Government TV stations played music and tried frantically to normalize a very abnormal situation. We stayed glued to the TV and could not process what was happening. Everybody was asking if Gorbachev was incapacitated, and if so, what was he suffering from? The lack of clarity and credibility added to the tense situation. For some reason, we were more bemused than frightened by the disappearance of the most heavily-guarded person in the world. All kinds of wild speculations ensued, since he had left healthy and in great shape for his vacation.

It turned out that a group of Gorbachev's closest friends attempted to seize power while he was away. Unfortunately for them, nobody believed their story, and the whole world stood behind Gorbachev and demanded his return. Yeltsin stood on top of a tank, with the army and the people, to denounce the coup. He demanded the return of Gorbachev to Moscow to tell his side of the story. Three putchists committed suicide, and the rest of the band got arrested without a fight.

Yeltsin used the opportunity to humiliate Gorbachev on live TV, asking him to sign a decree disbanding the communist party forever. I will never forget that painful scene, when Yeltsin walked across the room to Gorbachev's podium with that piece of paper, and vociferously ordered him to sign it. The members in the room burst into laughter, turning the whole meeting into a complete embarrassment for Gorbachev. To make matters worse, this was his first meeting with the parliament after returning from Crimea, where he had been held up by the putschists for three days.

The infamous video clip said it all: Yeltsin could not go any higher and Gorbachev any lower in standing in the eyes of the Soviets. Personally, it was one of the worst sights of my stay, given how much I admired the General Secretary. The poor man went from victim of the coup to culprit, because he had previously handpicked every one of the gang who tried to overthrow him. To drive that point home at that infamous first meeting with the congress, Yeltsin again vehemently and rudely demanded that Gorbachev read aloud the minutes of the plotters' last gathering before the coup.

During the same week, the parliament of Ukraine voted to create the Independent State of Ukraine, Belarusians elected their first president, and Moldova declared its independence. We were overwhelmed but captivated by these historic events that nobody had anticipated even in our wildest dreams.

When the dust cleared, Gorbachev came out swinging again, as if for the last time, and to the chagrin of many. He gave press conference after press conference and talked to all the leaders about working out the details of keeping the country together in a new Union to avert a tragedy. But he was fighting a lost cause, since everywhere else in the country, minds were already made up. The General Secretary became a shadow of himself as he soldiered on against all odds, clinging to his fading presidency.

While Gorbachev was dusting himself off after the coup attempt and Yeltsin's humiliation, several republics were plotting behind his back. Once they had recognized the independence of the three Baltic republics, the big three (the Russian Federation, Ukraine, and Belarus) led the way toward creating a commonwealth. Eleven of the twelve remaining republics started to hammer out the details of their future union despite a number of unknowns: fate of the Soviet military arsenal scattered around the Union; which currency or currencies to adopt; world market prices for internal commerce or a brokered trade structure.

In Moldova, the declaration of independence added to tensions with Transdniestra and between nationalists, who wanted to join the future commonwealth and those who wanted to join Romania. As poor as Moldova was, the president had to weigh a lot of potential pitfalls that an independence would generate, at least in the beginning. Moldova could not afford to pay for its oil, gas or even parts for its bus fleet from other republics or from abroad in dollars. Since it did not have much heavy industry, it would lose a lot during negotiations with the other republics that would become foreign countries after the agreement was signed. By now, Ukraine was already considering charging its partners in dollars, and at market value, something the different republics had never experienced before.

Things were going fast in every direction, creating an atmosphere of precariousness seen at the beginning of perestroika. Even time zones were revisited to reflect the real location of different cities, which caused a lot of confusion for travelers and those who called outside of their time zone at the post office. Average citizens did not know how to figure out what time would be in a given city, and had nowhere to turn for quick and reliable information. New passports were printed and checked at the numerous borders that were being erected every day.

It became clear to all that the country was soon going to fall without bullets, but less clear where all the different pieces might end up in the very near future. In the Soviets' minds, the idea of freedom outweighed the sea of numbing problems that would begin on day one of independence. So, in December 1991, after a meeting in Minsk (Belarus) and in Alma Ata (Kazakhstan), the independent republics agreed to form the Commonwealth of Independent States, without Gorbachev at its head. They decided to each mind their own business, but intensely collaborate in order to lessen the impact of the collapse of the old Soviet Union and the growing pains of their respective new self-governing countries.

On that Christmas Day, I had to endure the second most painful video clip, as I watched Gorbachev deliver his resignation speech. Even then, he talked about the independence of republics but within a Union State, and the importance of a referendum to decide the fate of the Union, not just through a meeting of elected officials. Many listened to his speech just to make sure they heard from the horse's mouth that the USSR was no more, not with sorrow as some of us did. The mighty motherland USSR, first in space, first in Berlin to defeat Hitler, and godmother of the Eastern bloc, had just disappeared in a blink of six short years under Gorbachev. Watching it live, in Russian, and right there in the Soviet Union was an exceptional experience that allowed me to get the full impact of the speech and all its implications for the Union and the rest of the world.

With this once-in-a-lifetime moment, I also came full circle in following my hero and concluding my education. I came to Moscow when perestroika was only eighteen months old, and graduated just three months after Gorbachev's premature exit. I wanted to, but could not, forgive him for the way our exhilarating journey ended: an earth-shattering end superficially attributed to a US president by some self-centered revisionists of history. The rest of the world does not even think about Reagan when it comes to the breakup of the Soviet Union.

So, what really happened? Who is to blame or to thank for the most important event of the 20th century? I was there, not the nostalgic pundits bent on brushing up Reagan's image. Here is my eyewitness account:

In March 1985, when Gorbachev took the helm of the Soviet Union, it presented conflicting images to different audiences. To the rest of the world, the USSR was a tightly-controlled, heavily-armed superpower, leading the entire Eastern bloc and many third world satellites, and as stable as a mountain. To the brain-washed Soviet citizens, no country in the world was better than the motherland; only the United States came in a distant second. To the successive leaders of the Union, facts gathered by their own KGB showed that the capitalist West trounced the communist East in every field but space and armaments, while the USSR slowly crawled toward an economic iceberg.

Gorbachev had a choice: feed his ego and keep his head in the sand like all of his predecessors, or try to radically change the Soviet Union, and therefore the world. He chose the latter in order to save his country from a looming economic disaster, and to also bring it into a respected fold of the international community. His foreign policy promoted peace and a nuclear- free world by the year 2000. He ended the war in Afghanistan, withdrew troops and weaponry from Eastern Europe, and signed arms reduction treaties with the US. Finally, he clearly stated that the questions in Eastern Europe would be solved by eastern Europeans, not Moscow.

The financial and moral burdens of the Warsaw pact countries and other communist nations around the world became too heavy to bear. Some readjustments were in order if the Soviet Union were to survive in the long run; Gorbachev took a step back to reassess all commitments and responsibilities. Because of his bold steps in foreign policy, the rest of the world liked and respected him. "We can do business with him," Prime Minister Thatcher once said.

The picture in domestic affairs was complicated and must have been depressing for a conscientious leader. There were many difficulties almost impossible to address without disturbing the accepted and comfortable stagnation of the passive Soviet citizenry. Gorbachev flatly told his fellow citizens that the country could not live this way anymore, and that it was his choice to do something about it to avert a looming tragedy. In his restructuring campaign, or perestroika, Gorbachev outlined the difficulties ahead and how he intended to address them. His litany of political, economic, and social changes disturbed many old-guard conservatives who dreaded losing their power and privileges. On the other hand, a lot of younger and pragmatic apparatchiks, along with many intrigued citizens, could not wait for the proposed changes.

Then and there, you had a split in the leadership that was supposed to work together to tackle the gigantic task of restructuring a country once called "the zoo of absurdity" by Joseph Brodsky, the Russian-born American 1987 Nobel laureate of literature. "A conversation with a Russian (Soviet) could be interesting if you are an anthropologist, and not if you are into politics or philosophy", he said. "Entire generations grew up without laws. Personal initiative was destroyed, basic instinct to act, killed. It got castrated."[38]

That is precisely why Gorbachev wanted a fundamental change, from the style of underwear produced in the Union to the way the people related their government, to each other and to the rest of the world. Unfortunately, we all know that profound changes are often unwelcomed, especially when the status quo (or the slow trip toward a disaster, in this case) is accepted as "the good old times."

Since democracy was the bedrock of his vision, Gorbachev began his campaign for change by laying down its foundation. Ironically, he did not have to look very far for references or guidance, because the constitution of the Soviet Union guaranteed ninety-eight per cent of the rights required for a successful democracy. These laws had simply been ignored, and nobody dared claim them; to do so one could risk the wrath of the government and end up in a hard labor camp or mental institution. Gorbachev began by implementing laws that were already on the books, starting with the basic freedoms a democratic society needs to function: freedom of speech, worship, assembly, and the press. People would finally be free to say what they thought, demand that their rights be

---

[38] *Courier International # 225 : 23 February - March 1, 1995.*

respected, and read and watch all the previously-censured books and movies. Citizens would be allowed to travel abroad. The new General Secretary even opened some of the most contentious top-secret archives in the history of the Union for the sake of glasnost (transparency).

Economically, Gorbachev pushed through sweeping laws that would drastically change the way the old planned economy functioned, so that it could work as a market-based one. For the first time in seventy years, the average Soviet citizen could own property, work part-time for himself, partner with foreign investors or even import or export goods for his or her own business. The government, or the communist party, backed off of its five-year plans that also imposed production targets from Moscow, and even let companies make their own local decisions. Everything was for sale or rent, even for foreigners who could not work, buy or rent property. The word "business," in the heavy Russian accent, was on every lip.

In domestic politics, straight elections with multiple candidates became reality. The privileged positions once reserved for big party bosses were up for grabs for many, instead of the lone communist party. The latter was to lose its overarching dominant role, having less and less influence in local decisions and at workplaces, where membership had previously been compulsory in order to get ahead in life.

Now, armed with perestroika and newly-generated freedoms, many republics, led by the three Baltic States (Lithuania, Latvia and Estonia), began asking for either autonomy or outright independence. Many of the fifteen republics had been forcefully integrated into the Union, contrary to the official tale of peaceful and willful adherence. In this new climate of freedom, their local governments passed laws that practically declared their sovereignty from Moscow and rendered the communist party powerless.

Instead of seriously addressing these issues that were popping up all over the country, Gorbachev made some speeches, but then sent tanks and Special Forces to quash peaceful demonstrators. This was his first mistake, and a contradiction to Statute #72 of the constitution, which asserted that republics had the right to leave the Soviet Union. It clearly states: "Each republic reserves the right to freely leave the Union of the Soviet Socialist Republics,"[39] although the mechanism to do so was less clear.

Sending troops to occupy government buildings, disperse demonstrators, and, in the process, kill many innocent freedom-seekers, was obviously not the right approach. It only galvanized demonstrators around the country and uncovered a crack in the system no one had anticipated.

These popular nationalist, pro-independence, and anti-Moscow sentiments turned into anti-Russian sentiments. Russians were living in big numbers among other nationalities far from the Russian Federation. These Russians and Ukrainians, who held leadership positions over native tribes and nationalities, were seen as foreigners and enemies overnight in the very places where they were born. Inability to speak the native dialect was the last straw, which expedited their forced exodus to safer regions. In some cases, these settlements later claimed their own autonomy or independence, sometimes with the protection of the Russian army.

It became obvious that this melting pot of different tribes, nationalities, and religions had been artificially engineered and was held together by coercion and the promise of a future heaven-on-earth called communism. Seventy years later, when Gorbachev awakened everybody with glasnost (transparence) and the freedom to express themselves, to travel, to critique, to compare and contrast, nobody wanted to touch the system, or neighbors of different tribes, with a ten-foot pole. As tribal, ethnic, political and border tensions rose and led to deaths and destruction, Gorbachev pushed back hard and categorically refused to compromise. Understandably, giving in to one demand would have opened the floodgates, but forcefully suppressing every claim of

---

[39] *Constitution (Main Law) of the USSR (adopted at the Seventh Extraordinary Session of the Supreme Soviet's ninth convocation on October 7, 1977). Moscow Law books 1986. P-22*

independence was also impossible, given the sheer number of them.

Gorbachev found himself in a stalemate not only with these independent movements, but also with nationalist movements, both bent on freeing themselves from Moscow. In Eastern Europe, labor movements and intellectuals started to push for democracy, bearing banners with Gorbachev's name on them as if to call on him to liberate them from their tyranny. He asserted that he supported freedom and democracy and would not send troops and tanks to prop up his communist colleagues as in the Prague's spring of 1968. His vision of freedom and democracy reverberated across Eastern Europe all the way to China, where students greeted him with signs proclaiming perestroika and democracy. By championing democracy, he was at odds with many tyrants who did not want to willfully open up their societies. His domestic changes fueled the fire in sister states of the Warsaw pact. Everyone envied the changing Soviet Union and started dreaming about their own liberation.

Meanwhile, the old guard was consistently blocking, if not actively sabotaging the latest reforms, which prompted Gorbachev to clear the deck and made more close enemies in the process. As if these problems were not enough, the economic measures he enacted were not delivering goods and services to a frustrated public. To the contrary, these reforms confused a now-disillusioned populace that had taken the chance to try the foreign notion of marketplace over a moribund, but stable and familiar one. Perestroika became a disaster economically, forcing seniors to beg in the streets, unemployment ranks to swell, a vicious Soviet mafia to arise, while the old barter system with Eastern Europe died. This nameless economic catastrophe that could not restock the shelves and provide cooking oil, sugar, or butter for the proud veterans of WWII, destroyed Gorbachev's credibility. Unhappy miners soon took to the streets and provoked a national strike, prompting Gorbachev to cave in to most of their demands, among them, guaranteeing the availability of soap so they could wash up after work.

By the summer of 1989, the microcosm of the USSR that was Eastern Europe was also at its breaking point, as basic freedoms, particularly labor rights and economic development were desperately needed. Gorbachev's push for democracy and peace, and his unwillingness to send tanks to other capitals in the East to save dictators, created a fertile ground for civil disobedience. It was not the will that was lacking in those societies.

After nearly ten years of struggle, Solidarnosc won an election and entered a coalition government in Poland. This crack in the system propelled others to press on for their own liberation. By October, the dice were cast, and the world witnessed the fall of Communist dominos, starting with the Iron Curtain itself – the Berlin wall. Bloodlessly or not, Eastern Europeans unchained themselves, one nation after another, under the watchful eyes of the Soviet republics.

Now all eyes were on Moscow, the spiritual leader of the communist bloc and the subsequent freedom trailblazer. Only God knows what was going through Gorbachev's mind after the fall of the Berlin wall and the liberation of millions of people. I wish I could ask him that question and get an honest answer. All that turmoil outside the borders of the Soviet Union happened at the same time a barrage of dire problems were crippling the country and further destroying Gorbachev's image and ability to deliver. The Soviet republics took note and doubled their efforts toward their everlasting goal of independence from big brother and the communist party in Moscow. Declarations of independence piled upon declarations of autonomy, which piled upon presidential elections, which piled upon rejections of the communist party, which piled upon laws of citizenship, which piled upon acts of local languages renouncing Russian as the official one. The tribes and nationalities that had become neighbors, not by choice but by design and Stalin's deportations, were now at each other's throats. The economy was in the tank, crime and corruption had never been so high, the anti-reformists were mad as hell at the changes, and the new leaders and their supporters were fuming at the pace of reforms.

With all the critical problems to resolve and Gorbachev at his weakest point, the disgruntled old guard dealt him the final blow in the form of an attempted coup. It is the three days of the attempted coup in August 1991 that sealed Gorbachev's fate as the President of the Soviet Union. The putsch was attempted by his own hand-picked men, a fact that seriously discredited his judgment and the relevance of the communist party.

After publicly standing on a tank to save Gorbachev, the country, and his own political fortunes, Yeltsin proceeded to clean house. He signed a decree outlawing the communist party and pushed Gorbachev to do the same. Surprisingly, Gorbachev balked and continued to hang on to a party that had just tried to depose him by force. That attitude cost him what little clout he had left as he struggled to convince the republics to sign on to his latest creation – the Commonwealth of Independent States, with him as President. Instead, Yeltsin and the others created it without him. Since they were all by now independent and had their respective presidents, they did not need him.

Left with no choice, my political hero pitifully resigned on Christmas night 1991. That night, he officially signed the death certificates of the "mighty" USSR and the cold war, after 74 years of wander.

What about Ronald Reagan's part in all of this? By asking Gorbachev to tear down the Berlin wall, Reagan could not, in his wildest dreams, have triggered the chain reaction I have just described. Let us never forget that, while the history revisionists would say Reagan was fighting to free Eastern Europe, in reality he was busy vetoing a bill meant to free black South Africans from apartheid. Fortunately, the veto was eventually overridden by a Congress that knew better. If Reagan was such a champion of freedom, why did he oppose freedom in South Africa, to preserve one of the worst examples of crimes against humanity? I challenge any revisionist to answer to that question first. Deep down, was Reagan a racist?

In fact, the ingredients for the fall of the USSR and the regimes in Eastern Europe, were parts and parcels of their communist constitutions themselves. They always were there in a latent stage, waiting for the right conditions to be set in motion. They were the few basic human rights and freedoms terribly lacking in communist countries, but written in their constitutions: Freedoms of speech, association, worship and the press. These were the vital components of the implosions that ensued in the Communist bloc, and Gorbachev alone delivered them on a silver platter, nobody else.

He hoped to preside over a superpower Union made up of loosely tied republics, that was free, prosperous, respected, and influential on the world stage. Given all the talents, natural resources, and resilience the country demonstrated during WWII, such a democratic Union could have been a force for good, instead of the ridiculous armed third-world giant it was. Internal interests were so divergent that only a civil war, mirroring the one the US fought, could have kept the Union together. Mr. Gorbachev would not and could not go down that route in the 20th century.

In Africa today, it is China and India that are "taking over" the cold warriors in investment and so called cooperation with "no strings attached". That is another story.

VI
Шесть

F. XTRA-FILES

In the tightly controlled empire, highly suspicious of everything and everybody; each student had a file populated with teachers' observations. That file would eventually follow foreign students as they go through grades and/or between towns. Here is what my Russian language teacher wrote, according to a secretary I implored, when the country imploded:

"Student Diallo T. H of the preparatory faculty for foreign citizens at the 'Red Banner of Labor' Agriculture Institute M.B. Frunze in Kishinev, on government scholarship for specialty 1507 – Veterinary Medicine.

Diallo T. H was born in Bamako in a family of civil servants. According to student's own words, dad held an administrative position in education and mom - a teacher. Diallo has four brothers and three sisters, two brothers are in elementary school and two others are students with one in France. One married sister lives in Senegal. The family is well off and owns some land. Diallo has been in France. He constantly keeps in touch with relatives. He finished High school in Bamako and did not work before coming to the USSR. He is fluent in French and speaks good English. Native language is Bambara.

He did not learn Russian before arriving to the USSR. The student has good language skills. He has mastered quite well all kinds of speech activities. He is a capable and inquisitive student. Studies seriously, never skipped a class. He studies regularly. He is very interested in natural sciences. By seriously studying, he sets a high standard of preparation for teachers. He is practically, always in good health. He never called in seek during the entire school year. He is a Muslim. His family is very pious, especially his dad. His religious vision however does not prevent him to accept many natural scientific and atheistic theories.

Outgoing student, he has a good sense of humor. He is the non-official leader of the group, even though there were opportunities to become the official one. He refused to be the leader of the class. He does not participate openly in many social events, in general, anything associated with competition and grades. It is the particularity of his character he says. He gets lost in front of a big crowd, but that could be explained by other reasons. He always portrays himself as a supporter of "total freedom, individualism, does not want to take part in anything associated with "collectivism", "socialist propaganda". He always stays away from open political actions, although History and Russian language classes show that these are questions that interest him very much. He is an eclectic when it comes to world vision. At the same time he has firmly rooted stereotypes of bourgeois morality and ideology. He thinks that the injustices of bourgeoisie are something immutable, impossible to fight, people need only to adapt. He thinks that money is the main determining factor in people's relationships. He is starting to review his visions under the influence of Soviet reality.

He is a decent and educated man. Disciplined in all that concerns education, he systematically works throughout the semester and never a trouble maker. He is always courteous and friendly with friends and teachers. He enjoys a good deal of authority in the group and Malian community.

He has a very strong self-esteem. With teachers, he behaves more like a colleague than student, although he always tries to observe subordination. He is a good athlete, loves football and swimming."

Olga G Nocik.

I would love to meet my teacher today and talk about what she wrote a generation ago, and also hear her take on what transpired since.

Made in the USA
Las Vegas, NV
17 February 2022

44085797R00164